Buying Time

A MAN is fed, not that he may be fed, but that he may work."
— EMERSON

"If he is to enjoy leisure and privacy, marry, buy books, travel and entertain his friends, a writer needs upwards of £5 a day net. If he is prepared to die young of syphilis for the sake of an adjective, he can do on under." — CYRIL CONNOLLY

"Money should circulate like rainwater." — THORNTON WILDER

Buying Time

AN ANTHOLOGY CELEBRATING 20 YEARS
OF THE LITERATURE PROGRAM
OF THE NATIONAL ENDOWMENT FOR THE ARTS

EDITED BY SCOTT WALKER

INTRODUCTION BY RALPH ELLISON

GRAYWOLF PRESS
SAINT PAUL, MINNESOTA

Publication of this volume is made possible through generous donations from
New York Community Trust and B. Dalton, Bookseller.

The Endowment would like to acknowledge the four people who have
served as Director of the Literature Program since its founding:
Carolyn Kizer, Leonard Randolph, David Wilk, and Frank Conroy.

The editor is grateful for the assistance of Helen Byers. Others who helped
considerably include Patricia Davis, Mary MacArthur, Amanda Urban,
Marie Behan, Adrianne Harun and Gail Wallis.

Published by Graywolf Press, a non-profit corporation
Post Office Box 75006, Saint Paul, Minnesota 55175

ISBN 0-915308-72-X
Library of Congress Catalog Card Number 85-80545

First Printing, 1985
9   8   7   6   5   4   3   2

Acknowledgments

JOHN ASHBERY: "Some Words," from *The Double Dream of Spring*, copyright ©
1976 by John Ashbery. Reprinted by permission of the author.

JOHN BERRYMAN: "Dream Song" #282 from *The Dream Songs* by John Berryman. Copyright © 1959, 1962, 1963, 1964, 1965, 1966, 1967, 1968, 1969 by John
Berryman. Reprinted by permission of Farrar, Straus & Giroux, Inc.

LOUISE BOGAN: "Night," from *The Blue Estuaries*, copyright © 1962, 1968 by
Louise Bogan. Published by The Ecco Press in 1977. Reprinted by permission of Farrar, Straus & Giroux, Inc.

PAUL BOWLES: "Monologue – Tangier 1975" first appeared in *The Threepenny
Review*. Copyright © 1984 by Paul Bowles. Reprinted by permission of the
author.

RITA MAE BROWN: from *Rubyfruit Jungle*, copyright © 1973 by Rita Mae Brown.
Reprinted by permission of the author.

RAYMOND CARVER: "Gazebo," from *What We Talk About When We Talk About
Love*, copyright © 1981 by Raymond Carver. Reprinted by permission of
Alfred A. Knopf, Inc.

LUCILLE CLIFTON: "The Poet" and "The Turning," from *An Ordinary Woman*,
copyright © 1974 by Lucille Clifton. Reprinted by permission of Curtis
Brown, Ltd.

Table of Contents

Editorial Note

T HE LITERATURE PROGRAM of the National
Endowment for the Arts has, since 1966, awarded nearly 1200
grants and awards in creative writing to an amazingly diverse
group of writers. The Federally funded program has recognized
writers, often quite early in their careers, who have gone on to win
the Nobel Prize, Pulitzer Prizes and every other major book award.
Fellowships have supported the creative endeavors of poets,
novelists, short story writers, critics, writers of creative nonfiction
and dramatists. Grants have been awarded to formalists, experi-
mental writers, neo-classicists, young writers, older ones just start-
ing out, writers who began their literary careers in prison, poets
who later became best-selling novelists, and writers from Florida
to Alaska and from Maine to California.

The Literature Program of the National Endowment for the
Arts, on behalf of the citizens of the United States, provides creative artists with the most valued of treasures: time to write.

Assistance to writers has come in many forms. Awards and fellowships granted since 1966 include a publication award for inclusion in the *American Literary Anthology* in 1967-1970, Distinguished
Service grants (later to become Senior Fellowships, awarded to
writers with a long record of distinguished achievement), Work-in-
Progress grants that allowed writers to complete projects, Discovery Awards that sought to recognize talented writers early in their

careers, and, most of all, Creative Writing Fellowships in poetry, fiction, creative nonfiction and drama.

Writers included in this volume represent nearly every kind of grant or award given and every year that awards and fellowships were made. The writers include a Nobel Laureate, several Pultizer Prize winners, and winners of National Book Critics Circle Awards, National Book Awards, both American Book Awards, Obie Awards, P.E.N. Faulkner Awards, as well as writers who have received another sort of reward – that of being read enthusiastically by a wide audience.

In most cases, the work selected for this anthology was written in the year the writers received their grant or award. We also have attempted to select work which we and the authors feel is among their strongest, but which has not been sufficiently recognized in other anthologies.

This anthology is a tribute to the Literature Program of the National Endowment for the Arts, to its grantees, to the human spirit, and to the vision of the American people who have chosen to support their creative artists by buying them time to explore, enliven and create.

s.w.

Introduction

RALPH ELLISON

TWENTY YEARS AGO the Congress of the United States established the National Endowment for the Arts as an independent agency of the Federal government. Its mission was to encourage and support America's arts and its creative talent by fostering excellence, diversity and vitality in the realm of the imagination. In carrying out its mission the Endowment would stimulate an appreciation of the arts in all sectors of the land by making available the finest examples of artistic creativity. And it would pursue its mission by facilitating a creative collaboration between the Federal and local governments, private foundations, business corporations and the general public. The Act of Congress which created the National Foundation for the Arts was remarkable for the breadth and flexibility of its conception and is of broad historical significance.

For the Endowment came as a long-deferred answer to questions that had perplexed the nation's leaders for close to two hundred years: what role should the imaginative arts play in the official affairs of a democratic society, and what role should the Federal government play in relation to America's art and artists? In the case of literature this volume comes as an answer to such questions, and the variety and high quality of the literary works presented here celebrate the success of the Endowment's ongoing effort. Indeed, it has carried out its mission with such verve that one suspects that if it were possible for certain of the nation's

Founding Fathers to read these writings they might well be amazed.

Amazed? Yes, and baffled – as much by the high quality of these examples of contemporary American literature as by the anthology's presentation of young along with well-established writers, the newly discovered along with those who preceded and inspired them. Also amazing would be the diversity of cultural and regional backgrounds from which the writers presented here have come, and the variety of their artistic styles and points of view. It is easy to speculate that the likes of John Adams and Benjamin Franklin would find in the very *idea* of such a collection a drastic reversal of their notions of the role the imaginative arts should (or shouldn't) play in the drama of American society. And that time-wrought reversal of their expectations might well be as startling – and as delightful – as that which occurs when, say, some drab and dejected creature of creepy obscure habit undergoes a metamorphosis through which it becomes before one's eyes a thing of brilliant color and soaring flight, stirring the mind with intimations of bomb-burst and rocket-flare.

In evaluating the role of the National Endowment for the Arts an historical perspective is instructive. For if being an American is, as Henry James put it, a "Complex fate," in the early days of our history being an American *artist* was perhaps the most complex and discouraging fate of all. And much of that complexity had to do with the Founding Fathers' uncertainty about the potential function of the arts in shaping American society. Not that they were unconcerned with the arts, but that, having achieved a successful revolution and mapped out the groundwork for the new nation, they were faced with a world of practical problems; problems which in their view called for military preparedness, statesmanship, a knowledge of law, and that variety of utilitarian skills today classified generally as "industrial arts and crafts." "First things first" was their guiding principle, and the fine arts seemed of a different order. For instance, George Washington believed that "only arts of a practical nature...would be esteemed" in the new republic, and suggested that because of the circumstance of its establishment the "genius" of the new society was "scientific rather than imaginative." Nevertheless the arts nagged him, and the first draft of his farewell address included a suggestion (later deleted at Alexander Hamilton's prompting) that the Federal government should promote literature and the arts.

So it wasn't that the Founding Fathers were unaware of the imaginative arts, but that they were baffled as to their proper role in the affairs of the new nation. As to the role of the arts in their *own* lives, they were less ambivalent. Washington was fond of theater, music and dancing; Jefferson was both an architect and a musician; Franklin was familiar with European arts, knew his way around the courts of Europe, and was the inventor of a musical instrument – the glass harmonica. He was also aware of the difficulties faced by America's imaginative artists, and in Constance Rourke's *The Roots of American Culture* he is quoted as having written Charles Wilson Peal (the struggling young painter who would become famous for his portraits of our Revolutionary leaders) that since "the arts have always traveled westward…there is no doubt of their flourishing hereafter on our side of the Atlantic."

It must be said, however, that this note of optimism was sounded in the spirit of exhilaration that followed the victorious Revolution, and that once the rigors attending the establishment of the new republic had set in Franklin consigned the role of the fine arts to a place in the nation's distant future. As Miss Rourke indicates, it was his opinion that:

> To America one school-master is worth a dozen poets, and the invention of a machine is of more importance than a masterpiece by Raphael. Nothing is good or beautiful but in the measure that it is useful: yet all things have a utility under particular circumstances. Thus poetry, painting, music (and the stage as their embodiment) are all necessary and proper gratifications of a refined state of society but objectionable at an earlier period, since their cultivation would make a taste for their enjoyment precede its means.

But while Franklin envisioned a possible role for the arts in the future, John Adams was strongly negative concerning their suitability in the life of a struggling democracy. Not only did he regard the imaginative arts as luxuries, but he viewed artists and writers with suspicion. Artists were, as he saw it, a lot of oddballs who "neglected their exercise" and destroyed their health for the sake of "reputation." It would seem that he saw artists as having nothing positive to contribute to the nation's welfare. But if artists – painters, sculptors and actors – were guilty of seeking "notoriety" and "celebration" above all else, those artists who identified themselves as men of letters were far worse. These were a type who demanded "a great deal of praise," a thing Adams saw as being in too short supply, even for statesmen. Nor was it simply a matter of writers being egotistical; they were by trait, as by trade, dishonest. Therefore if they were successful in arousing public interest in their creations it would be not because their work had inherent social value, but because they had managed to dupe "the people" into "bestowing their applause and adorations...on artifices and tricks."

The imaginative arts, as Adams saw them, were agencies of disorder – at least for a democratic republic – and as such they were a threat to be discouraged. For there was a possibility that the easily confused "people" would not only be seduced by such artistic ne'er-do-wells but would expect such distractions to be provided *gratis* by their hard-pressed government.

One hesitates to say it, and no disrespect is intended, but Adams' position regarding the arts and government seems to have counseled a position of "benign [if so mild a term applies] neglect." Nor is this said to saddle his illustrious shoulders with a mischievous oxymoron from our own contentious times. Nevertheless it *does* serve to describe Adams' sense of checkmate in the face of those questions now answered in the form of the National Endowment for the Arts. For in effect his attitude toward art and artists was as "discountenancing" as that held by Franklin and Noah Webster toward the slang and regional lingos that were taking root in the interaction between the English language and the diverse peoples and geography of the New World. Franklin and Webster took the vernacular as a threat to the proper English in which our documents of statehood were written – even though it had been transforming the mother tongue into an improvised catch-as-catch-can language long before the Revolution, and was becoming more distinctly and appallingly "American" than the nation in which it thrived. The conflict here was between the language in which the nation was conceived and that through which it would "improvise" its democratic identity – and that sportive, unruly action of language (more precisely of speech) was a clue to what was already happening, if at a much slower pace, to the imaginative arts, agriculture, architecture, engineering and the industrial techniques and processes.

Inspirited by the principles of democracy, and adapting rapidly to the New World scene, both arts and crafts were becoming "Americanized" and were actively Americanizing the new society. The fine arts were less vulnerable to that process, though not entirely. The disruption brought by the Revolution made for new alignments, and divorced from their roots and roles in European societies the fine arts blended with the folk arts that had been transplanted from Europe – Yes, and from the artistic tendencies brought to America by the slaves – and were quietly providing modes of artistic communication which worked, ironically, to help bond the nation's diverse peoples ever closer to the ideas and ideals of the nation's founders. Democracy allowed more choices for the individual, and Americans were, if they chose to be, heirs of all the arts. Thus they chose, willy-nilly, those artistic modes and techniques which struck their fancy.

History has proved the Founding Fathers to have been wise statesmen who dealt brilliantly with the disrelationships and incongruities released by the Revolution, but it is useful to recall that they were children of the Old World and at once English Colonials *and* American Revolutionaries. Men of Old World culture, they thought of the arts in terms of European society and associated the fine arts with artistocracy. For them the imaginative arts were an enhancement of monarchic culture that required an educated elite for their proper appreciation. Thus their dilemma.

But art, like love, is where one finds it; a fact which artists know instinctively, no matter what statesmen might think about it. In the broader sense art emerges wherever there are human communities, for art is an extension of human character, an exploration of human creative potential that is not only irresistible but necessary, both for the individual and for the cohesion of society. Where men go the arts go, and where men mingle the arts arise to work their magic. And even when disregarded as inessential they persist in traveling, from east to west or north to south, across land, sea or mountain. They travel, sometimes in disguise, with forms of labor. They travel with forms of religious worship. They travel with secular rites and with the games of children. Most of all, they travel with itinerant and expatriate artists – who, contrary to John Adams' misconception, are a type who sacrifice themselves *not* for fame but through sheer necessity and pleasure of artistic creation.

In the nation's beginnings Americans were more "made" than born. Like their society they were products both of conscious thought and improvisation; the thought which shaped them arose from the Old World and embodied itself in the new. And so with the arts. Here the fine arts became a source of modes and motives for vernacular improvisation (as in our music, literature and dance) to give expression to the unfolding American experience. Its products were often crude and comically self-derisive, but they helped to shape the new society by helping to clarify and make bearable the endless contentions of democracy, and they were the unconscious underside of the conscious political efforts that were being asserted to incarnate democracy. Thus the vernacular mingling of the fine and folk arts occurred unnoticed in the process of nation-building.

As the creation of the National Endowment for the Arts bears witness, it was not a question of *when* the arts should be given official recognition in the new society, so much as *how*, and by what method. For as we say, art gives creative expression to a society's ideals by allowing its members an objective unofficial view of themselves and their culture, and it makes possible communication across the barriers of social hierarchy. And by projecting free-wheeling definitions of the diversity and complexity of American experience it allows for a more or less peaceful adjustment between the claims of "inferiors" and "superiors" – a function of inestimable value to a society based, as is ours, upon the abstract ideal of social equality.

Time has allowed us to recognize relationships which Franklin and Adams stood too close to the chaos of the Revolution to see: that the arts are not merely forms of expression that are of concern to artists, but forms of freedom which allow the American people to gauge their progress as they move toward and away from the fulfillment of their democratic ideals. As Congress recognized in granting the National Endowment for the Arts its broad measure of independence, even artistic dissent is conducive to our social health, and it is for the well-being of the nation that the arts' value as agencies of social order has been recognized. In this volume the National Endowment for the Arts demonstrates that ongoing process of Americanization as it finds expression in literature.

May Sarton

PRISONER AT A DESK

IT IS NOT so much trying to keep alive
As trying to keep from blowing apart
From inner explosions every day.
I sit here, open to psychic changes,
Living myself as if I were a land,
Or mountain weather, the quick cycles
Where we are tossed from the ice age
To bursts of spring, to sudden torrents
Of rain like tears breaking through iron.
It is all I can do to keep tethered down.

No prisoner at a desk, but an ocean
Or forest where waves and gentle leaves
And strange wild beasts under the groves
And whales in all their beauty under the blue
Can gently rove together, still untamed,
Where all opens and breathes and can grow.

Whatever I have learned of good behavior
Withers before these primal powers.
Here at the center governess or censor
No longer has command. The soul is here,
Inviolable splendor that exists alone.

Prisoner at a desk? No, universe of feeling
Where everything is seen, and nothing mine
To plead with or possess, only partake of,
As if at times I could put out a hand
And touch the lion head, the unicorn.
Here there is nothing, no one, not a sound
Except the distant rumor, the huge cloud
Of archetypal images that feed me...

Look, there are finches at the feeder.
My parrot screams with fear at a cloud.
Hyacinths are budding. Light is longer.

Buying Time

John Ashbery

John Ashbery received the Pulitzer Prize, the National Book Award and a National Book Critics Circle Award for *Self-Portrait in a Convex Mirror* (1975). He received a publication award from the N.E.A. for work included in the *American Literary Anthology* in 1969 and 1970.

SOME WORDS

from the French of Arthur Cravan

LIFE IS NOT at all what you might think it to be
A simple tale where each thing has its history
    It's much more than its scuffle and anything goes
Both evil and good, subject to the same laws.
    Each hour has its color and forever gives place
Leaving less than yon bird of itself a trace.
In vain does memory attempt to store away
The scent of its colors in a single bouquet
Memory can but shift cold ashes around
When the depths of time it endeavors to sound.
    Never think that you may be allowed, at the end,
To say to yourself, "I am of myself the friend,"
Or make with yourself a last reconciliation.
You will remain the victim of your hesitation
You will forget today before tomorrow is here
And disavow yourself while much is still far from clear.
    The defunct days will offer you their images
Only so that you may read of former outrages
And the days to come will mar with their complaints
The splendor that in your honor dejected evening paints.
    Wishing to collect in your heart the feelings
Scattered in the meadows of misfortune's hard dealings
You will be the shepherd whose dog has run away
You will know even less whence comes your dismay

Than you know the hour your boredom first saw the light.
      Weary of seeking day you will relish the night
In night's dim orchards you will find some rest
The counsels of the trees of night are best
Better than those of the tree of knowledge, which corrupts us at birth
And which you allowed to flourish in the accursèd earth.
      When your most arduous labors grow pale as death
And you begin to inhale autumn's chilly breath
Winter will come soon to batter with his mace
Your precious moments, scattering them all over the place.
      You will always be having to get up from your chairs
To move on to other heartbreaks, be caught in other snares.
      The seasons will revolve on their scented course
Solar or devastated you will perforce
Be perfumed at their tepid passing, and not know
Whether their fragrance brings you joy or woe.
      At the moment when your life becomes a total shambles
You will have to resume your hopeless rambles
You have left everything behind and you still are eligible
And all alone, as the gulf becomes unbridgeable
You will have to earn your daily bread
Although you feel you'd be better off dead.
      They'll hurt you, and you'd like to put up some resistance
Because you know that your very existence
Depends on others as unworthy of you
As you are of God, and when it's time to review
Your wrongs, you will feel no pain, they will seem like a joke
For you will have ceased to suffer under their yoke.
      Whether you pass through fields, towns or across the sea
You will always retain your melancholy
And look after it; you will have to think of your career
Not live it, as in a game where the best player
Is he who forgets himself, and cannot say
What spurs him on, and makes him win the day.
      When weary henceforth of wishing to gaze
At the sinuous path of your spread-out days
You return to the place where your stables used to tower

You will find nothing left but some fetid manure
Your steeds beneath other horsemen will have fled
To autumn's far country, all rusted and red.
    Like an ardent rose in the September sun
You will feel the flesh sag from your limbs, one by one,
Less of you than of a pruned rosebush will remain,
That spring lies in wait for, to clothe once again.
    If you wish to love you won't know whom to choose
There are none whose love you'd be sorry to lose
Not to love at all would be the better part
Lest another seize and confiscate your heart.
    When evening descends on your deserted routes
You won't be afraid and will say, "What boots
It to worry and fret? To rail at my luck?
Since time my actions like an apple will pluck."
    You would like of yourself to curtail certain features
That you dislike, making allowances for this creature,
Giving that other one a chance to show his fettle,
Confining yet another behind bars of metal:
That rebel will soon become an armèd titan.
    Then let yourself love all that you take delight in
Accept yourself whole, accept the heritage
That shaped you and is passed on from age to age
Down to your entity. Remain mysterious;
Rather than be pure, accept yourself as numerous.
The wave of heredity will not be denied:
Best, then, on a lover's silken breast to abide
And be wafted by her to Nirvana's blue shoals
Where the self is abolished and renounces its goals.
    In you all things must live and procreate
Forget about the harvest and its sheaves of wheat
You are the harvest and not the reaper
And of your domain another is the keeper.
    When you see the lapsed dreams that childhood invents
Salute your adolescence and fold their tents
Virginal, tall and slim beside the jasmine tree
An adorable girl is plaiting tenderly

The bouquet of love, which will stick in your memory
As the final vision and the final story.
    Henceforth you will burn with lascivious fire
Accursèd passion will strum its lyre
At the charming crossroads where day is on the wane
As the curve of a hill dissolves in a plain.
    The tacit beauty of the sacred plateau
Will be spoiled for you and you will never know
Henceforth the peace a pious heart bestows
To the soul its gentle sister in whom it echoes;
Anxiety will have called everything into question
And you will be tempted to the wildest actions.
    Then let all fade at the edge of our days!
No God emerges to dream our destinies.
The days depart, only boredom does not retreat
It's like a path that flies beneath one's feet
Whose horizon shifts while as we trudge
The dust and mud stick to us and do not budge.
    In vain do we speak, provoke actions or think,
We are prisoners of the world's demented sink.
    The soft enchantments of our years of innocence
Are harvested by accredited experience
Our fondest memories soon turn to poison
And only oblivion remains in season.
    When, beside a window, one feels evening prevail
Who is there who can receive its slanting veil
And not regret day that bore it on its stream
Whether day was joy or under evil's regime
Drawing us to the one and deploring the other
Regretting the departure of all our brothers
And all that made the day, including its stains.
    Whoever you may be O man who complains
Not at your destiny, can you then doubt,
When the moment arrives for you to stretch out,
That remorse, a stinking jackal with subtle nose,
Will come at the end to devour your repose?
    ...Something gentle and something sad eftsoons

In the flanks of our pale and realistic noons
Holds with our soul a discourse without end
The curtain rises on the afternoon wind
Day sheds its leaves and now will soon be gone
And already my adulthood seems to mourn
Beside the reddish sunsets of the hollow vase
As gently it starts to deepen and slowly to increase.

John Berryman

John Berryman received a Pulitzer Prize for Poetry in 1965 for
77 Dream Songs, and a National Book Award for Poetry in
1969 for *His Toy, His Dream, His Rest*. He received a Distinguished Service Award from the N.E.A. in 1968.

from THE DREAM SONGS [282]

RICHARD & RANDALL, & one who never did,
two who will never cross this sea again,
& Delmore,
filled his pitted mind as the ship forged on
I hear the three freaks in their different notes
discussing more & more

our meaning to the Old World, theirs to us
which much we pondered in our younger years
and then coughed & sang
the new forms in which ancient thought appears
the altering bodies of the labile souls,
foes fang on fang.

The lovely friends, and friends the friends of friends,
pursuing insights to their journeys' ends
subtle & steadfast:
the wind blows hard from our past into our future
and we are that wind, except that the wind's nature
was not to last.

Louise Bogan

Louise Bogan's publications include *The Blue Estuaries: Poems 1923-1968*. She was, for many years, a reviewer and poetry editor of *The New Yorker*. She received a Distinguished Service Award in 1968.

NIGHT

THE COLD remote islands
And the blue estuaries
Where what breathes, breathes
The restless wind of the inlets,
And what drinks, drinks
The incoming tide;

Where shell and weed
Wait upon the salt wash of the sea,
And the clear nights of stars
Swing their lights westward
To set behind the land;

Where the pulse clinging to the rocks
Renews itself forever;
Where, again on cloudless nights,
The water reflects
The firmament's partial setting;

– O remember
In your narrowing dark hours
That more things move
Than blood in the heart.

Paul Bowles

Paul Bowles is the author of several novels (including *Shelter-ing Sky*) and collections of short stories (including *Collected Stories*). He received a Creative Writing Fellowship in 1978 and a Senior Fellowship in 1980.

MONOLOGUE – TANGIER 1975

I FIRST MET her just after she'd bought the big villa overlooking the valley Saudis have it now they've got most of the good properties I remember she asked Anton and me to tea we hadn't been married very long then she seemed very much inerested in him she'd seen him dance years ago in Paris before his accident and they talked about those days it was all very correct she had delicious petits fours strange how that impressed itself on my mind of course at that time you must remember we were frightfully poor living on the cheapest sort of food fortunately Anton was a fantastic cook or we should have starved he knew how to make a meal out of nothing at all I assure you well it wasn't a fortnight later that she invited us to lunch terribly formal a large staff everything perfect and afterward I remember we were having coffee and liqueurs beside the fireplace and she suddenly offered us this little house she had on the property there were several extra cottages hidden around you know guest houses but most of them were up above nearer the big house this one was way down in the woods far from everything except a duck pond I was absolutely stunned it was the last thing I should have expected of her then she took us down to see it very simple but charming tastefully furnished and a rather primitive kitchen and bath but there were heaps of flowers growing outside and lovely views from the windows we were enchanted of course you understand there was nothing to pay we were simply given the use of the house for as long as we wished I admit it was a very kind gesture for her to make although at the time I suspected that she had her eye on Anton I was quite wrong as it happened in any case having the house made an enormous difference to us it was a gift from the gods there was as a matter of fact one drawback for me Anton didn't seem to mind them but there were at least twenty peacocks in an enormous aviary in the woods not far away and some nights they'd scream you know how hair-raising the sound is especially in the middle of the night it took me weeks to get used to it lying there in the dark listening to those insane screams eventually I was able to sleep through it well once we'd moved in our hostess never came near us which was her privilege naturally but it did seem a bit peculiar at least she wasn't after Anton the months went by and we never caught sight of her you see we had a key to the gate at the bottom of the estate so we always used the lower road to come and go it was much easier than climbing up past the big house so of course in order for us to see her she'd have had to come down to our part of the property but she never ventured near us time went on then all at once we began to hear from various directions a strange rumor that whenever she spoke of us she referred to us as her squatters I was all for going up and having it out with her on the spot is that why you invited us here so you could ridicule us wherever you go but Anton said I'd got no proof it could simply be the typical sort of malicious gossip that seems to be everywhere in this place he said to wait until I heard it with my own ears well clearly she wasn't likely to say it in front of me then one morning I went out to take a little walk in the woods and what should I see but several freshly painted signs that had been put up along the paths all saying DEFENSE DE TOUCHER AUX FLEURS obviously they'd been put there for us there was no one else isn't it extraordinary the way people's minds work we didn't want her beastly flowers we'd never touched them I don't like cut flowers I much prefer to see them growing Anton said best pay no attention if we have words she'll put us out and he was right of course but it was very hard to take at all events you know she had lovers always natives of course what can one expect that's all right I'm not so narrow-minded I'd begrudge her that dubious pleasure but there are ways and ways of doing things you'd expect a woman of her age and breeding to have a certain amount of discretion that is she'd make everything as unnoticeable as possible but no not at all in the first place she allowed them to live with her quite as if they were man and wife and that gave them command over the servants which is unthinkable but worse she positively flourished those wretched lovers of hers in the face of the entire town never went out without the current incumbent if people didn't include him she didn't accept the invitation she was the sort of woman one couldn't imagine ever having felt embarrassment but she could have managed to live here without alienating half the Europeans you know in those days people felt strongly about such things natives couldn't even enter the restaurants it wasn't that she had lovers or even that her lovers were natives but that she appeared with them in public that was a slap in the face for the European colony and they didn't forgive it but she couldn't be bothered to care what anybody felt what I'm leading up to is the party we never caught a glimpse of her from one month to the next you understand and suddenly one day she came to call on us friendly as you please she said she had a favor to ask of us she was giving this enormous party she'd sent out two hundred invitations that had to be surrendered at the gate she said there were always too many gate-crashers at her parties the tourists would pay the guides to get them in and this time nobody was to get in excepting the ones she'd invited what she wanted us to do was to stand in a booth she'd built just outside the gate it had a little window and a counter Anton was to examine the invitations and give a sign to one of the policemen stationed outside to admit the holder I had a big ledger with all the names alphabetically listed and as Anton passed me the invitation I was to make a red check opposite the name she wanted to be sure later who had come and who hadn't I've got ten servants she said and not one of them can read or write it's discouraging then I thought of you and decided to ask this great favor of you is everything all right in your little house do you enjoy living here so of course we said oh yes everything is lovely we'd be glad to help you what fools we were it won't take long she said two hours at most it's a costume party drinks dinner and dancing by moonlight in the lower garden the musicians begin to play at half past seven after she'd gone I said to Anton two hundred invitations indeed she hasn't got twenty friends in this entire city well the night of the party came and we were up there in our little sentry-box working like coolies the sweat was pouring down my back sometimes a dozen people came all together half of them already drunk and they didn't at all like having to wait and be admitted one at a time they kept arriving on and on I thought they'd never stop coming at midnight we were still there finally I told Anton this is too much I don't care who comes I'm not going to stand here another minute and Anton said you're right and he spoke to the guard and said that's it no more people are coming don't let anybody else in and good night and so on and we went down to where the party was the costumes were very elaborate we stood for a few minutes at the end of the garden watching them dancing suddenly a tall man in robes with a false beard and a big turban came up to us I had no idea who he was but Anton claimed he recognized him at once anyway it was her lover if you please she'd sent him to tell us that if we were going to come to the party would we please go and put on our costumes as if we had any costume to put on I was staggered after getting us to stand for almost five hours in a suffocating little box she has the infernal gall to ask us to leave yes and not even the common courtesy to come and speak to us herself no she sends her native lover to do it I was starved there was plenty of food on the buffet but it was a hundred feet away from us at the other end of the garden when we got back down to our house I told Anton I hate that woman I know it's wrong but I really hate her to make things worse the next day she came down to see us again not as you might think to thank us far from that on the contrary she'd come to complain that we'd let in people who had no invitations what do you mean I cried look at the cards and look at the book they tally what are you talking about and she said the Duchesse de Saint Somethingorother was missing her evening bag where she'd put her emerald earrings and I said just what has that got to do with us will you please tell me well she said we'd left our post our post she called it as though we were in the army and after we'd gone some other people had

arrived and the police let them in Anton asked if they'd presented
their invitations well she said she hadn't been able to get hold of
that particular policeman so she didn't know but if we'd been there
it wouldn't have happened my dear lady I said do you realize we
were in that booth for five hours you told us it wouldn't take more
than two I hope you're aware of that well it's most unfortunate she
said I've had to call in the police that made me laugh eh bien madame I said since according to you it was the police who let the
thief in it ought to be very simple I don't see that we have anything
to do with it then she raised her voice all I can say is I'm sorry I
was foolish enough to count on you I shall know better another
time and she went out it was then that I said to Anton look we
can't go on living in this woman's house we've got to find somewhere else he was earning a little at that time working in an
export-import office practically nothing but enough to pay rent
on a small cottage he thought we should hang on there and hope
that things would return to normal but I began to go out by myself
nearly every day to look for somewhere we could move to this
turned out later to have been very useful at least I'd seen a good
many houses and knew which ones were possible you see the party
was only the prelude to the ghastly thing that happened less than
a month afterward one night some teenage hoodlums got into the
big house the lover had gone to Marrakech for the weekend so she
was alone yes she made the servants sleep in cabins in the upper
garden she was alone in the house and you know these people
they're always convinced that Europeans must have vast sums of
money hidden about the premises so they tortured her all night
long trying to make her tell where it was she was beaten and
burned and choked and cut and both her arms were broken she
must have screamed I should think but maybe they covered her
face with pillows at all events no one heard a thing the maids found
her in the morning she was alive but she died in hospital that afternoon we knew nothing about it until the police suddenly arrived
two days later and said the property was being padlocked and
everybody had to leave immediately meaning the servants and gar-
deners and us so out we went with all our things it was terrible
but as Anton said at least we lived for more than a year without

paying rent he always insisted on seeing the positive side of things in a way that was helpful later when I heard the details I was frightfully upset because you see the police traced the hooligans through a gold cigarette case and some other things they'd taken the night they tortured her and then it was discovered that they also had the Duchess's evening bag one of the criminals had arrived late the night of the party and slipped in with a group of Spaniards after Anton and I had left the gate and of course that gave him the opportunity of examining the house and grounds for the break-in later so I felt terribly guilty of course I knew it wasn't my fault but I couldn't keep myself from thinking that if we'd only stayed on a little longer she'd still have been alive I was certain at first that the lover had had some part in it you see he never left her side she wouldn't hear of it and all at once he goes off to Marrakech for a weekend no it seemed too pat it fitted too well but apparently he had nothing to do with it besides he'd had every chance to make off with whatever he wanted and never had touched a thing so he must have been fairly intelligent at least he knew better than to bite the hand that was feeding him except that in the end he got nothing for his good behavior poor wretch I've tried to think back to that night and sometimes it seems to me that in my sleep maybe I did hear screams but I'd heard those blasted peacocks so many times that I paid no attention and now it makes my blood run cold to think that perhaps I actually did hear her calling for help and thought it was the birds except that the big house was so far away she'd have had to be screaming from a window that looked over the valley so I keep telling myself I couldn't possibly have heard her they wouldn't have let her get near a window but it's upsetting all the same

Rita Mae Brown

Rita Mae Brown's published writings include *Rubyfruit Jungle, Southern Discomfort* and, most recently, *Sudden Death*, which appeared on *The New York Times* bestseller list. She received a Creative Writing Fellowship in 1978.

from RUBYFRUIT JUNGLE

THE SUMMER of my revenge was also the summer that the crops died and Jennifer died too. Jennifer was Leroy's real mother. She was tall with a face like those ladies in Sunday School books. Her eyes were so big that when you looked at her that's all you could see. I called her Aunt Jenna although she wasn't really my aunt, but then none of them were my family. That summer was full of bad things, and it started with Ep's getting trimmed with a knife.

Couple of days after I got Earl good, Ep, Jennifer's husband, came in the house covered with blood. It ran down his face and matted in the thick, curly, blond hair on his huge chest. Jennifer screamed when she saw him, and Florence ran to the kitchen for a bowl of cold water. For all her faults, Florence was always the first to grasp what was needed in any situation. My dad Carl hadn't come home yet so just us kids and the women were there – with Ep soaking in blood and looking so mad I thought his brains would fry. Leroy's eyes almost fell out of his head when he looked at his old man all busted up. Ep didn't notice the two of us standing there, staring. Ted eased his father down into a chair and Florence came back into the room with basin, rags and an air of command. "Put your head back, Ep, and let me get the blood off your face. Molly, go in the pantry and get gauze and merthiolate. Leroy, go pump more water for your father. Jennifer, you sit down, you lookin' pale as a ghost. Now, Ep, hold still. I know it hurts, but you just hold still. It ain't gonna hurt nearly as bad as when you got stuck in the first place."

Ep gave in and let his hands hang back, wincing each time the rag touched his wounds. He didn't get busted, he got carved. "Ep," Jennifer said low, "honey, what happened? You went and lost your temper again, didn't you?"

Ep's anger started to drain away and he answered quietly, "Yes, I went and lost my head but I couldn't help it and I didn't have one drink, I swear, not one drink."

Florence gave him a dirty look but kept on with her business. "Molly, go over to your Aunt Jenna and get her to show you how to make a butterfly stitch out of adhesive tape. Make a lot, he's got holes in him as big as mouths."

Leroy padded back into the room and sat a bowl of water on the oil tablecloth. "Hey, Pop, you get him, the guy that got you? You get him, Pop?"

"Leroy, I wish you wouldn't ask those questions with such joy in your face," Jennifer pleaded. She looked old, so old sometimes, and this was one of those times. The color seemed to have left her face and hidden somewhere. The lines around the top of her upper lip were drawn and it made her look strange. She was about two weeks away from having another baby. She looked like a grandmother that swallowed a weather balloon, and Carrie said that Jennifer was only thirty-three years old.

"What was the fight about this time?" she asked.

"Fought about the boys with that bastard, Layton." That word made me cringe. How come whenever a person was bad they called him a bastard? My face went hot and I didn't dare look up from my butterfly bandages for fear someone would see my color. "Layton he come on into the shop all puffed up like a banty rooster about his son, Phil. Phil got an appointment to West Point he says; then he gives me this sly look and asks how my boys doing. Well, I told him both Ted and Leroy going to the Point too. After all, I'm a veteran, got a purple heart and they ain't gonna refuse my boys when they are ready to go. They can't turn away sons of men shot up in the war. So Layton he roars laughing and says that being the son of a fool got shot up in the war don't mean they can go to so high a place as West Point. He says everyone on the hill knows my boys are so dumb they don't know their ass from their elbow. Well Jenna, I couldn't stand it no more. I told him his son Phil don't deserve to belong to the army, that pansy sits down to piss... we got into it after that and I laid him to whaleshit. Then he pulls a toadsticker on me and well, there's not more to tell."

"There's a lot more to tell," Florence intervened. "The cops gonna come down here and haul you off if you gonna get in fights like trash. How'd you leave Layton? You didn't kill him, I hope?"

"Nah, I didn't kill him though I'd have liked to wrung his neck until his tongue hit the ground. Carl came by the shop on his way home and broke it up. He's down there now making some kind of peace with Layton. You know Carl's so good-natured he can get anyone feeling good again. He sent me home because I wasn't any help."

Jennifer got up to check the snap beans cooking on the stove. Ep looked at the floor and studied his dusty shoes. "Honey," he called out, "our boys ain't stupid. They'll do good, you wait. Seeing them do good will make me feel better than pounding on Layton anyway."

Jennifer turned from the bubbling water and walked back in the room to give him a kiss. "Sure, they'll do all right, but I don't think fighting is an example for them." A sheepish grin took over Ep's face, and he put his hand on her bloated belly and kissed her hand.

Carl came through the door and made a big show out of tossing his gray worker's cap on the coat rack. He made it and we all gave a cheer. Under his arm he had a big piece of meat wrapped in greasy butcher's paper. His gold tooth in front glittered as he smiled. "Lamb stew tonight, folks. It was left over after the day and I brought it home. So get out the carrots and celery, we're gonna have lamb stew." Carrie sidled over to Carl and whispered in his ear. He patted her on the shoulder and told her everything was fine.

I ran over and jumped up high to put my arms around his neck. "Come on, Daddy, swing me in a circle till I get dizzy."

"All right, pilot to copilot, here we go-o-o." Carl worked hard and his robust, muscular body already had a taint of early age about it, different from Jennifer's but bowed some way.

After my swing, he went over to Ep and asked him how he was doing. Ep looked up to Carl the way boys look up to their fathers even though Carl was only ten years older than Ep.

"Supper's on the way, gang. Clear off this table and get these bloody rags out of the way," Carrie announced later. The stew was brought steaming to the table and Leroy and I fought for a place next to Carl. Jennifer and Ep kept looking at each other over the table and Florence ran her mouth more than usual but there was no edge in her voice this time. She wanted to smooth things out. Leroy forgot to steal meat off my plate and Carrie laughed at everything Carl said. Carl talked more than I remembered him ever doing. He told stories about Sure Mike the burly man he worked for at the butcher shop, and he joked about the president of the United States. The grownups laughed at those jokes more than anything but they didn't make sense to me. In school they told us that the president was the best man in the whole country but I knew my father was the best man in the whole country; the country didn't know it, that's all. So I guessed it was okay for Carl to make fun of the president. Anyway, how did I know the president was for real? I never saw him, just pictures in the paper and they can make those up. How do you know someone is real if you don't see him?

Jennifer was losing weight instead of gaining it like you're supposed to do when you have a baby but she was so close to having the baby that no one paid much attention except Carrie. When it came time for Jennifer to go to the George Street Hospital, things seemed regular enough. She had the baby, named Carl after Dad, but the baby only lived two days. She didn't come home. The grownups paid less attention to us than usual. Coming in from the outhouse, I stopped on the porch and heard Florence, Carrie, and Ep. It was a hot, sticky night. Leroy was on the porch spitting watermelon seeds, so we both sat and listened.

Ep's voice sounded like a fuzzy radio show. He sounded worse than when he got cut up. "Carrie, she never told me about no pains. She never told me anything. If she'd let me know how she was feeling, I'd have got her to a doctor."

Florence answered him in a calm voice that was even stern, "My daughter, Jennifer, never was one to put herself first. She figured doctors ran too high and whatever was the matter with her had to do with the baby, so it'd be soon gone. Don't blame yourself, Ep. She did what she thought was right and God knows with all of us working we can't make hardly enough to keep going. She was thinking about that."

"I'm her husband. She should have told me. It's my duty to know."

Carrie came in on it. "Women often get ailments they keep from their men. Jennifer was quieter than most that way. She mentioned to me that she had pains but how were any of us to know she's shot through with cancer? She didn't know. You don't know things like that."

"She's going to die. I know she's going to die. When it's all through you like that, you can't live."

"No, there's no way she can live. These things are in the hands of the Lord." Florence was resolute. Fate was fate. If God wanted Jennifer then he would have her. Carrie seconded the motion. "'The Lord giveth and the Lord taketh away.' It's not our business, these things, birth and death. We have to keep going on."

Leroy looked at me and clutched my arm. "Molly, Molly, what does it mean that Mom's got cancer? What are they talking about? Tell me what they're talking about."

"I don't know, Leroy. They say Aunt Jenna's gonna die." My throat hurt, there was a burning lump in it and I held onto Leroy's hand and whispered, "Don't let them know we heard. Nothin' we can do except stay out of their way and see what happens. Maybe it's a mistake and she'll be home soon. People make mistakes sometimes." Leroy started to cry and I took him out by the lima beans so nobody would hear either of us. Leroy sobbed, "I don't want my mom to die." He cried himself sick and then fell asleep. Even the mosquitoes didn't bother him. After a while Carrie called us to come in, so I got him up and half carried fat, lumpy Leroy back to the house to his little iron bed. Leroy slept in the same room with Ted, and I slept with Carrie and Carl in my own bed. I'd rather have been in there with Leroy, but people said it wasn't right, but that made no sense to me at all, especially tonight. "Mom, let me stay in here with Leroy, just for tonight, Mom, please?"

"No, you're not sleeping in here with the boys and Ted big enough so his voice is changing. You come where you belong. When you get older you'll understand." She hauled me off and I took one last look at poor Leroy, eyes red and swollen and groggy. He was too tired to protest and fell back into a stupor.

He must have told Ted because next day Ted was more withdrawn than usual and his eyes looked red too.

Within a week Jenna was gone. The funeral was jammed with the entire population of the Hollow, and people were impressed with the flowers. Ep busted himself on the casket. He got the best there was and nobody could talk him out of it. If his wife was going to be dead, then she was going to be dead right, he said. Florence took charge of everything. Leroy, Ted and I were banished during the preparations and that was fine with us. Everybody got all dressed up to honor the dead. Leroy wore a bow tie, Ted wore a string tie, and Daddy and Ep had long ties on and coats that didn't match their trousers, but coats just the same. Carrie rigged me in a horrible dress full of itchy crinolines and patent leather shoes. At least Jennifer was beyond being tormented by itchy dresses. I thought I was worse off than the corpse. The service went on and on, the preacher got carried away with himself over the casket as he talked about the joys of heaven. When they lowered the gleaming box into the ground, Florence swooned and gasped, "My baby." Carl grabbed her and held her up. Ep had Ted and Leroy by the hand, and he never moved a muscle. He stared straight into that hole and never said a word. Leroy was trying hard not to start bawling again, and I stared at the cowlick on back of his slicked-down hair so as not to start crying myself and show up for a big sissy. The dress didn't help none, it's easier to cry in a dress anyway.

After the casket was in the ground we all went back to the house.

Neighbors and relatives from as far away as Harrisburg had come and they brought food. I don't know why, because no one felt like eating. Ep received people with a pained dignity, and Florence almost enjoyed the attention she was getting as mother of the deceased but it was mixed with sorrow. So much of what Florence did was mixed that way.

Once it got dark, people started to clear out and finally we were left to ourselves. Carrie set the table to try to get us kids to eat. Carl passed the fruit bread and put a hunk on my plate. "The candied cherries are cut up in little red pieces. Take a bite, it's real good."

"I don't wanna eat, Daddy. I'm not hungry." I pushed the food around on my plate to make it look as though I'd had some. After a proper amount of time the table was cleared and we went off to bed.

Before going to my room I went into Leroy and Ted's room. Between their two beds, on the wall, hung an embroidered, fancy piece of satin from the casket. "Mother" it said with red roses embroidered on it. Leroy was under the covers, his enormous eyes were all that showed. Ted was sitting up in bed.

"Hey, you guys, hey, I came on in to say goodnight. Your sign is pretty up there. Maybe tomorrow we can go down to the pond or something. Maybe the three of us can do something."

Ted looked at me like an old man. "Sure. They said I don't have to go to the Esso station tomorrow. I'll go down to the pond with you."

Leroy didn't say anything and started crying again. "I want my mother. They said God took her away. That's a crock of shit. God don't do evil things like that and if he does then I don't like him. If he's so good then let him bring my mother back." He screeched on like that and Carrie came hustling into the room. She sat down on the bed and held Leroy to soothe him. She gave him that line of crap about God and how we don't know what his plans are because we are only people and people are morons compared to God Almighty. Leroy stopped crying. Carrie rose and told me to "come on to bed and leave the boys alone." Leroy gave me a look, but I could only hold up my hands because she was dead set against me staying there. Ted slouched down on his bed, closed his eyes and and looked one hundred years old. Carrie switched off the naked light bulb and there wasn't another sound.

I didn't stay in bed too long. I couldn't sleep thinking about Aunt Jenna there under the ground. What would happen if she'd open her eyes and see only dark and feel satin from the coffin? That'd scare her enough to kill her all over again. How do they know dead people don't open their eyes and see? They don't know nothing about being dead. Maybe they should have sat her in a chair along with other dead people. But I'd seen a very dead cow once and that made my thoughts worse. Was Aunt Jenna gonna swell up like that cow and turn black and smell and get full of maggots? I couldn't think about that, it tore my stomach right off its moorings. That's animals, same thing doesn't happen to people, does it? That's gonna happen to me someday, too? No, not me. I ain't dying. I don't care what they say, I ain't dying. I'm not lying on my back under the ground in everlasting darkness. Not me. I'm not closing my eyes. If I close my eyes, I might not open them. Carrie was asleep so I crawled out of bed and crept down the hall covered with peeling green wallpaper with white gardenias on it. I was planning to hotfoot it out on the porch and watch the stars but I never made it because Ep and Carl were in the living room and Carl was holding Ep. He had both arms around him and every now and then he'd smooth Ep's hair or put his cheek next to his head. Ep was crying just like Leroy. I couldn't make out what they were saying to each other. A couple times I could hear Carl telling Ep he had to hang on, that's all anybody can do is hang on. I was afraid they were going to get up and see me so I hurried back to my room. I'd never seen men hold each other. I thought the only things they were allowed to do was shake hands or fight. But if Carl was holding Ep maybe it wasn't against the rules. Since I wasn't sure, I thought I'd keep it to myself and never tell. I was glad they could touch each other. Maybe all men did that after everyone went to bed so no one would know the toughness was for show. Or maybe they only did it when someone died. I wasn't sure at all and it bothered me.

The next morning the sky was black with thunderclouds, and

we had to spend the whole day in the house. The rain poured down and the leak by the kitchen table opened up again so Ted went out with shingles to patch it. After the storm the sky stayed dark but across the horizon was a brilliant rainbow. We all stared in silence for a long time, then went back inside. Ep stayed on the porch to look at the rainbow. Leroy bet me I couldn't find a pot of gold at the end, and I told him that was a stupid bet because the rainbow was enough.

Raymond Carver

Raymond Carver's most recent books are a volume of poetry, *Where Water Comes Together with Other Water*, and a short story collection, *Cathedral*. In 1983 he received the Mildred and Harold Strauss Living Award. He received a Discovery Award in 1970 and a Creative Writing Fellowship in 1980.

GAZEBO

THAT MORNING she pours Teacher's over my belly and licks it off. That afternoon she tries to jump out the window.

I go, "Holly, this can't continue. This has got to stop."

We are sitting on the sofa in one of the upstairs suites. There were any number of vacancies to choose from. But we needed a suite, a place to move around in and be able to talk. So we'd locked up the motel office that morning and gone upstairs to a suite.

She goes, "Duane, this is killing me."

We are drinking Teacher's with ice and water. We'd slept awhile between morning and afternoon. Then she was out of bed and threatening to climb out the window in her undergarments. I had to get her in a hold. We were only two floors up. But even so.

"I've had it," she goes. "I can't take it any more."

She puts her hand to her cheek and closes her eyes. She turns her head back and forth and makes this humming noise.

I could die seeing her like this.

"Take what?" I go, though of course I know.

"I don't have to spell it out for you again," she goes. "I've lost control. I've lost pride. I used to be a proud woman."

She's an attractive woman just past thirty. She is tall and has long black hair and green eyes, the only green-eyed woman I've ever known. In the old days I used to say things about green eyes, and she'd tell me it was because of them she knew she was meant for something special.

And didn't I know it!

I feel so awful from one thing and the other.

I can hear the telephone ringing downstairs in the office. It has been ringing off and on all day. Even when I was dozing I could hear it. I'd open my eyes and look at the ceiling and listen to it ring and wonder at what was happening to us.

But maybe I should be looking at the floor.

"My heart is broken," she goes. "It's turned to a piece of stone. I'm no good. That's what's as bad as anything, that I'm no good anymore."

"Holly," I go.

WHEN WE'D FIRST moved down here and taken over as managers, we thought we were out of the woods. Free rent and free utilities plus three hundred a month. You couldn't beat it with a stick.

Holly took care of the books. She was good with figures, and she did most of the renting of the units. She liked people, and people liked her back. I saw to the grounds, mowed the grass and cut weeds, kept the swimming pool clean, did the small repairs.

Everything was fine for the first year. I was holding down another job nights, and we were getting ahead. We had plans. Then one morning, I don't know. I'd just laid some bathroom tile in one of the units when this little Mexican maid comes in to clean. It was Holly had hired her. I can't really say I'd noticed the little thing before, though we spoke when we saw each other. She called me, I remember, Mister.

Anyway, one thing and the other.

So after that morning I started paying attention. She was a neat little thing with fine white teeth. I used to watch her mouth.

She started calling me by my name.

One morning I was doing a washer for one of the bathroom faucets, and she comes in and turns on the TV as maids are like to do. While they clean, that is. I stopped what I was doing and stepped outside the bathroom. She was surprised to see me. She smiles and says my name.

It was right after she said it that we got down on the bed.

"HOLLY, YOU'RE STILL a proud woman," I go. "You're still number one. Come on, Holly."

She shakes her head.

"Something's died in me," she goes. "It took a long time for it to do it, but it's dead. You've killed something, just like you'd took an axe to it. Everything is dirt now."

She finishes her drink. Then she begins to cry. I make to hug her. But it's no good.

I freshen our drinks and look out the window.

Two cars with out-of-state plates are parked in front of the office, and the drivers are standing at the door, talking. One of them finishes saying something to the other, and looks around at the units and pulls his chin. There's a woman there too, and she has her face up to the glass, hand shielding her eyes, peering inside. She tries the door.

The phone downstairs begins to ring.

"Even a while ago when we were doing it, you were thinking of her," Holly goes. "Duane, this is hurtful."

She takes the drink I give her.

"Holly," I go.

"It's true, Duane," she goes. "Just don't argue with me," she goes.

She walks up and down the room in her underpants and her brassiere, her drink in her hand.

Holly goes, "You've gone outside the marriage. It's trust that you killed."

I get down on my knees and I start to beg. But I am thinking of Juanita. This is awful. I don't know what's going to happen to me or to anyone else in the world.

I go, "Holly, honey, I love you."

In the lot someone leans on a horn, stops, and then leans again. Holly wipes her eyes. She goes, "Fix me a drink. This one's too watery. Let them blow their stinking horns. I don't care. I'm moving to Nevada."

"Don't move to Nevada," I go. "You're talking crazy," I go.

"I'm not talking crazy," she goes. "Nothing's crazy about Nevada. You can stay here with your cleaning woman. I'm moving to Nevada. Either there or kill myself."

"Holly!" I go.

"Holly *nothing*!" she goes.

She sits on the sofa and draws her knees up to under her chin.

"Fix me another pop, you son of a bitch," she goes. She goes, "Fuck those horn-blowers. Let them do their dirt in the Travelodge. Is that where your cleaning woman cleans now? Fix me another, you son of a bitch!"

She sets her lips and gives me her special look.

DRINKING'S FUNNY. When I look back on it, all of our important decisions have been figured out when we were drinking. Even when we talked about having to cut back on our drinking, we'd be sitting at the kitchen table or out at the picnic table with a six-pack or whiskey. When we made up our minds to move down here and take this job as managers, we sat up a couple of nights drinking while we weighed the pros and the cons.

I pour the last of the Teacher's into our glasses and add cubes and a spill of water.

Holly gets off the sofa and stretches on out across the bed.

She goes, "Did you do it to her in this bed?"

I don't have anything to say. I feel all out of words inside. I give her the glass and sit down in the chair. I drink my drink and think it's not ever going to be the same.

"Duane?" she goes.

"Holly?"

My heart has slowed. I wait.

Holly was my own true love.

THE THING with Juanita was five days a week between the hours of ten and eleven. It was in whatever unit she was in when she was making her cleaning rounds. I'd just walk in where she was working and shut the door behind me.

But mostly it was in 11. It was 11 that was our lucky room.

We were sweet with each other, but swift. It was fine.

I think Holly could maybe have weathered it out. I think the thing she had to do was really give it a try.

Me, I held on to the night job. A monkey could do that work. But things here were going downhill fast. We just didn't have the heart for it anymore.

I stopped cleaning the pool. It filled up with green gick so that the guests wouldn't use it anymore. I didn't fix any more faucets or lay any more tile or do any of the touch-up painting. Well, the truth is we were both hitting it pretty hard. Booze takes a lot of time and effort if you're going to do a good job with it.

Holly wasn't registering the guests right, either. She was charging too much or else not collecting what she should. Sometimes she'd put three people to a room with only one bed in it, or else she'd put a single in where the bed was king-size. I tell you, there were complaints, and sometimes there were words. Folks would load up and go somewhere else.

The next thing, there's a letter from the management people. Then there's another, certified.

There's telephone calls. There's someone coming down from the city.

But we had stopped caring, and that's a fact. We knew our days were numbered. We had fouled our lives and we were getting ready for a shake-up.

Holly's a smart woman. She knew it first.

THEN THAT SATURDAY morning we woke up after a night of rehashing the situation. We opened our eyes and turned in bed to take a good look at each other. We both knew it then. We'd reached the end of something, and the thing was to find out where new to start.

We got up and got dressed, had coffee, and decided on this talk. Without nothing interrupting. No calls. No guests.

That's when I got the Teacher's. We locked up and came upstairs here with ice, glasses, bottles. First off, we watched the color TV and frolicked some and let the phone ring away downstairs. For food, we went out and got cheese crisps from the machine.

There was this funny thing of anything could happen now that we realized everything had.

"WHEN WE WERE just kids before we married?" Holly goes. "When we had big plans and hopes? You remember?" She was sitting on the bed, holding her knees and her drink.

"I remember, Holly."

"You weren't my first, you know. My first was Wyatt. Imagine. Wyatt. And your name's Duane. Wyatt and Duane. Who knows what I was missing all those years? You were my everything, just like the song."

I go, "You're a wonderful woman, Holly. I know you've had the opportunities."

"But I didn't take them up on it!" she goes. "I couldn't go outside the marriage."

"Holly, please," I go. "No more now, honey. Let's not torture ourselves. What is it we should do?"

"Listen," she goes. "You remember the time we drove out to that old farm place outside of Yakima, out past Terrace Heights? We were just driving around? We were on this little dirt road and it was hot and dusty? We kept going and came to that old house, and you asked if could we have a drink of water? Can you imagine us doing that now? Going up to a house and asking for a drink of water?"

"Those old people must be dead now," she goes, "side by side out there in some cemetery. You remember they asked us in for cake? And later on they showed us around? And there was this gazebo there out back? It was out back under some trees? It had a little peaked roof and the paint was gone and there were these weeds growing up over the steps. And the woman said that years before, I mean a real long time ago, men used to come around and play music out there on a Sunday, and the people would sit and listen. I thought we'd be like that too when we got old enough.

Dignified. And in a place. And people would come to our door."

I can't say anything just yet. Then I go, "Holly, these things, we'll look back on them too. We'll go, 'Remember the motel with all the crud in the pool?'" I go, "You see what I'm saying, Holly?"

But Holly just sits there on the bed with her glass.

I can see she doesn't know.

I move over to the window and look out from behind the curtain. Someone says something below and rattles the door to the office. I stay there. I pray for a sign from Holly. I pray for Holly to show me.

I hear a car start. Then another. They turn on their lights against the building and, one after the other, they pull away and go out into the traffic.

"Duane," Holly goes.

In this, too, she was right.

Lucille Clifton

Lucille Clifton is the Poet Laureate of Maryland and the author of 19 children's books as well as many collections of poetry. She received a Discovery Award in 1970 and a Creative Writing Fellowship in 1973.

THE POET

i beg my bones to be good but
they keep clicking music and
i spin in the center of myself
a foolish frightful woman
moving my skin against the wind and
tap dancing for my life.

TURNING

turning into my own
turning on in
to my own self
at last
turning out of the
white cage, turning out of the
lady cage
turning at last
on a stem like a black fruit
in my own season
at last

Robert Creeley

Robert Creeley is a fine prose writer as well as a poet, whose most recent work is his *Collected Poems*. He received a Creative Writing Fellowship for Poetry in 1981.

MOTHER'S VOICE

IN THESE few years
since her death I hear
mother's voice say
under my own, I won't

want any more of that.
My cheekbones resonate
with her emphasis. Nothing
of not wanting only

but the distance there from
common fact of others
frightens me. I look out
at all this demanding world

and try to put it quietly back,
from me, say, thank you,
I've already had some
though I haven't

and would like to
but I've said no, she has,
it's not my own voice anymore.

It's higher as hers was
and accommodates too simply
its frustrations when
I at least think I want more
and must have it.

Robert Duncan

Robert Duncan has had a long career as a poet and writer. His books include *Roots & Branches, Bending the Bow* and *Ground Work: Before the War*. In 1966, he received a publication award for work included in the American Literary Anthology; in 1967 a Work-in-Progress grant; and in 1980 a Senior Fellowship.

Variations On

TWO DICTA OF WILLIAM BLAKE:

> *Mental things alone are real.*
> *The Authors are in Eternity.*

I

THE AUTHORS are in eternity.
Our eyes reflect
prospects of the whole radiance
between you and me

where we have lookd up
        each from his being.
And I am the word "each".
And you are the word "his".

        Each his being
a single glance the authors see
        as part of the poetry of what is, what
we suffer. You talkd of "freedom",
        and I saw
how foreign I am from me,

saw the spark struck from the black rock,

saw I was not free to obey
and for a moment might have been free.

I had only to reach up,
restore our hands touching,
speak the words direct the authors struck.

You are the black rock, you are the spark,

eternally.

2

How long dare I withhold myself
my Lord withholds.

I shy a glance that he too shies.
The authors of the look
write with our eyes
broken phrases of their book.

Why is it you?
Because my senses swarm,
I fear what harm?

"Compulsion" you spoke of then
that makes us men less than Man,
moved as we are. Move my hand,
bright star,
if you are there, author out of the light.

Why could I not move my hand?
Why can I not move my hand?
waiting, a word in a moving sentence,
just at the point where
the authors reveal (but their revelation
is everywhere) the book.

I recognized in you my own presence
beyond touch, within being.
What could I reach, reacht as I was?

The authors are in eternity.

3

I am the author of the authors
and I am here. I do not dare
rescue myself in you
or you in me. Such a dark trouble
stirs in every act.
For what do I know of from where I come?
and others shall attend me
when I am gone.

What I am is only a factor of what I am.
The authors of the author
before and after
wait for me to restore
(I had only to touch you then)
the way to the eternal
sparks of desire.

4

Come, eyes, see more than you see!
For the world within and the outer world
rejoice as one. The seminal brain
contains the lineaments of eternity.

5

Mental things alone are real.

There is no mental thing unrealized.

To be a man – but we are men
who are of one mind. For the flower of nerves
and tissue in the skull
calls, O messengers of the boundaries,
        eyes of every cell,   touch, touch,
complete me such a world as I contain

        where angels move like waves,
            convulsive energies,
lighting ways in me you do not see,
        have not seen them.

They were there for they are here.
        You overlookt or, seeing them,
changed focus and dismisst them.

        O fearful eyes,
O cells that are all doubt and reckoning,
        accommodation's slaves!

You've only to restore what I know to sight
        to realize the flash
that was eternity – a world –
        in the heart's delight.

6

For the heart, my sister,
is likewise a dark organ, an inner
        suitor, my brother, a part
            of the whole yearning.

And there must have been a flood of,
        an up-rush, a change in pulse.
For when we see an answer,
        as the young man in moving answerd,

in leaning forward toward rapture
    where Charles Olson read,
answerd, or disturbd, some question

  — the poet's voice, a whole beauty of the man Olson,
     lifting us up into

where the disturbance is, where the words
    awaken
sensory chains between being and being,
    inner acknowledgments
of the fiery masters — there
    like stellar bees my senses swarmd.

Here, again, I have come close upon what harm?
    where the honey is,
charmd by the consideration of his
    particular form,

as by lines in the poem charmd.

7

There was the event there was.

    That is

recomposed in the withholding.

The whole of time waits like a hand
    trembling upon the edge of another hand,
    trembling upon the edge of not caring,
    trembling upon the edge of its eternal answer

    That is

not ours in the withholding.

We wait, two Others, outside ever
   our eternal being

That is

here, in this sad tableau too,
   (for us, unwilling actors)
   rapture.

The authors are in eternity

That is

in thought intensely between us,
restraint that acknowledges

   the lover's kiss.

Stanley Elkin

Stanley Elkin's published writing includes *Searches & Seizures, The Franchiser, George Mills* (winner of the National Book Critics Circle Award for fiction) and, most recently, *Stanley Elkin's Magic Kingdom*. He received a Creative Writing Fellowship in 1972.

THE CONVENTIONAL WISDOM

ELLERBEE HAD BEEN having a bad time of it. He'd had financial reversals. Change would slip out of his pockets and slide down into the crevices of other people's furniture. He dropped deposit bottles and lost money in pay phones and vending machines. He overtipped in dark taxicabs. He had many such financial reversals. He was stuck with Super Bowl tickets when he was suddenly called out of town and with theater and opera tickets when the ice was too slick to move his car out of his driveway. But all this was small potatoes. His portfolio was a disgrace. He had gotten into mutual funds at the wrong time and out at a worse. His house, appraised for tax purposes at many thousands of dollars below its replacement cost, burned down, and recently his once flourishing liquor store, one of the largest in Minneapolis, had drawn the attentions of burly, hopped-up and armed deprivators, ski-masked, head-stockinged. Two of his clerks had been shot, one killed, the other crippled and brain damaged, during the most recent visitation by these marauders, and Ellerbee, feeling a sense of responsibility, took it upon himself to support his clerks' families. His wife reproached him for this, which led to bad feeling between them.

"Weren't they insured?"

"I don't know, May. I suppose they had some insurance but how much could it have been? One was just a kid out of college."

"Whatshisname, the vegetable."

"Harold, May."

"What about whosis? He was no kid out of college."

"George died protecting my store, May."

"Some protection. The black bastards got away with over four-teen hundred bucks." When the police called to tell him of the very first robbery, May had asked if the men had been black. It hurt Ellerbee that this should have been her first question. "Who's going to protect you? The insurance companies red-lined that lousy neighborhood a year ago. We won't get a penny."

"I'm selling the store, May. I can't afford to run it anymore."

"Selling? Who'd buy it? *Selling!*"

"I'll see what I can get for it," Ellerbee said.

"Social Security pays them benefits," May said, picking up their quarrel again the next day. "Social Security pays up to the time the kids are eighteen years old, and they give to the widow, too. Who do you think you are, anyway? We lose a house and have to move into one not half as good because it's all we can afford, and you want to keep on paying the salaries not only of two people who no longer work for you, but to pay them out of a business that you mean to sell! Let Social Security handle it."

Ellerbee, who had looked into it, answered May. "Harold started with me this year. Social Security pays according to what you've put into the system. Dorothy won't get three hundred a month, May. And George's girl is twenty. Evelyn won't even get that much."

"Idealist," May said. "Martyr."

"Leave off, will you, May? I'm responsible. I'm under an obligation."

"Responsible, under an obligation!"

"Indirectly. God damn it, yes. Indirectly. They worked for me, didn't they? It's a combat zone down there. I should have had security guards around the clock."

"Where are you going to get all this money? We've had financial reverses. You're selling the store. Where's this money coming from to support three families?"

"We'll get it."

"*We'll* get it? There's no we'll about it, Mister. *You'll.* The stocks are in joint tenancy. You can't touch them, and I'm not signing a thing. Not a penny comes out of my mouth or off my back."

"All right, May," Ellerbee said. "I'll get it."

In fact Ellerbee had a buyer in mind — a syndicate that specialized in buying up businesses in decaying neighborhoods — liquor and drugstores, small groceries — and then put in ex-convicts as personnel, Green Berets from Vietnam, off-duty policemen, experts in the martial arts. Once the word was out, no one ever attempted to rob these places. The syndicate hiked the price of each item at least 20 percent — and got it. Ellerbee was fascinated and appalled by their strong-arm tactics. Indeed, he more than a little suspected that it was the syndicate itself which had been robbing him — all three times his store had been held up he had not been in it — to inspire him to sell, perhaps.

"We read about your trouble in the paper," Mr. Davis, the lawyer for the syndicate, had told him on the occasion of his first robbery. The thieves had gotten away with $300 and there was a four-line notice on the inside pages. "Terrible," he said, "terrible. A fine old neighborhood like this one. And it's the same all over America today. Everywhere it's the same story. Even in Kansas, even in Utah. They shoot you with bullets, they take your property. Terrible. The people I represent have the know-how to run businesses like yours in the spoiled neighborhoods." And then he had been offered a ridiculous price for his store and stock. Of course he turned it down. When he was robbed a second time, the lawyer didn't even bother to come in person. "Terrible. Terrible," he said. "Whoever said lightning doesn't strike twice in the same place was talking through his hat. I'm authorized to offer you ten thousand less than I did the last time." Ellerbee hung up on him.

Now, after his clerks had been shot, it was Ellerbee who called the lawyer. "Awful," the lawyer said. "Outrageous. A merchant shouldn't have to sit still for such things in a democracy."

They gave him even less than the insurance people had given him for his underappraised home. Ellerbee accepted, but decided it was time he at least hint to Davis that he knew what was going on. "I'm selling," he said, "because I don't want anyone else to die."

"Wonderful," Davis said, "wonderful. There should be more Americans like you."

He deposited the money he got from the syndicate in a separate account so that his wife would have no claims on it and now, while he had no business to go to, he was able to spend more time in the hospital visiting Harold.

"How's Harold today, Mrs. Register?" he asked when he came into the room where the mindless quadraplegic was being cared for. Dorothy Register was a red-haired young woman in her early twenties. Ellerbee felt so terrible about what had happened, so guilty, that he had difficulty talking to her. He knew it would be impossible to visit Harold if he was going to run into his wife when he did so. It was for this reason, too, that he sent the checks rather than drop them off at the apartment, much as he wanted to see Hal's young son, Harold, Jr., in order to reassure the child that there was still a man around to take care of the boy and his young mother.

"Oh, Mr. Ellerbee," the woman wept. Harold seemed to smile at them through his brain damage.

"Please, Mrs. Register," said Ellerbee, "Harold shouldn't see you like this."

"Him? He doesn't understand a thing. You don't understand a thing, do you?" she said, turning on her husband sharply. When she made a move to poke at his eyes with a fork he didn't even blink. "Oh, Mr. Ellerbee," she said, turning away from her husband, "that's not the man I married. It's awful, but I don't feel anything for him. The only reason I come is that the doctors say I cheer him up. Though I can't see how. He smiles that way at his bedpan."

"Please, Mrs. Register," Ellerbee said softly. "You've got to be strong. There's little Hal."

"I know," she moaned, "I know." She wiped the tears from her eyes and sniffed and tossed her hair in a funny little way she had which Ellerbee found appealing. "I'm sorry," she said. "You've been very kind. I don't know what I would have done, what *we* would have done. I can't even thank you," she said helplessly.

"Oh don't think about it, there's no need," Ellerbee said quickly. "I'm not doing any more for you than I am for George Lesefario's widow." It was not a boast. Ellerbee had mentioned the older woman because he didn't want Mrs. Register to feel compromised. "It's company policy when these things happen," he said gruffly.

Dorothy Register nodded. "I heard," she said, "that you sold your store."

He hastened to reassure her. "Oh now listen," Ellerbee said, "you mustn't give that a thought. The checks will continue. I'm getting another store. In a very lovely neighborhood. Near where we used to live before our house burned down."

"Really?"

"Oh yes. I should be hearing about my loan any time now. I'll probably be in the new place before the month is out. Well," he said, "speaking of which, I'd better get going. There are some fixtures I'm supposed to look at at the Wine and Spirits Mart." He waved to Harold.

"Mr. Ellerbee?"

"Mrs. Register?"

The tall redhead came close to him and put her hands on his shoulders. She made that funny little gesture with her hair again and Ellerbee almost died. She was about his own height and leaned forward and kissed him on the mouth. Her fingernails grazed the back of his neck. Tears came to Ellerbee's eyes and he turned away from her gently. He hoped she hadn't seen the small lump in his trousers. He said goodbye with his back to her.

The loan went through. The new store, as Ellerbee had said, was in one of the finest neighborhoods in the city. In a small shopping mall, it was flanked by a good bookstore and a fine French restaurant. The Ellerbees had often eaten there before their house burned to the ground. There was an art cinema, a florist, and elegant haberdashers and dress shops. The liquor shop, called High Spirits, a name Ellerbee decided to keep after he bought the place, stocked, in addition to the usual gins, Scotches, bourbons, vodkas, and blends, some really superior wines, and Ellerbee was forced to become something of an expert in oenology. He listened to his customers – doctors and lawyers, most of them – and in this way was able to pick up a good deal.

The business flourished – doing so well that after only his second month in the new location he no longer felt obliged to stay open on Sundays – though his promise to his clerks' families, which he kept, prevented him from making the inroads into his extravagant debt that he would have liked. Mrs. Register began to come to the store to collect the weekly checks personally. "I thought I'd save you the stamp," she said each time. Though he enjoyed seeing her – she looked rather like one of those splendid wives of the successful doctors who shopped there – he thought he should discourage this. He made it clear to her that he would be sending the checks.

Then she came and said that it was foolish, his continuing to pay her husband's salary, that at least he ought to let her do something to earn it. She saw that the suggestion made him uncomfortable and clarified what she meant.

"Oh no," she said, "all I meant was that you ought to hire me. I was a hostess once. For that matter I could wait on trade."

"Well, I've plenty of help, Mrs. Register. Really. As I may have told you, I've kept on all the people who used to work for Anderson." Anderson was the man from whom he'd bought High Spirits.

"It's not as though you'd be hiring additional help. I'm costing you the money anyway."

It would have been pleasant to have the woman around, but Ellerbee nervously held his ground. "At a time like this," he said, "you ought to be with the boy."

"You're quite a guy," she said. It was the last time they saw each other. A few months later, while he was examining his bank statements, he realized that she had not been cashing his checks. He called her at once.

"I can't," she said. "I'm young. I'm strong." He remembered her fierce embrace in her husband's hospital room. "There's no reason for you to continue to send me those checks. I have a good job now. I can't accept them any longer." It was the last time they spoke.

And then he learned that George's widow was ill. He heard about it indirectly. One of his best customers — a psychiatrist — was beeped on the emergency Medi-Call he carried in his jacket, and asked for change to use Ellerbee's pay phone.

"That's not necessary, Doc," Ellerbee said, "use the phone behind my counter."

"Very kind," the psychiatrist said, and came back of the counter. He dialed his service. "Doctor Potter. What have you got for me, Nancy? What? She did *what*? Just a minute, let me get a pencil. — Bill?" Ellerbee handed him a pencil. "Lesefario, right. I've got that. Give me the surgeon's number. Right. Thanks, Nancy."

"Excuse me, Doctor," Ellerbee said. "I hadn't meant to listen, but Lesefario, that's an unusual name. I know an Evelyn Lesefario."

"That's the one," said the medical man. "Oh," he said, "you're *that* Ellerbee. Well, she's been very depressed. She just tried to kill herself by eating a mile of dental floss."

"I HOPE she dies," his wife said.

"*May!*" said Ellerbee, shocked.

"It's what she wants, isn't it? I hope she gets what she wants."

"That's harsh, May."

"Yes? Harsh? You see how much good your checks did her? And another thing, how could she afford a high-priced man like Potter on what *you* were paying her?"

He went to visit the woman during her post-operative convalescence, and she introduced him to her sister, her twin she said, though the two women looked nothing alike and the twin seemed to be in her seventies, a good dozen years older than Mrs. Lesefario. "This is Mr. Ellerbee that my husband died protecting his liquor store from the niggers."

"Oh yes?" Mrs. Lesefario's sister said. "Very pleased. I heard so much about you."

"Look what she brought me," Mrs. Lesefario said, pointing to a large brown paper sack.

"Evelyn, don't. You'll strain your stitches. I'll show him." She opened the sack and took out a five-pound sack of sugar.

"Five pounds of sugar," the melancholic woman said.

"You don't come empty-handed to a sick person," her sister said.

"She got it at Kroger's on special. Ninety-nine cents with the coupon," the manic-depressive said gloomily. "She says if I don't like it I can get peach halves."

Ellerbee, who did not want to flaunt his own gift in front of her sister, quietly put the dressing gown, still wrapped, on her tray table. He stayed for another half hour, and rose to go.

"Wait," Mrs. Lesefario said. "Nice try but not so fast."

"I'm sorry?" Ellerbee said.

"The ribbon."

"Ribbon?"

"On the fancy box. The ribbon, the string."

"Oh, your stitches. Sorry. I'll get it."

"I'm a would-be suicide," she said. "I tried it once, I could try it again. You don't bring dangerous ribbon to a desperate, unhappy woman."

In fact Mrs. Lesefario did die. Not of suicide, but of a low-grade infection she had picked up in the hospital and which festered along her stitches, undermining them, burning through them, opening her body like a package.

The Ellerbees were in the clear financially, but his wife's reactions to Ellerbee's efforts to provide for his clerks' families had soured their relationship. She had discovered Ellerbee's private account and accused him of dreadful things. He reminded her that it had been she who had insisted he would have to get the money for the women's support himself — that their joint tenancy was not to be disturbed. She ignored his arguments and accused him further. Ellerbee loved May and did what he could to placate her.

"How about a trip to Phoenix?" he suggested that spring. "The store's doing well and I have complete confidence in Kroll. What about it, May? You like Phoenix, and we haven't seen the folks in almost a year."

"Phoenix," she scoffed, "the *folks*. The way you coddle them. Any other grown man would be ashamed."

"They raised me, May."

"They raised you. Terrific. They aren't even your real parents. They only adopted you."

"They're the only parents I ever knew. They took me out of the Home when I was an infant."

"Look, you want to go to Phoenix, go. Take money out of your secret accounts and go."

"Please, May. There's no secret account. When Mrs. Lesefario died I transferred everything back into joint. Come on, sweetheart, you're awfully goddamn hard on me."

"Well," she said, drawing the word out. The tone was one she had used as a bride, and although Ellerbee had not often heard it since, it melted him. It was her signal of sudden conciliation, cute surrender, and he held out his arms and they embraced. They went off to the bedroom together.

"You know," May said afterwards, "it *would* be good to run out to Phoenix for a bit. Are you sure the help can manage?"

"Oh, sure, May, absolutely. They're a first-rate bunch." He spoke more forcefully than he felt, not because he lacked confidence in his employees, but because he was still disturbed by an image he had had during climax. Momentarily, fleetingly, he had imagined Mrs. Register beneath him.

In the store he was giving last-minute instructions to Kroll, the man who would be his manager during their vacation in Phoenix.

"I think the Californias," Ellerbee was saying. "Some of them beat several of even the more immodest French. Let's do a promotion of a few of the better Californias. What do you think?"

"They're a very competitive group of wines," Kroll said. "I think I'm in basic agreement."

Just then three men walked into the shop.

"Say," one called from the doorway, "you got something like a Closed sign I could hang in the door here?" Ellerbee stared at him. "Well you don't have to look at me as if I was nuts," the man said. "Lots of merchants keep them around. In case they get a sudden toothache or something they can whip out to the dentist. All right, if you ain't you ain't."

"I want," the second man said, coming up to the counter where

Ellerbee stood with his manager, "to see your register receipts."

"What is this?" Kroll demanded.

"No, don't," Ellerbee said to Kroll. "Don't resist." He glanced toward the third man to see if he was the one holding the gun, but the man appeared merely to be browsing the bins of Scotch in the back. Evidently he hadn't even heard the first man, and clearly he could not have heard the second. Conceivably he could have been a customer. "Where's your gun?" Ellerbee asked the man at the counter.

"Oh gee," the man said, "I almost forgot. You got so many things to think about during a stickup – the traffic flow, the timing, who stands where – you sometimes forget the basics. Here," he said, "here's my gun, in your kisser," and he took an immense handgun from his pocket and pointed it at Ellerbee's face.

Out of the corner of his eye Ellerbee saw Kroll's hands fly up. It was so blatant a gesture Ellerbee thought his manager might be trying to attract the customer's attention. If that was his idea it had worked, for the third man had turned away from the bins and was watching the activity at the counter. "Look," Ellerbee said, "I don't want anybody hurt."

"What's he say?" said the man at the door who was also holding a pistol now.

"He don't want nobody hurt," the man at the counter said.

"Sure," said the man at the door, "it's costing him a fortune paying all them salaries to the widows. He's a good businessman all right."

"A better one than you," the man at the counter said to his confederate sharply. "He knows how to keep his mouth shut."

Why, they're white, Ellerbee thought. They're *white* men! He felt oddly justified and wished May were there to see.

"The register receipts," the man at the counter coaxed. Ellerbee's cash register kept a running total on what had been taken in. "Just punch Total Tab," the man instructed Kroll. "Let's see what we got." Kroll looked at Ellerbee and Ellerbee nodded. The man reached forward and tore off the tape. He whistled. "Nice little place you got here," he said.

"What'd we get? What'd we get?" the man at the door shouted.

Ellerbee cleared his throat. "Do you want to lock the door?" he asked. "So no one else comes in?" He glanced toward the third man.

"What, and have you kick the alarm while we're fucking around trying to figure which key opens the place?" said the man at the door. "You're cute, you're a cutie. What'd we get? Let's see." He joined the man at the counter. "Holy smoke! Jackpot City! We're into four figures here." In his excitement he did a foolish thing. He set his revolver down on top of the appetizer table. It lay on the tins of caviar and smoked oysters, the imported cheeses and roasted peanuts. The third man was no more than four feet from the gun, and though Ellerbee saw that the man had caught the robber's mistake and that by taking one step toward the table he could have picked up the pistol and perhaps foiled the robbery, he made no move. Perhaps he's one of them, Ellerbee thought, or maybe he just doesn't want to get involved. Ellerbee couldn't remember ever having seen him. (By now, of course, he recognized all his repeat customers.) He still didn't know if he were a confederate or just an innocent bystander, but Ellerbee had had enough of violence and hoped that if he *were* a customer he wouldn't try anything dumb. He felt no animus toward the man at all. Kroll's face, however, was all scorn and loathing.

"Let's get to work," the man said who had first read the tape, and then to Kroll and Ellerbee, "Back up there. Go stand by the aperitifs."

The third man fell silently into step beside Ellerbee.

"Listen," Ellerbee explained as gently as he could, "you won't find that much cash in the drawer. A lot of our business is Master Charge. We take personal checks."

"Don't worry," the man said who had set his gun down (and who had taken it up again). "We know about the checks. We got a guy we can sell them to for — what is it, Ron, seventeen cents on the dollar?"

"Fourteen, and why don't you shut your mouth, will you? You want to jeopardize these people? What do you make it?"

Ellerbee went along with his sentiments. He wished the bigmouth would just take the money and not say anything more.

"Oh, jeopardize," the man said. "How jeopardized can you get? These people are way past jeopardized. About six hundred in cash, a fraction in checks. The rest is all credit card paper."

"Take it," Ron said.

"You won't be able to do anything with the charge slips," Kroll said.

"Oh yeah?" Ron's cohort said. "This is modern times, fellow. We got a way we launder Master Charge, BankAmericard, all of it."

Ron shook his head and Ellerbee glanced angrily at his manager.

The whole thing couldn't have taken four minutes. Ron's partner took a fifth of Chivas and a bottle of Lafitte '47. He's a doctor, Ellerbee thought.

"You got a bag?"

"A bag?" Ellerbee said.

"A bag, a paper bag, a doggy bag for the boodle."

"Behind the counter," Ellerbee said hopelessly.

The partner put the cash and the bottle of Chivas into one bag and handed it to Ron, and the wine, checks, and credit charges into a second bag which he held on to himself. They turned to go. They looked exactly like two satisfied customers. They were almost at the door when Ron's partner nudged Ron. "Oh, yeah," Ron said, and turned back to look at them. "My friend, Jay Ladlehaus, is right," he said, "you know too much."

Ellerbee heard two distinct shots before he fell.

When he came to, the third man was bending over him. "You're not hurt," Ellerbee said.

"Me? No."

The pain was terrific, diffuse, but fiercer than anything he had ever felt. He saw himself covered with blood. "Where's Kroll? The other man, my manager?"

"Kroll's all right."

"He is?"

"There, right beside you."

He tried to look. They must have blasted Ellerbee's throat away, half his spinal column. It was impossible for him to move his head. "I can't see him," he moaned.

"Kroll's fine." The man cradled Ellerbee's shoulders and neck and shifted him slightly. "There. See?" Kroll's eyes were shut. Oddly, both were blackened. He had fallen in such a way that he seemed to lie on both his arms, retracted behind him into the small of his back like a yogi. His mouth was open and his tongue floated in blood like meat in soup. A slight man, he seemed strangely bloated, and one shin, exposed to Ellerbee's vision where the trouser leg was hiked up above his sock, was discolored as thundercloud.

The man gently set Ellerbee down again. "Call an ambulance," Ellerbee wheezed through his broken throat.

"No, no. Kroll's fine."

"He's not conscious." It was as if his words were being mashed through the tines of a fork.

"He'll be all right. Kroll's fine."

"Then for *me*. Call one for *me*."

"It's too late for you," the man said.

"For Christ's sake, will you!" Ellerbee gasped. "I can't move. You could have grabbed that hoodlum's gun when he set it down. All right, you were scared, but some of this is your fault. You didn't lift a finger. At least call an ambulance."

"But you're dead," he said gently. "Kroll will recover. You passed away when you said 'move'."

"Are you crazy? What are you talking about?"

"Do you feel pain?"

"What?"

"Pain. You don't feel any, do you?" Ellerbee stared at him. "Do you?"

He didn't. His pain was gone. "Who are you?" Ellerbee said.

"I'm an angel of death," the angel of death said.

"You're — "

"An angel of death."

Somehow he had left his body. He could see it lying next to Kroll's. "I'm dead? But if I'm dead — you mean there's really an afterlife?"

"Oh boy," the angel of death said.

THEY WENT to Heaven.

Ellerbee couldn't have said how they got there or how long it took, though he had the impression that time had passed, and distance. It was rather like a journey in films — a series of quick cuts, of montage. He was probably dreaming, he thought.

"It's what they all think," the angel of death said, "that they're dreaming. But that isn't so."

"I could have dreamed you said that," Ellerbee said, "that you read my mind."

"Yes."

"I could be dreaming all of it, the holdup, everything."

The angel of death looked at him.

"Hobgoblin...I could..." Ellerbee's voice — if it was a voice — trailed off.

"Look," the angel of death said, "I talk too much. I sound like a cabbie with an out-of-town fare. It's an occupational hazard."

"What?"

"*What?* Pride. The proprietary air. Showing off death like a booster. Thanatopography. 'If you look to your left you'll see where...Julius Cæsar de dum de dum...Shakespeare da da da.... And dead ahead our Father Adam heigh ho — ' The tall buildings and the four-star sights. All that Bædeker reality of plaque place and high history. The Fields of Homer and the Plains of Myth. Where whosis got locked in a star and all the Agriculture of the Periodic Table — the South Forty of the Universe, where Hydrogen first bloomed, where Lithium, Berylium, Zirconium, Niobium. Where Lead failed and Argon came a cropper. The furrows of gold, Bismuth's orchards....Still think you're dreaming?"

"No."

"Why not?"

"The language."

"Just so," the angel of death said. "When you were alive you had a vocabulary of perhaps seventeen or eighteen hundred words. Who am I?"

"An eschatological angel," Ellerbee said shyly.

"One hundred percent," the angel of death said. "Why do we do that?"

"To heighten perception," Ellerbee said, and shuddered.

The angel of death nodded and said nothing more.

When they were close enough to make out the outlines of Heaven, the angel left him and Ellerbee, not questioning this, went on alone. From this distance it looked to Ellerbee rather like a theme park, but what struck him most forcibly was that it did not seem – for Heaven – very large.

He traveled as he would on Earth, distance familiar again, volume, mass, and dimension restored, ordinary. (*Quotidian*, Ellerbee thought.) Indeed, now that he was convinced of his death, nothing seemed particularly strange. If anything, it was all a little familiar. He began to miss May. She would have learned of his death by this time. Difficult as the last year had been, they had loved each other. It had been a good marriage. He regretted again that they had been unable to have children. Children – they would be teenagers now – would have been a comfort to his widow. She still had her looks. Perhaps she would remarry. He did not want her to be lonely.

He continued toward Heaven and now, only blocks away, he was able to perceive it in detail. It looked more like a theme park than ever. It was enclosed behind a high milky fence, the uprights smooth and round as the poles in subway trains. Beyond the fence were golden streets, a mixed architecture of minaret-spiked mosques, great cathedrals, the rounded domes of classical synagogues, tall pagodas like holy vertebræ, white frame churches with their beautiful steeples, even what Ellerbee took to be a storefront church. There were many mansions. But where were the people?

Just as he was wondering about this he heard the sound of a gorgeous chorus. It was making a joyful noise. "Oh dem golden slippers," the chorus sang, "Oh dem golden slippers." It's the Heavenly Choir, Ellerbee thought. They've actually got a Heavenly Choir. He went toward the fence and put his hands on the smooth posts and peered through into Heaven. He heard laughter and caught a glimpse of the running heels of children just disappearing around the corner of a golden street. They all wore shoes.

Ellerbee walked along the fence for about a mile and came to gates made out of pearl. The Pearly Gates, he thought. There are actually Pearly Gates. An old man in a long white beard sat behind them, a key attached to a sort of cinch that went about his waist. "Saint Peter?" Ellerbee ventured. The old man turned his shining countenance upon him. "Saint Peter," Ellerbee said again, "I'm Ellerbee."

"I'm Saint Peter," Saint Peter said.

"Gosh," Ellerbee said, "I can't get over it. It's all true."

"What is?"

"Everything. Heaven. The streets of gold, the Pearly Gates. You. Your key. The Heavenly Choir. The climate."

A soft breeze came up from inside Heaven and Ellerbee sniffed something wonderful in the perfect air. He looked toward the venerable old man.

"Ambrosia," the Saint said.

"There's actually ambrosia," Ellerbee said.

"You know," Saint Peter said, "you never get tired of it, you never even get used to it. He does that to whet our appetite."

"You eat in Heaven?"

"We eat manna."

"There's actually manna," Ellerbee said. An angel floated by on a fleecy cloud playing a harp. Ellerbee shook his head. He had never heard anything so beautiful. "Heaven is everything they say it is," he said.

"It's paradise," Saint Peter said.

Then Ellerbee saw an affecting sight. Nearby, husbands were reunited with wives, mothers with their small babes, daddies with their sons, brothers with sisters — all the intricate blood loyalties and enlisted loves. He understood all the relationships without being told — his heightened perception. What was most moving, however, were the old people, related or not, some just lifelong friends, people who had lived together or known one another much the greater part of their lives and then had lost each other. It was immensely touching to Ellerbee to see them gaze fondly into one another's eyes and then to watch them reach out and touch the patient, ancient faces, wrinkled and even withered but, Ellerbee could tell, unchanged in the loving eyes of the adoring beholder. If there were tears they were tears of joy, tears that melded inextricably with tender laughter. There was rejoicing, there were Hosannas, there was dancing in the golden streets. "It's wonderful," Ellerbee muttered to himself. He didn't know where to look first. He would be staring at the beautiful flowing raiments of the angels – There are actually raiments, he thought, there are actually angels – so fine, he imagined, to the touch that just the caress of the cloth must have produced exquisite sensations not matched by anything in life, when something else would strike him. The perfectly proportioned angels' wings like discrete Gothic windows, the beautiful halos – There are actually halos – like golden quoits, or, in the distance, the lovely green pastures, delicious as fairway – all the perfectly banked turns of Heaven's geography. He saw philosophers deep in conversation. He saw kings and heroes. It was astonishing to him, like going to an exclusive restaurant one has only read about in columns and spotting, even at first glance, the celebrities one has read about, relaxed, passing the time of day, out in the open, up-front and sharing their high-echelon lives.

"This is for keeps?" he asked Saint Peter. "I mean it goes on like this?"

"World without end," Saint Peter said.

"Where's…"

"That's all right, say His name."

"God?" Ellerbee whispered.

Saint Peter looked around. "I don't see Him just….Oh, wait. *There!*" Ellerbee turned where the old Saint was pointing. He shaded his eyes. "There's no need," Saint Peter said.

"But the aura, the light."

"Let it shine."

He took his hand away fearfully and the light spilled into his eyes like soothing unguents. God was on His throne in the green pastures, Christ at His right Hand. To Ellerbee it looked like a picture taken at a summit conference.

"He's beautiful. I've never… It's ecstasy."

"And you're seeing Him from a pretty good distance. You should talk to Him sometime."

"People can talk to Him?"

"Certainly. He loves us."

There were tears in Ellerbee's eyes. He wished May no harm, but wanted her with him to see it all. "It's wonderful."

"We like it," Saint Peter said.

"Oh, I do too," Ellerbee said. "I'm going to be very happy here."

"Go to Hell," Saint Peter said beatifically.

HELL WAS the ultimate inner city. Its stinking sulfurous streets were unsafe. Everywhere Ellerbee looked he saw atrocities. Pointless, profitless muggings were commonplace; joyless rape that punished its victims and offered no relief to the perpetrator. Everything was contagious, cancer as common as a cold, plague the quotidian. There was stomachache, headache, toothache, earache. There was angina and indigestion and painful third-degree burning itch. Nerves like a hideous body hair grew long enough to trip over and lay raw and exposed as live wires or shoelaces that had come undone.

There was no handsomeness, no beauty, no one walked upright, no one had good posture. There was nothing to look at – although it was impossible to shut one's eyes – except the tumbled kaleidoscope variations of warted deformity. This was one reason, Ellerbee supposed, that there was so little conversation in Hell. No one could stand to look at anyone else long enough. Occasionally two or three – lost souls? gargoyles? devils? demons? – of the damned, jumping about in the heat first on one foot then the other, would manage to stand with their backs to each other and perhaps get out a few words – a foul whining. But even this was rare and when it happened that a sufferer had the attention of a fellow sufferer he could howl out only a half-dozen or so words before breaking off in a piercing scream.

Ellerbee, constantly nauseated, eternally in pain, forever befouling himself, longed to find something to do, however tedious or make-work or awful. For a time he made paths through the smoldering cinders, but he had no tools and had to use his bare feet, moving the cinders to one side as a boy shuffles through fallen leaves hunting something lost. It was too painful. Then he thought he would make channels for the vomit and excrement and blood. It was too disgusting. He shouted for others to join him in work details – "Break up the fights, pile up the scabs" – and even ministered to the less aggravated wounds, using his hands to wipe away the gangrenous drool since there was no fabric in Hell, all clothing consumed within minutes of arrival, flesh alone inconsumable, glowing and burning with his bones slow as phosphor. Calling out, suggesting in screams which may have been incoherent, all manner of pointless, arbitrary arrangements – that they organize the damned, that they count them. Demanding that their howls be synchronous.

No one stopped him. No one seemed to be in charge. He saw, that is, no Devil, no Archfiend. There were demons with cloven feet and scaly tails, with horns and pitchforks – They actually have horns, Ellerbee thought, there are actually pitchforks – but these seemed to have no more authority than he had himself, and when they were piqued to wrath by their own torment the jabs they made at the human damned with their sharp arsenal were no more painful – and no less – than anything else down there.

Then Ellerbee felt he understood something terrible – that the abortive rapes and fights and muggings were simply a refinement of his own attempts to socialize. They did it to make contact, to be friendly.

He was free to wander the vast burning meadows of Hell and to scale its fiery hills – and for many years he did – but it was much the same all over. What he was actually looking for was its Source, Hell's bright engine room, its storm-tossed bridge. It had no engine room, there was no bridge, its energy, all its dreadful combustion coming perhaps from the cumulative, collective agony of the inmates. Nothing could be done.

He was distracted, as he was sure they all were – "Been to Heaven?" he'd managed to gasp to an old man whose back was on fire and the man had nodded – by his memory of Paradise, his long-distance glimpse of God. It was unbearable to think of Heaven in his present condition, his memory of that spectacular place poisoned by the discrepancy between the exaltation of the angels and the plight of the damned. It was the old story of the disappointment of rising expectations. Still, without his bidding, thoughts of Paradise force-fed themselves almost constantly into his skull. They induced sadness, rage.

He remembered the impression he'd had of celebrity when he'd stood looking in at Heaven from beyond the Pearly Gates, and he thought to look out for the historic bad men, the celebrated damned, but either they were kept in a part of Hell he had not yet seen or their sufferings had made them unrecognizable. If there were great men in Hell he did not see them and, curiously, no one ever boasted of his terrible deeds or notoriety. Indeed, except for the outbursts of violence, most of the damned behaved, considering their state, in a respectable fashion, even an exemplary one. Perhaps, Ellerbee thought, it was because they had not yet abandoned hope. (There was actually a sign: "Abandon Hope, All Ye Who Enter Here." Ellerbee had read it.)

For several years he waited for May, for as long, that is, as he could remember her. Constant pain and perpetual despair chipped away at most of the memories he had of his life. It was possible to recall who and what he had been, but that was as fruitless as any other enterprise in the dark region. Ultimately, like everything else, it worked against him – Hell's fine print. It was best to forget. And that worked against him too.

He took the advice written above Hellgate. He abandoned hope, and with it memory, pity, pride, his projects, the sense he had of injustice – for a little while driving off, along with his sense of identity, even his broken recollection of glory. It was probably what they – whoever they were – wanted. Let them have it. Let them have the straight lines of their trade wind, trade route, through street, thrown stone vengeance. Let them have everything. Their pastels back and their blues and their greens, the recollection of gratified thirst, and the transient comfort of a sandwich and beer that had hit the spot, all the retrospective of good weather, a good night's sleep, a good joke, a good tune, a good time, the entire mosaic of small satisfactions that made up a life. Let them have his image of his parents and friends, the fading portrait of May he couldn't quite shake, the pleasure he'd had from work, from his body. Let them have all of it, his measly joy, his scrapbook past, his hope, too.

Which left only pure pain, the grand vocabulary they had given him to appreciate it, to discriminate and parse among the exquisite lesions and scored flesh and violated synapses, among the insulted nerves, joints, muscle and tissue, all the boiled kindling points of torment and the body's grief. That was all he was now, staggering Hiroshima'd flesh – a vessel of nausea, a pail of pain.

He continued thus for several years, his amnesia willed – There's Free Will, Ellerbee thought – shuffling Hell in his rote aphasia, his stripped self a sealed environment of indifference. There were years he did not think the name Ellerbee.

And even *that* did not assuage the panic of his burning theater'd, air raid warning'd, red alert afterlife. (And that was what they wanted, and he knew it, wanting as much as they did for him to persist in his tornado watch condition, fleeing with others through the crimped, cramped streets of mazy, refugee Hell, dragging his disaster-poster avatar like a wounded leg.) He existed like one plugged into superb equipment, interminably terminal – and changed his mind and tried it the other way again, taking back all he had surrendered, Hell's Indian giver, and dredged up from where he had left them the imperfect memories of his former self. (May he saw as she had once been, his breastless, awkward, shapeless childhood sweetheart.) And when that didn't work either – he gave it a few years – he went back to the other way, and then back again, shifting, quickly tiring of each tack as soon as he had taken it, changing fitfully, a man in bed in a hot, airless room rolling position, aggressively altering the surfaces of his pillow. If he hoped – which he came to do whenever he reverted to Ellerbee – it was to go mad, but there was no madness in Hell – the terrific vocabulary of the damned, their poet's knack for rightly naming everything which was the fail-safe of Reason – and he could find peace nowhere.

He had been there sixty-two years, three generations, older now as a dead man than he had been as a living one. Sixty-two years of nightless days and dayless nights, of aggravated pain and cumulative grief, of escalated desperation, of not getting used to it, to any of it. Sixty-two years Hell's greenhorn, sixty-two years eluding the muggers and evading the rapists, all the joyless joy riders out for a night on his town, steering clear of the wild, stampeding, horizontal avalanche of the damned. And then, spinning out of the path of a charging, burning, screaming inmate, he accidentally backed into the smoldering ruin of a second. Ellerbee leaped away as their bodies touched.

"Ellerbee?"

Who? Ellerbee thought wildly. Who?

"Ellerbee?" the voice repeated.

How? Ellerbee wondered. How can he know me? In this form, how I look…

Ellerbee peered closely into the tormented face. It was one of the men who had held him up, not the one who had shot him but his accomplice, his murderer's accomplice. "Ladlehaus?" It was Ellerbee's vocabulary which had recognized him, for his face had changed almost completely in the sixty-two years, just as Ellerbee's had, just as it was Ladlehaus's vocabulary which had recognized Ellerbee.

"It is Ellerbee, isn't it?" the man said.

Ellerbee nodded and the man tried to smile, stretching his wounds, the scars which seamed his face, and breaking the knitting flesh, lined, caked as stool, braided as bowel.

"I died," he said, "of natural causes." Ellerbee stared at him. "Of leukemia, stroke, Hodgkin's disease, arteriosclerosis. I was blind the last thirteen years of my life. But I was almost a hundred. I lived to a ripe old age. I was in a Home eighteen years. Still in Minneapolis."

"I suppose," Ellerbee said, "you recall how *I* died."

"I do," Ladlehaus said. "Ron dropped you with one shot. That reminds me," he said. "You had a beautiful wife. May, right? I saw her photograph in the Minneapolis papers after the incident. There was tremendous coverage. There was a TV clip on the Six O'clock News. They interviewed her. She was – " Ellerbee started to run. "Hey," the accomplice called after him. "Hey, wait."

He ran through the steamy corridors of the Underworld, plunging into Hell's white core, the brightest blazes, Temperature's moving parts. The pain was excruciating, but he knew that it was probably the only way he would shake Ladlehaus so he kept running. And then, exhausted, he came out the other side into an area like shoreline, burning surf. He waded through the flames lapping about his ankles and then, humiliated by fatigue and pain, he did something he had never done before.

He lay down in the fire. He lay down in the slimy excrement and noxious puddles, in the loose evidence of their spilled terror. A few damned souls paused to stare at him, their bad breath dropping over him like an awful steam. Their scabbed faces leaned down toward him, their poisoned blood leaking on him from imperfectly sealed wounds, their baked, hideous visages like blooms in nightmare. It was terrible. He turned over, turned face down in the shallow river of pus and shit. Someone shook him. He didn't move. A man straddled and penetrated him. He didn't move. His attacker groaned. "I can't," he panted, "I can't — I can't see myself in his *blisters*." That's why they do it, Ellerbee thought. The man grunted and dismounted and spat upon him. His fiery spittle burned into an open sore on Ellerbee's neck. He didn't move. "He's dead," the man howled. "I think he's dead. His blisters have gone out!"

He felt a pitchfork rake his back, then turn it in the wound it had made as if the demon were trying to pry foreign matter from it.

"Did he die?" Ellerbee heard.

He had Free Will. He wouldn't move.

"Is he dead?"

"How did he do it?"

Hundreds pressed in on him, their collective stench like the swamps of men dead in earthquake, trench warfare — though Ellerbee knew that for all his vocabulary there were no proper analogies in Hell, only the mildest approximations. If he didn't move they would go away. He didn't move.

A pitchfork caught him under the armpit and turned him over.

"He's dead. I think so. I think he's dead."

"No. It can't be."

"I think."

"How? How did he do it?"

"Pull his cock. See."

"No. Make one of the women. If he isn't dead maybe he'll respond."

An ancient harridan stooped down and rubbed him between her palms. It was the first time he had been touched there by a woman in sixty-two years. He had Free Will, he had Free Will. But beneath her hot hands his penis began to smoke.

"Oh God," he screamed. "Leave me alone. Please," he begged. They gazed at him like teammates over a fallen player.

"Faker," one hissed.

"Shirker," said another scornfully.

"He's not dead," a third cried. "I told you."

"There's no death here."

"World without end," said another.

"Get up," demanded someone else. "Run. Run through Hell. Flee your pain. Keep busy."

They started to lift him. "Let go," Ellerbee shouted. He rolled away from a demon poking at him with a pitchfork. He was on his hands and knees in Hell. Still on all fours he began to push himself up. He was on his knees.

"Looks like he's praying," said the one who had told him to run.

"No."

"Looks like it. I think so."

"How? What for?"

And he started to pray.

"Lord God of Ambush and Unconditional Surrender," he prayed. "Power Play God of Judo Leverage. Grand Guignol, Martial Artist — "

The others shrieked, backed away from him, cordoning Ellerbee off like a disaster area. Ellerbee, caught up, ignoring them, not even hearing them, continued his prayer.

"Browbeater," he prayed, "Bouncer Being, Boss of Bullies — this is Your servant, Ellerbee, sixty-two-year fetus in Eternity, tot, toddler, babe in Hell. Can You hear me? I know You exist because I saw You, avuncular in Your green pastures like an old man on a picnic. The angeled minarets I saw, the gold streets and marble temples and all the flashy summer palace architecture, all the gorgeous glory locked in Receivership, Your zoned Heaven in Holy Escrow. The miracle props – harps and Saints and popes at tea. All of it – Your manna, Your ambrosia, Your Heavenly Host in their summer whites. So can You *hear* me, pick out my voice from all the others in this din bin? Come on, come on, Old Terrorist, God the Father, God the Godfather! The conventional wisdom is we can talk to You, that You love us, that – "

"I can hear you."

A great awed whine rose from the damned, moans, sharp cries. It was as if Ellerbee alone had not heard. He continued his prayer.

"I hear you," God repeated.

Ellerbee stopped.

God spoke. His voice was pitchless, almost without timbre, almost bland. "What do you want, Ellerbee?"

Confused, Ellerbee forgot the point of his prayer. He looked at the others who were quiet now, perfectly still for once. Only the snap of localized fire could be heard. God was waiting. The damned watched Ellerbee fearfully. Hell burned beneath his knees. "An explanation," Ellerbee said.

"For openers," God roared, "I made the heavens and the earth! Were you there when I laid the foundations of the firmament? When I – "

Splinters of burning bone, incandescent as filament, glowed in the gouged places along Ellerbee's legs and knees where divots of his flesh had flared and fallen away. "An *explanation*," he cried out, "an *explanation!* None of this what-was-I-doing-when-You-pissed-the-oceans stuff, where I was when You colored the nigger and ignited Hell. I wasn't around when You elected the affinities. I wasn't there when You shaped shit and fashioned cancer. Were *You* there when I loved my neighbor as myself? When I never stole or bore false witness? I don't say when I never killed but when I never even raised a hand or pointed a finger in anger? Where were You when I picked up checks and popped for drinks all round? When I shelled out for charity and voted Yes on the bond issues? So no Job job, no nature in tooth and claw, please. An explanation!"

"You stayed open on the Sabbath!" God thundered.

"I what?"

"You stayed open on the Sabbath. When you were just getting started in your new location."

"You mean because I opened my store on Sundays? That's why?"

"You took My name in vain."

"I took..."

"That's right, that's right. You wanted an explanation, I'll give you an explanation. You wanted I/Thou, I'll give you I/Thou. You took It in vain. When your wife was nagging you because you wanted to keep those widows on the payroll. She mocked you when you said you were under an obligation and you said, 'Indirectly. G-d damn it, yes. Indirectly.' 'Come on, sweetheart,' you said, 'you're awfully g-ddamn hard on me.'"

"That's why I'm in Hell? *That's* why?"

"And what about the time you coveted your neighbor's wife? You had a big boner."

"I coveted no one, I was never unfaithful, I practically chased that woman away."

"You didn't honor your father and mother."

Ellerbee was stunned. "I did. I *always* honored my father and mother. I loved them very much. Just before I was killed we were planning a trip to Phoenix to see them."

"Oh, *them*. They only adopted you. I'm talking about your natural parents."

"I was in a Home. I was an *in*fant!"

"Sure, sure," God said.

"And *that's* why? *That's* why?"

"You went dancing. You wore zippers in your pants and drove automobiles. You smoked cigarettes and sold the demon rum."

"These are Your reasons? *This* is Your explanation?"

"You thought Heaven looked like a theme park!"

Ellerbee shook his head. Could this be happening? This pettiness signaled across the universe? But anything could happen, everything could, and Ellerbee began again to pray. "Lord," he prayed, "Heavenly Father, Dear God – maybe whatever is is right, and maybe whatever is is right isn't, but I've been around now, walking up and down in it, and *ev*erything is true. There is nothing that is not true. The philosopher's best idea and the conventional wisdom, too. So I am praying to You now in all humility, asking Your forgiveness and to grant one prayer."

"What is it?" God asked.

Ellerbee heard a strange noise and looked around. The damned, too, were on their knees – all the lost souls, all the gargoyles, all the demons, kneeling in fire, capitulate through Hell like a great ring of the conquered.

"What is it?" He asked.

"To kill us, to end Hell, to close the camp."

"Amen," said Ellerbee and all the damned in a single voice.

"Ha!" God scoffed and lighted up Hell's blazes like the surface of a star. Then God cursed and abused Ellerbee, and Ellerbee wouldn't have had it any other way. *He*'d damned him, no surrogate in Saint's clothing but the real McCoy Son of a Bitch God Whose memory Ellerbee would treasure and eternally repudiate forever, happily ever after, world without end.

But everything was true, even the conventional wisdom, perhaps especially the conventional wisdom – that which had made up Heaven like a shot in the dark and imagined into reality halos and Hell, gargoyles, gates of pearl, and the Pearl of Great Price, that had invented the horns of demons and cleft their feet and conceived angels riding clouds like cowboys on horseback, their harps at their sides like goofy guitars. Everything. Everything was. The self and what you did to protect it, learning the house odds, playing it safe – the honorable percentage baseball of existence.

Forever was a long time. Eternity was. He would seek out Ladlehaus, his murderer's accomplice, let bygones be bygones. They would get close to each other, close as family, closer. There was much to discuss in their fine new vocabularies. They would speak of Minneapolis, swap tales of the Twin Cities. They would talk of Ron, of others in the syndicate. And Ladlehaus had seen May, had caught her in what Ellerbee hoped was her grief on the Six O'clock News. They would get close. And one day he would look for himself in Ladlehaus's glowing blisters.

Louise Erdrich

Louise Erdrich won the National Book Critics Circle Award
in 1985 for *Love Medicine*, her first novel. She is also the author
of *Jacklight*, a collection of poetry. She received a Creative
Writing Fellowship in 1983.

FLESH AND BLOOD

from LOVE MEDICINE

THERE WAS surely no reason I should go up
that hill again. For days, for weeks after I heard Sister Leopolda
was dying, I told myself I was glad. I told myself good riddance
to her puckered mind. Boiling jars that morning, pouring syrup,
I told myself what she deserved. The jars were hot. She deserved
to be packed in one alive. But as soon as I imagined that, I pitied
her in the jar, balled up in her black rag, staring through the glass.
I was always that way. Through the years I had thought up many
various punishments I would like to commit on the nun who'd
cracked my head and left a scar that was tight and cold in my palm,
a scar that ached on Good Friday and throbbed in the rain. But
every time I thought of her damned, I relented. I saw her kneeling,
dead faced, without love.

I stood in my kitchen packing apples in jars, pouring the boiling
syrup and cinnamon over them. I knew what I knew. She had gone
streadily downshill. In the past years of her life it was canes, chairs,
confinement. They said she prayed to herself twenty-four hours at
a stretch. There were some who touched the hem of her garment
to get blessed. As if she were the saint. Bag of bones! I knew the
truth. She had to pray harder than the others because the Devil
still loved her far better than any on that hill. She walked the sor-
rowful mysteries one year with bloody feet. There were those who
kept the gravel stones she bled on. I wouldn't. I knew the Devil

drove her toward grace with his persistence. She got famous. Like Saint Theresa, she lived for many weeks on Sacred Hosts.

But I hadn't seen her visiting the sick nor raising the sad ones up. No everyday miracles for her. Her talent was the relishment of pain, foaming at the mouth, and it was no surprise to me that lately there had been a drastic disarrangement of her mind.

I heard that she was kept in her little closet now. Confined. I heard she had an iron spoon that she banged on the bedstead to drive away spirits. Sparks flew up her walls. They had to keep her room very clean, I heard, otherwise she licked off the windowsills. She made meals of lint. They didn't dare let a dust ball collect beneath her bed. I knew why this had happened. I knew it was the heat. The prolonged heat of praying had caused her brain to boil. I also knew what they did not know about her appetite for dust.

She ate dust for one reason: to introduce herself to death. So now she was inhabited by the blowing and the nameless.

Packing apples in my jars, I came to the last. I was thinking of her with such concentration that I poured the syrup on my hand.

"Damn buzzard!" I screamed, as if she'd done it. And she might have. Who knew how far the influence spread?

I slipped my apron off and hung it on a chair. A sign perhaps. My hand was scalded. I hardly noticed. I was going up the hill.

"I'll visit her," I said, to hear it said out loud. "I'll bring Zelda."

That was one thing I had not expected of myself. Deciding that I'd bring the girl along with me, I realized another reason. I would visit Leopolda not just to see her, but to let her see me. I would let her see I had not been living on wafers of God's flesh but the fruit of a man. Long ago she had tried for my devotion. Now I'd let her see where my devotion had gone and where it had got me. For by now I was solid class. Nector was tribal chairman. My children were well behaved, and they were educated too.

I went to the wardrobe and pulled out the good wool dress I would wear up the hill, even on a day this hot. Royal plum, they called the color of it in the Grand Forks clothing shop. I had paid down twenty dollars for it and worn it the day they swore Nector to the chair with me beside him.

It was a good dress, manufactured, of a classic material. It was the kind of solid dress no Lazarre ever wore.

Zelda was sixteen, older than I was when I took on the nun and pulled the demon from her sleeve. Zelda was older in age but not in mind; that is, she did not know what she wanted yet, whereas my mind had made itself up once I walked down the hill. Fourteen years, that was all the older I was at that time, yet I was a woman enough to snare Nector Kashpaw. But Zelda still floundered, even with her advantages, and sometimes I found her staring in a quiet mood across the field.

This morning, however, she had been working in the garden as supervisor of the younger ones. As always, she had kept clean.

"Where are you going?" she asked, coming in the door. "You're wearing your dress."

"I'm wearing it," I said, "to visit the nuns. I want you to come along with me, so hurry up and change."

"All right!" She was glad to go up there anytime. She was friendly with a few of them, and could be found at Holy Mass any day of the week. Yet she had not decided to go any special route.

It did not take her long. She wore a pressed white blouse and plaid skirt. With her money from the potato fields she had bought herself anklets. Her saddle shoes were polished clean white. I would never have believed this was the granddaughter of Ignatius Lazarre, that sack of brew. There was even a ribbon in her hair, which she put up every night in pinned coils to get the curl.

So we went. It was a long enough walk, and the road was hot when we came out of the woods. I had my dress on, so I did not let myself sweat. The hill was covered with dust. Dust hung gray, in shifting bands, around the white convent walls. There had been no rain that fall, and the fields were blowing through the town. But we walked. We passed the place on the road where Nector had tried to throw me. We had passed this place many times before without me thinking of Nector, but today I was remembering everything.

"This is where I met your father," I told Zelda. For all I knew, it was the place we made Gordon as well, but I never exactly said that.

"Your father could not keep away from me," I suddenly bragged. I suppose I said that to put some other expression on my daughter's face. She was getting that serious glazed-over stare, as if she had to look down the well of her soul. But now she started, and went red.

"Don't give me that cow look," I said to her shocked face. "Maybe you're a little backwards about men, but your time will come."

She wouldn't look at me after that.

"How come we're visiting?" she asked, after we walked a bit farther.

"Take them some apples," I said. In my hand I held a jar of fresh canned crabs. I had planted the tree myself twelve years before, and for a long time it was the only apple tree on the reservation. Then the nuns had planted two on their hill. But those trees hardly bore yet. Mine was established.

"And also," I told Zelda, "to see the old nun who was my teacher. That's Leopolda."

"I never knew she was your teacher," said Zelda. "She's pretty old."

"Well she's sick now, too," I said. "That's why we're going to see her."

We came to the door. The lawn had shrunk back, to make room for a parking lot. Large square hedges went off to either side. The walls still blazed with cheap whitewash as before, but now most of the cracks were filled and the birds' nests were knocked down. The old convent had got a few fresh nuns and come up in the world.

I rang the bell. It made a deep and costly sound in the hall. I heard the knock of thick black shoes, the rustle of heavy cloth, and a slight wind caught me. I had imagined coming back here many times to this door, and always it was the carved bone of Leopolda's face that met me, not Dympna, who opened the door and plumply smiled. She had only three teeth left, now, in her wide pale face. Two were on the top and one was on the bottom. That, and her eyes so red and blank, gave her the look of a great rabbit.

I realized the strangeness of what was happening. Over twenty years had passed since I'd set foot in this place and been worshiped on the couch of the Superior as a saint. Twenty years since Leopolda had speared me with her bread poker. Twenty years while I also came up in the world.

"We are here to see Sister Leopolda," I said.

"Come in! Come in!" The rabbit seemed pleased and eyed my jar. "Are these apples from your tree?"

"Yes." I offered them.

"This must be your mother," Dympna decided. Zelda nodded. The nun did not recognize me. "Please come upstairs."

She took the apples from my hands and led us down the hall. We went up a flight of brown tile stairs that I remembered. We went down a shorter hall and stopped at the very end. All her grown life, Leopolda had lived in the same room.

Dympna tapped. There was silence.

"Maybe she's asleep," said Zelda.

"I am not asleep," the voice said, very low, so we hardly heard it from our side.

"Please go in," said Dympna, "she'll be expecting you now."

So Dympna left us, and we stood by the door as it fell, opening slowly into the dim camphor-ball air of Leopolda's room. I stepped in first, Zelda following. I saw nothing but the bed sheets, so white they almost glowed. Leopolda was among them. As my eyes grew accustomed to the light I made her out, a small pile of sticks wrapped in a white gown.

Not even the kindling to start a fire, I thought.

"It's dark in here," I said.

She did not answer.

"I came to visit you."

Still, silence.

"I brought my daughter. Zelda Kashpaw."

"I don't know who you are," she finally said.

"Marie."

I opened the curtains a crack. A beam of light came through. I saw her clearly, wrapped in sheets and shawls, and I was so surprised at what I saw that I let the curtain fall back. She had shriveled on the stick bones. Her arms were thin as ropes. And her hair. The hair shocked me first, because I never thought of nuns as having any, and then for the strangeness of it. Her hair was pure white and sprang out straight and thin from her skull like the floss of dandelions. I was almost afraid to breathe, as if the hair would float off. The rest of her, too, was frail as a dead plant.

"Marie!" she said suddenly. Her voice went deep and hoarse. "Star of the Sea! You'll shine when we burn off the salt!"

"At least you have not forgot me." I groped for a chair and sat. Zelda stood at the foot of the bed watching the two of us. At first I was relieved. I was expecting that the nun would rave at us or have taken complete absence of her senses. But it seemed that her mind was still clear. Just her body was affected. I started feeling sorry for her, so dried up and shriveled. That was always my mistake. For I grasped her hand like a common consoling friend and felt, immediately, the grim forbidding strength of her, un-diminished all these years.

"Oh no, I never forgot you," she said, and squeezed my hand still tighter. "I knew you would come back."

I was not going to let her get a hold on me, especially as I knew she had her mind now. I pulled away.

"I felt sorry for you," I said.

But this only made her laugh, a dry crackle like leaves crushed underfoot.

"I feel sorry for you too, now that I see."

It was dim. She saw nothing, unless she had the vision of a night thing, which I doubted even with the miracle of her strength.

"Why?" I asked. Solid in my good dress, I was proud and could ask. But the dress was what she picked up and threw in my face.

"So poor that you had to cut an old Easter shroud up and sew it," she said, pointing. Her finger was a stick of glass.

"You're blind," I said. "It's no shroud, it's good wool."

"It's purple."

How she noticed the color of it I don't know. I guess she took me all in like I did her when the light came through the crack in the curtains.

"I suppose you had brats with the Indian," she went on, ignoring

Zelda, "sickly and mean. It turns out that way with them."

"Look here," I said, "this is my daughter."

Anyone could see Zelda wasn't sick, or mean, and she was perfectly dressed. The nun did seem to take a certain interest. She turned to Zelda, who stood quietly at her feet in a soft shadow. She looked at Zelda standing there. Moments passed. Then Leopolda suddenly shifted and turned back to me.

"Yes," she whispered. "Similar. Very much the same."

"Of course," I said, settling myself, although I knew Zelda and me were not the same at all. "And I have four more at home, just about full-grown like Zelda here."

"How do you feed them?" The nun looked down the long spear of her nose.

"I don't have a problem with that," I said. "My husband is chairman of this tribe."

I paused to let that sink inside her skull.

"Sometimes they bring him to Washington," I said.

The nun just watched me. Her eyes were two steady lightless beams.

"Once a senator came to our house," I went on. "They went hunting in the woods, but they never got anything. Another time…"

But she had already started making her dry noise, her laughter, and her mouth gaped black and wide.

"…he ate supper with the governor," I said.

"So you've come up in the world," she mocked, using my thoughts against me. "Or your husband has, it sounds like, not you, Marie Lazarre."

"Marie Kashpaw," I said. "He is what he is because I made him."

I felt my daughter's gaze train on me, but what I said was true, and Zelda knew it. She had seen me drag him back from the bootlegger's house. She had seen me sitting all night by the door with an ax handle so he would not wander off in search of liquor. She had seen me ration him down, mixing his brandy with water, until he came clean. So she knew the truth of what I said.

"No doubt," said the nun. "You had a certain talent." Her

breath was like a small wind stirring the dust, and I remembered
her hands on my back, rubbing a buttery ointment into the scalding burns that she herself had put there. The scar in my hand began
to itch. I'd had a talent, it was true.

"I got out of here alive," I said. "I had to have a talent to do
that."

I could feel Zelda stiffen in bewilderment at what I said.

This time when the nun laughed it was deep and harsh, like dry
twigs breaking in her chest, and it ended in a coughing fit that
turned her face bright blue as any time I'd seen her in a rage.

"You're sick," I said, pouring the pity in my voice, "sicker than
a dog. I'm sorry for you."

"I'm sorry for you," she said immediately, again, "now that I
see you're going to suffer in hell."

But I had my answer on the tip of my tongue.

"Why should I go there?" I said. "I've been good to my neighbors. I fed my children from my own mouth. I kept Nector from
hurting himself."

"Ah —" she began. I cut her off.

"You're the one. So proud of shredding your feet! Getting worshiped as a saint! While all the time you're measly and stingy to
the sick at your door. I heard!"

Again her face was darkening. Zelda reached forward in alarm.
But I wasn't finished.

"I quit that when I walked down the hill. Dust, it was dust. I
saw that clear. The meek will inherit the earth!"

The nun drew a racking breath.

"I don't want the earth," she said.

Then she did something that showed me that, for all the conversation we had, she wasn't right in the head after all. She pulled the
bed sheet over her and dived beneath the covers. She surfaced
quickly with the heavy black spoon in her fist. And then she began
to beat on the spools of the iron bedstead, knocking flakes of white
paint off, making an unholy racket. She beat and she beat. Zelda
put her hands over her ears. I did also. We hollered at her to stop,
but she beat the louder. No one came. I'd had enough. I reached

over and grabbed the end of the spoon.

Again, I'd forgotten she had the strength of the grave. She snatched it easily back to herself.

"They all try that," she said.

"Oh yes?"

And then I knew what I had come there for. It came to me with the touch of iron. I wanted that spoon.

I wanted that spoon because it was a hell-claw welded smooth. It was the iron poker that she'd marked me with, flattened. It had power. It was like her soul boiled down and poured in a mold and hardened. That was the shape of it. If I had that spoon I'd have her to stir in my pot. I'd have her to whack the bannock, fry the fish, lift out the smoking meat. Every time I held the spoon handle I'd know that she was nothing but a ghost, a black wind. I'd have her helpless in the scar of my palm.

I would get that spoon.

I watched it. The spoon was large, black, seasoned, but I could still see myself turned upside down in its face, as if it was made of shining silver.

"I came here to get your blessing," I told her.

Leopolda glared at me, the spoon tight in her claw. She looked suspiciously at Zelda, who smiled in her ignorance.

"Bless my girl too," I said. "She might have a vocation."

There was interest. I was certain. She was hooked by the thought.

"God will decide that."

"Your blessing might help her."

She finally nodded.

Here was my plan: I would let her give Zelda the blessing, and then I would kneel before her to receive my blessing too. But just as she prayed over my head, I would lunge forward, taking her off-balance. I would go straight for the spoon, snatch it from her, have it, take it back home up the sleeve of my royal-plum dress that was certainly no shroud.

Zelda went down on her knees, and the nun's hand went up. I thought Leopolda would be a good half hour at her blessing prayer, so much did she enjoy this chance. Her right hand made numerous signs of the cross or rested skeletal on the hair of my girl. Her left hand gripped the spoon forgetfully. But she did not put it down.

I was about to make some move to get this over, when Leopolda came to the end of her speech and wound it up. She made a few parting waves overhead, and Zelda staggered to her feet. I kneeled down then, at the side of the bed, and rested my folded hands on the coverlet in good reaching distance.

Kneeling there, I was surprised how it affected me.

My heart was beating in my throat. It was like I had gone back years and years to the old Marie who was spoken to by the dark. It was like I had come full circle to that rough girl, again, for one last fight with Leopolda before she swirled off and was nothing.

When I smiled into her face she smiled back. It was the huge bleached grin of a skull. She lifted her hand.

But it was not the right hand of her blessing she lifted. It was the other hand, the left hand, still gripping the iron spoon. The hand went up. Our eyesights locked. She lifted half out of bed, with her deathly strength, to give herself the leverage she needed to connect a heavy blow.

I went up with her, drawn by her gaze, knowing her intention as if she spoke it. The arm smacked down, but I somehow had grasped her wrist, and now we leaned into each other, balanced by hate.

"Down!" she said.

"No!"

And then, with my other hand, I tried to take the spoon from her weakened grip. But she clung to the iron handle with both hands and kept grinning into my face. I grinned back at her, just to even things, and that was when I felt she got the better of me, for suddenly my face stretched and the air around me flattened. On her breath, in which I kneeled, was the smell of turned earth. Her gaze, in which I struggled, was a deep square hole. Her strength was the strict progress of darkness.

"Hold on!" I yelled, frightened, for it seemed just as if I was falling fast into her eyes and would be covered up by flowers and clods of earth unless she pulled me back.

And she did pull. She stood me up, and then I sat down on the bed with her. Once I was there I let go of the spoon. It dropped heavily on her starved breast and lay as spent of power as she.

Her body was so shallow I could hardly tell if she breathed, the covering of her bones so frail I could see the heart pumping in her breast.

I sat with her a long while, in silence.

The earth was so mild and deep. By spring she would be placed there, alone, and there was no rescue. There was nothing I could do after hating her all these years.

WE WERE QUIET walking back down the hill, through the woods. The path in the trees was shadowy and almost cold after the blaze of road. The sun flickered in the brush. Each leaf balanced in the air. Watching Zelda walk in front of me, so sure of herself and thin, with a cutting edge, with a mind that wasn't made up, with pure white anklets and careful curls, I felt an amazement. I remembered the year I carried her. It was summer. I sat under the clothesline, breathing quiet so she would move, feeling the hand or foot knock just beneath my heart. We had been in one body then, yet she was a stranger. We were not as close now, yet perhaps I knew her better.

Her black hair swung calmly with each step. She looked so young.

"I might go up there someday," she said, "up the hill."

"And stay with them?"

"Yes."

That did not surprise me. Yet I felt a sinking surge, a regret, a feeling like I should clutch her by the shoulders, although it plagued me that she couldn't make up her mind. "Don't make any hasty decision about your life," I said.

"I should get a job like Gordie did!"

"No! You shouldn't!"

I was on the verge of saying how I needed her, at the house, but I didn't say it. After all, I thought, she should be free to go.

As we came through the woods to the field, I heard Nector's shotgun. The boys were hunting ducks at the slough. The house looked quiet. I could see Aurelia moping in the yard with Eugene and Patsy, the little ones I left in her care. No doubt she wanted to be hunting with the boys and June.

"Go on after them," I said, as we walked in the yard. Aurelia got up and ran. She did not have to be convinced. She liked a boy down the road, a friend of Gordie's. She never had trouble making up her mind.

Zelda went in the house before me, to change to her overhalls. I stood in the yard. Nector was not home. I picked up the baby I was keeping for a young girl across the road, because he cried when he saw me. I looked over at the door.

Zelda was standing there, shadowy, behind the screen.

"Hurry up and change," I said. The cow was bawling.

But she didn't move when I told her to move. She said nothing. It gripped me in the throat that there was something wrong.

As if he would protect us, I kept the baby in my arms. I walked up the steps and stood on the other side of the screen. She looked at me, steady, and then I pulled the handle toward me.

"Here, Mama," she said, handing me the letter.

I stood in the kitchen, with the letter in my hand, not moving.

"Go on," I said, "change."

So she went. I opened the paper and I read.

Dear Marie,

Can't see going on with this when every day I'm going down even worse. Sure I loved you once, but all this time I am seeing Lulu also. Now she pressured me and the day has come I must get up and go. I apologize. I found true love with her. I don't have a choice. But that doesn't mean Nector Kashpaw will ever forget his own.

I folded the paper back up and put it in my dress pocket. Zelda stepped back into the room.

"Where did you get this?" I asked her.

"Under the sugar jar."

She pointed at the table and then we both looked, as if the table would tell us what to do next. I concentrated very hard on what I saw. The box of spoons. The butter plate. The can of salt. Somehow these things looked more full of special meaning than the sugar jar. It was just smooth clear glass, decent and familiar in the sunlight, half full. I looked back at Zelda. We gazed at each other. Her eyes were wide, staring, but I wasn't sure if she had read the letter or just been scared by the oddness of a piece of paper with my name on it, sitting on that table. I couldn't tell.

"Listen to that cow," I said. I felt my heart bang hard. My throat shut. I wouldn't have been able to say another word.

Zelda listened. She turned slowly, put her hands in her pockets, and walked outside. I went into the other room with the baby and sat on the bed. The paper crackled in my pocket. I needed the quiet. I could hear Patsy humming outside the window. She was safe. The cow went still. The rest of them were occupied. I could think.

What should I think first? It seemed like it didn't matter. So I didn't know what to think, because of course I knew it mattered, and yet there was nothing to think about. I remembered how Mary Bonne, who lived in town, found her husband in their own bed with a La Chien woman. She went back in her kitchen, took a knife off the wall, and even thought to sharpen the blade on her stone before she went back and cut them. She only gave them a few cuts, but there was blood. I thought the sight of Lamartine's blood would do me good. I saw her face, painted up and bold, and I thought I would cut it right off her neck.

Yet really, I wasn't angry. I didn't even feel like I was inside my body. For I fed the child until it was full and slept, a dead weight in my arms, and I never noticed. I was wondering how I could raise the children without their father. I thought of Eli, how he had gone quieter and hardly came out of the woods anymore. He would not come around. He never thought of women. He was like a shy animal himself when he got trapped in a house.

Then I said right out loud in that bedroom, "He's a man!"

But that didn't make any sense. It meant nothing. That all men were like Nector wasn't true. I thought of Henry Lamartine. Before he was killed on the tracks, he surely knew his wife went with anybody in the bushes. When she had the boys, all colors of humans, he could tell they were not his. He took care of them. I understood Henry, and I felt for him as I sat. I knew why he had parked his Dodge square on the tracks and let the train bear down.

He must have loved her. But I wouldn't park myself on the tracks for Nector.

"I'd see him in hell first," I said to the room. I realized the child was very heavy and put him on the bed. My arms ached. My throat was tight and dry. I saw that Patsy had come in the door and thrown herself on the bed, limp and exhausted as a doll made of rags. She was sleeping too. The afternoon was getting on, and I was still sitting there without having thought what I should do next.

"I should peel the potatoes," I told myself. No doubt they would bring in a duck at least.

So I went in the kitchen and sat down with a bowl of potatoes. I had peeled enough potatoes in my life so far to feed every man, woman, child of the Chippewas. Still I had more of them to go. It was calming to remove the rough skin, the eye sprouts, and get down to the smooth whiteness. I ate a raw slice. I would eat a raw potato like some people ate an apple. Zelda helped me cook at night. She would fry up the potatoes. After I peeled enough of them I went to the door and called her.

And then, when she never answered, I knew that she was gone. I knew that she read the letter. She had gone after Nector.

It wasn't hard to figure. What else would she do?

I went back in the house and sat down with the potatoes, and I cursed the girl for doing what she did. I should have done it. I should have gone to Lamartine's and dragged him out of her bed and beat him hard with a stick. And after I beat him and he was lying on the floor, I should have turned around and made the La- martine miserable.

Yet in time, as I calmed down, I knew I'd thought better of go- ing there for a reason. A good reason. The letter said that he loved her. I began peeling more potatoes, I don't know what for, but now I'd struck the comfortless heart I could not ignore. He loved the Lamartine, which was different from all the other things he did that caused me shame and disconvenienced my life. Him loving her, him finding *true love with her*, was what drove me to peel all the potatoes in that house.

I heard Aurelia, June, and the boys coming in the yard, fighting over whose turn it was to clean the birds. I guess they all cleaned their goose. I heard them behind the barn for awhile. I put some potatoes on to boil. My hands hurt, full of acids, blistered by the knife. I was like a person in a dream, but my oldest boy never noticed.

Gordie came in with a tough goose.

"It should have flew higher than that," he said. "I got it on the wing."

He looked around at the dishpans and the washtubs of peeled potatoes. Three empty gunnysacks were laying on the floor, crumpled like drawers a man had stepped out of in haste.

"Why'd you do that?" he said.

I only looked at him. I shrugged. He shrugged. He was Nector's son. I thought to myself, he wouldn't go after Nector and bring him home. I was sure Gordie wouldn't do that, even though, like with Zelda, there was a time we had been in the same body. He wouldn't go, even though I had nursed him. We were closer when I carried him, when we never knew each other, I thought now. I did not trust him.

"It's too hot in here for more fire," I said. "Make one outside and roast your birds. I'm washing my floor."

"At night?" he said.

The sun was going down very fast.

"You heard me."

He went out and made a fire in the backyard where we had an old fieldstone range made to cook on in the summer. They all stayed out there. I fed Patsy a mashed potato. I fed her milk. I let the baby play and roll across the floor. I sat and watched them while I decided how I would wash the floor. I looked at my linoleum carefully, all the worn spots and cracks, all the places where the tin stripping had to be hammered flat. It was one of my prides to keep that floor shined up. Under the gray swirls and spots and leaves of the pattern, I knew there was tar paper and bare wood that could splinter a baby's feet. I knew, because I bought and paid for and put down that linoleum myself. It was a good solid covering, but under it the boards creaked.

THERE WASN'T any use in thinking. I put the baby to sleep. I filled the tin bucket with hot water and spirits. I hauled the potatoes out of my way. Then I took up my brush. Outside they were talking. They had a fire. They could stay there. I never went down on my knees to God or anyone, so maybe washing my floor was an excuse to kneel that night. I felt better, that's all I know, as I scrubbed off the tarnished wax and dirt. I felt better as I recognized myself in the woman who kept her floor clean even when left by her husband.

I had been on a high horse. Now I was kneeling. I was washing the floor in my good purple dress. I never did laugh at myself in any situation, but I had to laugh now. I thought of cutting up a shroud. The nun was clever. She knew where my weakness had been.

But I was not going under, even if he left me. I could leave off my fear of ever being a Lazarre. I could leave off my fear, even of losing Nector, since he was gone and I was able to scrub down the floor.

I took my wax. I started polishing a little at a time.

Love had turned my head away from what was going on between my husband and Lamartine. There was something still left that Nector could hurt me with, and now I hurt for love and not because the old hens would squawk.

They would say Marie Kashpaw was down in the dirt. They would say how her husband had left her for dirt. They would say I got all that was coming, head so proud. But I would not care if Marie Kashpaw had to wear an old shroud. I would not care if Lulu Lamartine ended up the wife of the chairman of the Chippewa Tribe. I'd still be Marie. Marie. Star of the Sea! I'd shine when they stripped off the wax!

I had to laugh. I heard the dogs. I had waxed myself up to the table. I knew that I was hearing Nector and Zelda come home, walking in the yard. I wrung my rag out. I had waxed myself in.

I thought of the letter in my pocket. Then I thought very suddenly of what this Marie who was interested in holding on to Nector should do. I took the letter. I did what I never would expect of myself. I lifted the sugar jar to put the letter back. Then I thought. I put the sugar down and picked up the can of salt. This was much more something I would predict of Marie.

I folded the letter up, exactly as it had been found, and I put it beneath the salt can. I did this for a reason. I would never talk about this letter but instead let him wonder. Sometimes he'd look at me, I'd smile, and he'd think to himself: salt or sugar? But he would never be sure.

I sat down in a chair. I put my legs in another chair, off the floor, and I waited for him to walk up the steps. When he did, I let him come. Step by step. I let him listen to hear if I was inside. I let him open the door. Only when we saw each other did I stop him.

"I just put the wax down," I said. "You have to wait."

He stood there looking at me over that long, shiny space. It rolled and gleamed like a fine lake between us. And it deepened. I saw that he was about to take the first step, and I let him, but halfway into the room his eyes went dark. He was afraid of how deep this was going to become. So I did for Nector Kashpaw what I learned from the nun. I put my hand through what scared him. I held it out there for him. And when he took it with all the strength of his arms, I pulled him in.

Carolyn Forché

Carolyn Forché's books of poetry include *Gathering the Tribes*, which won the Yale Younger Poets Prize, and *The Country Between Us*, the 1981 Lamont Poetry Selection of the Academy of American Poets. She was awarded Creative Writing Fellowships in 1977 and 1984.

THE MEMORY OF ELENA

WE SPEND our morning
in the flower stalls counting
the dark tongues of bells
that hang from ropes waiting
for the silence of an hour.
We find a table, ask for *paella*,
cold soup and wine, where a calm
light trembles years behind us.

In Buenos Aires only three
years ago, it was the last time his hand
slipped into her dress, with pearls
cooling her throat and bells like
these, chipping at the night —

As she talks, the hollow
clopping of a horse, the sound
of bones touched together.
The *paella* comes, a bed of rice
and *camarones*, fingers and shells,
the lips of those whose lips
have been removed, mussels
the soft blue of a leg socket.

This is not *paella*, this is what
has become of those who remained
in Buenos Aires. This is the ring
of a rifle report on the stones,
her hand over her mouth,
her husband falling against her.

These are the flowers we bought
this morning, the dahlias tossed
on his grave and bells
waiting with their tongues cut out
for this particular silence.

1977

Maria Irene Fornes

Maria Irene Fornes has won six Obie awards for playwriting and direction, including the 1982 Sustained Achievement Award for her more than twenty years of contributions to Off-Broadway Theater. She received a Creative Writing Fellowship in Drama in 1974.

from FEFU AND HER FRIENDS

NEW ENGLAND, SPRING 1935

PART I: Noon. The living room. The entire audience watches from the auditorium.

PART II: Afternoon. The lawn, the study, the bedroom, the kitchen. The audience is divided into four groups. Each group is guided to the spaces. These scenes are performed simultaneously. When the scenes are completed the audience moves to the next space and the scenes are performed again. This is repeated four times until each group has seen all four scenes.

PART III: Evening. The living room. The entire audience watches from the auditorium.

PART I

FEFU: I'm strange, Christina. But I am fortunate in that I don't mind being strange. It's hard on others sometimes. But not that hard. Is it, Cindy. Those who love me, love me precisely because

I am the way I am. *[To Cindy.]* Isn't that so? *[Cindy nods and shakes her head.]*

CINDY: I would love you even if you weren't the way you are.

FEFU: You wouldn't know it was me if I weren't the way I am.

CINDY: I would still know it was you underneath.

FEFU: *[To Christina.]* You see? – There are some good things about me. – I'm never angry for example.

CHRISTINA: But you make everyone else angry.

[Fefu thinks a moment.]

FEFU: No.

CHRISTINA: You've made me furious.

FEFU: I know. And I might make you angry again. Still I would like it if you liked me. – You think it unlikely.

CHRISTINA: I don't know.

FEFU: ...We'll see. *[Fefu goes to the doors. She stands there for a moment before she speaks.]* I still like men better than women. – I envy them. I like being like a man. Thinking like a man. Feeling like a man. – They are well together. Women are not. *[Christina puts her glass to her mouth.]* I'm driving you to alcohol. *[Fefu looks outside. She speaks reflectively.]* Look at them. They are checking the new grass mower....Out in the fresh air and the sun, while we sit here in the dark....Men have natural strength. Women have to find their strength, and when they do find it, it comes forth with bitterness and it's erratic....Women are restless with each other. They are like live wires...either chattering to keep themselves from making contact, or else, if they don't chatter, they avert their eyes...like Orpheus...as if a god once said "and if they shall recognize each other, the world will be blown apart." They are always eager for the men to arrive. When they do, they can put themselves at rest, tranquilized and in a mild stupor. With the men they feel safe. The danger is gone. That's the closest they can be to feeling wholesome. Men are muscle that covers the raw nerve. They are the insulators. The danger is gone, but the price is the mind and the spirit. ...High price. – Why? – What is feared? – Hmm. Well... – Do you know? Perhaps the heavens would fall. – Have I offended you again?

CHRISTINA: No. I too have wished for that trust men have for each other. The faith the world puts in them and they in turn put in the world. I know I don't have it.

FEFU: Hmm. Well, I have to see how my toilet is doing. *[Fefu goes to the landing and exits. She puts her head out.]* Plumbing is more important than you think.

[Christina falls off her chair in a mock faint. Cindy smiles.]

CINDY: What do you think?

.   .   .

CINDY: He shot. Julia and the deer fell. The deer was dead...dying. Julia was unconscious. She had convulsions...like the deer. He died and she didn't. I screamed for help and the hunter came and examined Julia. He said, "She is not hurt." Julia's forehead was bleeding. He said, "It is a surface wound. I didn't hurt her." I know it wasn't he who hurt her. It was someone else. He went for help and Julia started talking. She was delirious. Apparently there was a spinal nerve injury but the doctors are puzzled because it doesn't seem her spine was hurt when she fell. She hit her head and she suffered a concussion but that would not affect the spinal nerve. So there seems to be no reason for the paralysis. She blanks out and that is caused by the blow on the head. It's a scar in the brain. It's called the petit mal.

[Fefu enters. She remains by the door.]

CHRISTINA: What was it she said?
CINDY: Hmm?...
CHRISTINA: When she was delirious.
CINDY: When she was delirious? That she was persecuted. – That they tortured her....That they had tried her and that the shot was her execution. That she recanted because she wanted to live.... That if she talked about it...to anyone...she would be tortured further and killed. And I have not mentioned this before because ...I fear for her.
CHRISTINA: It doesn't make any sense, Cindy.
CINDY: It makes sense to me.

PART II

IN THE LAWN

There is a bench. A game of croquet is set on the grass. Fefu and Emma eat apples and play croquet.

FEFU: You always bring joy to me.

EMMA: Thank you.

FEFU: I thank you. *[Fefu becomes distressed. She sits.]* I am in constant pain. I don't want to give in to it. If I do I am afraid I will never recover....It's not physical, and it's not sorrow. It's very strange Emma. I can't describe it, and it's very frightening....It is as if normally there is a lubricant...not in the body...a spiritual lubricant ...it's hard to describe...and without it, life is a nightmare, and everything is distorted. – A black cat started coming to my kitchen. He's awfully mangled and big. He is missing an eye and his skin is diseased. At first I was repelled by him, but then, I thought, this is a monster that has been sent to me and I must feed him. And I fed him. One day he came and shat all over my kitchen. Foul diarrhea. He still comes and I still feed him. – I am afraid of him. *[Emma kisses Fefu.]* How about a little lemonade?

EMMA: Yes.

IN THE BEDROOM

A plain unpainted room. Perhaps a room that was used for storage and was set up as a sleeping place for Julia. There is a mattress on the floor. To the right of the mattress there is a small table, to the left is Julia's wheelchair. There is a sink on the wall. There are dry leaves on the floor although the time is not fall. The sheets are linen. Julia lies in bed covered to her shoulders. She wears a white hospital gown. Julia hallucinates. However, her behavior should not be the usual behavior attributed to a mad person. It should be rather still and luminous. There will be aspects of her hallucination that frighten her, but hallucinating itself does not.

JULIA: They clubbed me. They broke my head. They broke my will. They broke my hands. They tore my eyes out. They took my voice away. They didn't do anything to my heart because I didn't bring my heart with me. They clubbed me again, but my head did not fall off in pieces. That was because they were so good and they felt sorry for me. The judges. You didn't know the judges? — I was good and quiet. I never dropped my smile. I smiled to everyone. If I stopped smiling I would get clubbed because they love me. They say they love me. I go along with that because if I don't...

[With her fingers she indicates her throat being cut and makes the sound that usually accompanies that gesture.]

JULIA: I told them the stinking parts of the body are the important ones: the genitals, the anus, the mouth, the armpits. All important parts except the armpits. And who knows, maybe the armpits are important too. That's what I said. He said that all those parts must be kept clean and put away. He said that women's entrails are heavier than anything on earth and to see a woman running creates a disparate and incongruous image in the mind. It's anti-æsthetic. Therefore women should not run. Instead they should strike positions that take into account the weight of their entrails. Only if they do, can they be æsthetic. He said, for example, Goya's Maja. He said Rubens' women are not æsthetic. Flesh. He said that a woman's bottom should be in a cushion, otherwise it's revolting. He said that there are exceptions. Ballet dancers are exceptions. They can run and lift their legs because they have no entrails. Isadora Duncan had entrails, that's why she should not have danced. But she danced and for this reason became crazy. She wasn't crazy.

[She moves her hand as if guarding from a blow.]

JULIA: She was. He said that I had to be punished because I was getting too smart. I'm not smart. I never was. Neither is Fefu smart. They are after her too. Well, she's still walking!

[She guards from a blow. Her eyes closed.]

JULIA: Wait! I'll say my prayer. I'm saying it.

[She mumbles. She opens her eyes with caution.]

JULIA: You don't think I'm going to argue with them do you. I repented. I told them exactly what they wanted to hear. They killed me. I was dead. But I repented and they said, "Live but crippled. And if you tell…"

[She repeats the throat-cutting gesture.]

JULIA: Why do you have to kill Fefu, for she's only a joker? "Not kill, cure. Cure her." Will it hurt?

[She whimpers.]

JULIA: Oh, dear, dear, my dear, they want your light. Your light my dear. Your precious light. Oh dear, my dear.

[Her head moves as if slapped.]

JULIA: Not cry. I'll say my prayer. I'll say it. Right now. Look.

[She sits up.]

JULIA: The human being is of the masculine gender. The human being is a boy as a child and grown up he is a man. Everything on earth is for the human being, which is man. To nourish him. – There are evil things on earth for man also. For him to fight with, and conquer and turn its evil into good. So that it too can nourish him. – There are Evil Plants, Evil Animals, Evil Minerals, and Women are Evil. – Woman is not a human being. She is: 1-A mystery. 2-Another species. 3-As yet undefined. 4-Unpredictable; therefore wicked and gentle and evil and good which is evil. – If a man commits an evil act, he must be pitied. The evil comes from outside him, through him and into the act. Woman generates the evil herself. – God gave man no other mate but woman. The oxen is good but it is not a mate for man. The sheep is good but it is not a mate for man. The mate for man is woman and that is the cross man must bear. – Man is not spiritually sexual, he therefore can enjoy sexuality. His sexuality is physical which means his spirit is pure. Women's spirit is sexual. That is why after coitus they dwell in nefarious feelings. Because that is their natural habitat. That is why it is difficult for them to return to the human world. Their sexual feelings remain with them till they die. And they take those feelings with them to the afterlife where they corrupt the heavens, and they are sent to hell where through suffering they may shed those feelings and return to earth as man.

[Her head moves as if slapped.]

JULIA: Don't hit me. Didn't I just say my prayer?

[A smaller slap.]

JULIA: I believe it.

[She lies back.]

JULIA: They say when I believe the prayer I will forget the judges. And when I forget the judges I will believe the prayer. They say both happen at once. And all women have done it. Why can't I?

[Sue enters with a bowl of soup on a tray.]

SUE: Julia, are you asleep?

[Short pause.]

JULIA: No.
SUE: I brought your soup.
JULIA: Put it down. I'm getting up in a moment.

[Sue puts the soup down.]

SUE: Do you want me to help you?
JULIA: No, I can manage. Thank you, Sue.

[Sue goes to the door.]

SUE: You're all right?
JULIA: Yes.
SUE: I'll see you later.
JULIA: Thank you, Sue.

[Sue exits. Julia closes her eyes. As soon as each audience group leaves, the tray is removed, if possible through a back door.]

IN THE KITCHEN

A fully equipped kitchen. There is a table and chairs and a high cutting table. On a counter next to the stove there is a tray with three soup bowls, three spoons and a ladle. On the cutting table there are two empty glasses. Soup is heating on a burner. A kettle with water sits on an unlit burner. In the refrigerator there is an ice tray with wooden sticks in each cube and two pitchers; one with water, one with lemonade. In one of the cabinets there are three complete sets of dishes and other utensils used in the scene. Paula sits at the table. She is writing on a pad. Sue leans on the cutting table. She is waiting for the soup to heat.

PAULA: I have it all figured out.

SUE: What?

PAULA: A love affair lasts seven years and three months.

SUE: It does?

PAULA: *[Reading.]* 3 months of love. 1 year saying: It's all right. This is just a passing disturbance. 1 year trying to understand what's wrong. 2 years knowing the end has come. 1 year finding the way to end it. After the separation, 2 years trying to understand what happened. 7 years, 3 months. *[No longer reading.]* At any point the sequence might be interrupted by another love affair that has the same sequence. That is, it's not really interrupted, the new love affair relegates the first one to a second plane and both continue their sequence at the same time.

[Sue looks over Paula's shoulder.]

SUE: You really added it up.

PAULA: Sure.

SUE: What do you want to drink?

PAULA: Water. *[Sue takes the water pitcher from the refrigerator and fills the two glasses.]* The old love affair may fade, so you are not aware the process goes on. A year later it may surface and you might find yourself figuring out what's wrong with the new one while trying to end the old one.

SUE: So how do you solve the problem?

PAULA: Celibacy?

SUE: *[Going to the refrigerator with the pitcher.]* Celibacy doesn't solve anything.

PAULA: That's true.

SUE: *[Taking out the ice tray with the sticks.]* What's this? *[Paula shakes her head.]* Dessert? *[Paula shrugs her shoulders. Sue takes an ice cube and places it against her forehead.]* For a headache. *[She takes another cube and moves her arms in a judo style.]* Eskimo wrestling. *[She places one stick behind her ear.]* Brain cooler. That's when you're thinking too much. You could use one. *[She tries to put the ice cube behind Paula's ear. They wrestle and laugh. She puts the stick in her own mouth. She takes it out to speak.]* This is when you want to keep chaste. No one will kiss you. *[She puts it back in to demonstrate. Then takes it out.]* That's good for celibacy. If you walk around with one of these in your mouth for seven years you can keep all your sequences straight. Finish one before you start the other. *[She puts the ice cube in the tray and looks at it.]* A frozen caterpillar. *[She puts the tray away.]*

PAULA: You're leaving that ice cube in there?

SUE: I'm clean. *[She pours soup in three bowls, brings the tray to the table and places a bowl and spoon in front of Paula.]* So what else do you have on love? *[Sue places another bowl and spoon on the table and sits.]*

PAULA: Well, the break-up takes place in parts. The brain, the heart, the body, mutual things, shared things. The mind leaves but the heart is still there. The heart has left but the body wants to stay. The body leaves but the things are still at the apartment. You must come back. You move everything out of the apartment but the mind stays behind. Memory lingers in the place. Seven years later, perhaps seven years later, it doesn't matter any more. Perhaps it takes longer. Perhaps it never ends.

SUE: It depends.

PAULA: Yup. It depends.

SUE: Something's bothering you.

PAULA: No.

SUE: *[Taking the tray.]* I'm going to take this to Julia.

PAULA: Go ahead.

[As Sue exits, Cecilia enters.]

CECILIA: May I come in?

PAULA: Yes…Would you like something to eat?

CECILIA: No, I ate lunch.

PAULA: I didn't eat lunch. I wasn't very hungry.

CECILIA: I know.

PAULA: Would you like some coffee?

CECILIA: I'll have tea.

PAULA: I'll make some.

CECILIA: No, you sit. I'll make it. *[Cecilia looks for tea. Paula also looks, finds it and gives it to Cecilia.]*

PAULA: Here it is.

CECILIA: *[She lights the burner.]* I've been meaning to call you. *[Paula walks to the table.]*

PAULA: It doesn't matter. I know you're busy.

CECILIA: Still I would have called you but I really didn't find the time.

PAULA: Don't worry.

CECILIA: I wanted to see you again. I want to see you often.

PAULA: There's no hurry. Now we know we can see each other.

CECILIA: Yes, I'm glad we can.

PAULA: I have thought a great deal about my life since I saw you. I have questioned my life. I can't help doing that. It's been many years and I wondered how you see me now.

CECILIA: You're the same.

PAULA: I felt small in your presence…I haven't done all that I could have. All I wanted to do. Our lives have gone in such different directions I cannot help but review what those years have been for me. I gave up, almost gave up. I have missed you in my life….I became lazy. I lost the drive. You abandoned me and I kept going. But after a while I didn't know how to. I didn't know how to go on. I knew why when I was with you. To give you pleasure. So we could laugh together. So we could rejoice together. To bring beauty to the world….Now we look at each other like strangers. We are guarded. I speak and you don't understand my words. Time has changed you more than it has changed me. You have forgotten. I remember every day.

[Fefu enters. Taking two glasses.]

FEFU: Emma and I are having a hell of a game of croquet. *[Taking the lemonade pitcher from the refrigerator.]* You want to join us?…No. You're having a serious conversation.

PAULA: Very serious. *[Paula smiles at Cecilia in a conciliatory manner.]* Too serious.

FEFU: *[As she exits.]* Come.

PAULA: I'm sorry. Let's go play croquet. – I'm not reproaching you.

CECILIA: *[Reaching for Paula's hand.]* I know. I've missed you too.

[They exit. As soon as the audience leaves, the props are reset.]

P<small>ART</small> III

The living room. It is dusk. There are flowers in the bar. Emma enters, checks the lights in the room on her hand, looks around the room and goes upstairs. The rest enter through the rear. Cecilia, Sue and Julia are last. Cecilia enters speaking.

CECILIA: Well, we each have our own system of receiving information, placing it, responding to it. That system can function with such a bias that it could take any situation and translate it into one formula. That is, I think, the main reason for stupidity or even madness, not being able to tell the difference between things.

FEFU: Like?

CECILIA: Like…this person is screaming at me. He's a bully. I don't like being screamed at. Another person screams, or the same person in a different situation is screaming and they have a good reason. You know you have done something that justly provokes them to scream. They are two different things. Often that distinction is not made.

SUE: I see.

CECILIA: We cannot survive in a vacuum. We must be part of a community, perhaps 10, 100, 1000. It depends on how strong you are. But even the strongest will need a dozen, three, even one who sees, thinks and feels as they do. The greater the need for that kind of reassurance, the greater the number that we need to identify with. Some need to identify with the whole nation. Then, the greater the number, the more limited the number of responses and thoughts. A common denominator must be reached. Thoughts, emotions that fit all, have to be limited to a small number. That is, I feel, the concern of the educator – to teach how to be sensitive to the differences, in ourselves as well as outside ourselves, not to supervise the memorization of facts. *[Emma's head appears in the doorway to the stairs.]* Otherwise the unusual in us will perish. As we grow we feel we are strange and fear any thought that is not shared with everyone.

JULIA: As I feel I am perishing. My hallucinations are madness, of course, but I wish I could be with others who hallucinate also. I would still know I am mad but I would not feel so isolated. – Hallucinations are real, you know. They are not like dreams. They are as real as all of you here. I have actually asked to be hospitalized so I could be with other nuts. But the doctors don't want to. They can't diagnose me. That makes me even more isolated. *[There is a moment's silence.]* You see, right now, it's an awful moment because you don't know what to say or do. If I were with other people who hallucinate they would say, "Oh yeah. Sure. It's awful. Those dummies, they don't see anything." *[The others begin to relax.]* It's not so bad, really. I can laugh at it....Emma is ready. We should start. *[The others are hesitant. She speaks to Fefu.]* Come on.

FEFU: Sure. *[Fefu begins to move the table. Others help move the table and enough furniture to clear a space in the center. They form a semi-circle facing upstage.]* All right. I start. Right?

CINDY: Right.

[Emma sits on the steps. Only her head and legs are visible.]

FEFU: I talk about the stifling conditions of primary school education, etc....etc....The project...I know what I'm going to say but I don't want to bore you with it. We all know it by heart. Blah blah blah blah. And so on and so on. And so on and so on. Then I introduce Emma...And now Miss Emma Blake. *[They applaud. Emma shakes her head.]* What.

EMMA: Paula goes next.

FEFU: Does it matter?

EMMA: Of course it matters. Dra-ma-tur-gia. It has to build. I'm in costume.

FEFU: Oh. And now, ladies and gentlemen, Miss Paula Cori will speak on Art as a Tool for Learning. And I tell them the work you have done at the Institute, community centers, essays, etc. Miss Paula Cori.

[They applaud. Paula goes to center.]

PAULA: Ladies and gentlemen, I, like my fellow educator and colleague, Stephany Beckmann...

FEFU: I am not an educator.

PAULA: What are you?

FEFU: ...a do-gooder...a girl scout.

PAULA: Well, like my fellow girl scout Stephany Beckmann I say blah blah blah blah blah blah blah and I offer the jewels of my wisdom and experience, which I will write down and memorize, otherwise I would just stand there and stammer and go blank. And even after I memorize it I'm sure I will just stand there and stammer and go blank.

EMMA: I'll work with you on it.

PAULA: However, after our other colleague Miss Emma Blake works with me on it... *[In imitation of Emma she brings her hands together and opens her arms as she moves her head back and speaks.]* My impulses will burst forth through a symphony of eloquence.

EMMA: Breathe...in... *[Paula inhales slowly.]* And bow. *[Paula bows. They applaud. She comes up from the bow.]*

.   .   .

CINDY: I'm O.K. — And how's your love life?

JULIA: Far away...I have no need for it.

CINDY: I'm sorry.

JULIA: Don't be. I'm very morbid these days. I think of death all the time.

PAULA: *[Standing in the doorway.]* Anyone for coffee? *[They raise their hands.]* Anyone take milk? *[They raise their hands.]*

JULIA: Should we go in?

PAULA: I'll bring it out. *[Paula exits.]*

JULIA: I feel we are constantly threatened by death, every second, every instant, it's there. And every moment something rescues us. Something rescues us from death every moment of our lives. For every moment we live we have to thank something. We have to be grateful to something that fights for us and saves us. I have felt lifeless and in the face of death. Death is not anything. It's being lifeless and I have felt lifeless sometimes for a brief moment, but I have been rescued by these...guardians. I am not sure who these guardians are. I only know they exist because I have felt their absence. I think we have come to know them as life, and we have become familiar with certain forms they take. Our sight is a form they take. That is why we take pleasure in seeing things, and we find some things beautiful. The sun is a guardian. Those things we take pleasure in are usually guardians. We enjoy looking at the sunlight when it comes through the window. Don't we? We as people, are guardians to each other when we give love. And then of course we have white cells and anti-bodies protecting us. Those moments when I feel lifeless have occurred, and I am afraid one day the guardians won't come in time and I will be defenseless. I will die... for no apparent reason.

[Pause. Paula stands in the doorway with a bottle of milk.]

PAULA: Anyone take rotten milk? *[She smiles. No one laughs.]* I'm kidding. This one is no good but there's more in there... *[Remaining in good spirits.]* Forget it. It's not a good joke.

JULIA: It's good.

PAULA: In there it seemed funny but here it isn't. It's a kitchen joke. *[Paula shrugs her shoulders.]* ...Bye...*[She exits.]*

JULIA: *[After her.]* It is funny, Paula. *[To Cindy.]* It was funny.

CINDY: It's all right, Paula doesn't mind.

JULIA: I'm sure she minds. I'll go see... *[Julia starts to go. Paula appears in the doorway.]*

PAULA: Hey, who was the lady I saw you with? – That was no lady. That was my rotten wife. That one wasn't good either, was it? *[Exiting.]* Emma....That one was no good either.

·   ·   ·

SUE: I was terribly exhausted and run down. I lived on coffee so I could stay up all night and do my work. And they used to give us these medical check-ups all the time. But all they did was ask how we felt and we'd say "Fine," and they'd check us out. In the meantime I looked like a ghost. I was all bones. Remember Susan Austin? She was very naïve and when they asked her how she felt,

she said she was nervous and she wasn't sleeping well. So she had
to see a psychiatrist from then on.
EMMA: Well, she was crazy.
SUE: No, she wasn't. – Oh god, those were awful days....Remember Julie Brooks?
EMMA: Sure.
SUE: She was a beautiful girl.
EMMA: Ah yes, she was gorgeous.

[Paula comes down as soon as possible and stands on the landing.]

SUE: At the end of the first semester they called her in because she
had been out with 28 men and they thought that was awful. And
the worst thing was that after that, she thought there was something wrong with her.
CINDY: She was a nymphomaniac, that's all.

[They are amused.]

SUE: She was not. She was just very beautiful so all the boys
wanted to go out with her. And if a boy asked her to go have a
cup of coffee she'd sign out and write in the name of the boy. None
of us did of course. All she did was go for coffee or go to a movie.
She was really very innocent.
EMMA: And Gloria Schuman? She wrote a psychology paper the
faculty decided she didn't write and they called her in to try to
make her admit she hadn't written it. She insisted she wrote it and
they sent her to a psychiatrist also.
JULIA: Everybody ended going to the psychiatrist.

[Fefu exits through the foyer.]

EMMA: After a few visits the psychiatrist said: Don't you think you
know me well enough now that you can tell me the truth about
the paper? He almost drove her crazy. They just couldn't believe
she was so smart.
SUE: Those were difficult times.
PAULA: We were young. That's why it was difficult. On my first
year I thought you were all very happy.
EMMA: Oh god.

PAULA: I had been so deprived in my childhood that I believed the rich were all happy. During the summer you spent your vacations in Europe or the Orient. I went to work and I resented that. But then I realized that many lives are ruined by poverty and many lives are ruined by wealth. I was always able to manage. And I think I enjoyed myself as much when I went to Revere Beach on my day off as you did when you visited the Taj Mahal. Then when I stopped feeling envy, I started noticing the waste. I began feeling contempt for those who, having everything a person can ask for, make such a mess of it. I resented them because they were not better than the poor. If you have all you need you should be generous. If you can afford to go to school your mind should be better. If you didn't have to fight for your place on earth you should be nobler. But I saw them cheating and grabbing like the kids in the slums, or wasting away with self-indulgence. And I saw them be plain stupid. If there is a reason why some are rich while others starve it must be so they put everything they have at the service of others. They should take the responsibility of everything that happens in the world. They are the only ones who can influence things. The poor don't have the power to change things. I think we should teach the poor and let the rich take care of themselves. I'm sorry, I know that's what we're doing. That's what Emma has been doing. I'm sorry...I guess I feel it's not enough. *[Paula sobs.]* I'll wash my face. I'll be right back. *[She starts to go.]* I think highly of all of you. *[She exits.]*

. . .

FEFU: You have given up!
JULIA: I get tired! I get exhausted! I am exhausted!
FEFU: What is it you see? *[Julia doesn't answer.]* What is it you see! Where is it you go that tires you so?
JULIA: I can't spend time with others! I get tired!
FEFU: What is it you see!
JULIA: You want to see it too?
FEFU: No, I don't. You're nuts, and willingly so.
JULIA: You know I'm not.
FEFU: And you're contagious. I'm going mad too.

JULIA: I try to keep away from you.

FEFU: Why?

JULIA: I might be harmful to you.

FEFU: Why?

JULIA: I am contagious. I can't be what I used to be.

FEFU: You have no courage.

JULIA: You're being cruel.

FEFU: I try to swallow my feelings but I can't. They choke me. I want to rest, Julia. How does a person rest. I want to put my mind at rest. I am frightened. *[Julia looks at Fefu.]* Don't look at me. *[She covers Julia's eyes with her hand.]* I lose my courage when you look at me.

JULIA: May no harm come to your head.

FEFU: Fight!

JULIA: May no harm come to your will.

FEFU: Fight, Julia!

JULIA: I have no life left.

FEFU: Fight, Julia!

JULIA: May no harm come to your hands.

FEFU: I need you to fight.

JULIA: May no harm come to your eyes.

FEFU: Fight with me!

JULIA: May no harm come to your voice.

FEFU: Fight with me!

JULIA: May no harm come to your heart.

[Christina enters. Fefu sees Christina, releases Julia. To Christina.]

FEFU: Now I have done it. Haven't I. You think I'm a monster. *[To Julia.]* Forgive me if you can. *[Julia nods.]*

JULIA: I forgive you.

[Fefu gets the gun.]

CHRISTINA: What in the world are you doing with that gun?

FEFU: I'm going to clean it.

CHRISTINA: I think you better not.

FEFU: I think you're silly.

[Cecilia appears on the landing. She is ready to go.]

CHRISTINA: I don't care if you shoot yourself. I just don't like the mess you're making.

[Fefu starts to go to the lawn and turns.]

FEFU: I enjoy betting it won't be a real bullet. You want to bet?
CHRISTINA: No. *[Fefu exits. Christina goes to Julia.]* Are you all right?
JULIA: Yes.
CHRISTINA: Can I get you anything?
JULIA: Water. *[Cecilia goes to the bar for water.]* Put some sugar in it. Could I have a damp cloth for my forehead? *[Christina goes toward the kitchen.]* I didn't tell her anything. Did I? I didn't.
CECILIA: About what?
JULIA: She knew. *[There is the sound of a shot. Christina and Cecilia run out. Julia puts her hand to her forehead. Her hand goes down slowly. There is blood on her forehead. Her head falls back. Fefu enters holding a dead rabbit in her arms. She stands behind Julia.]*
FEFU: I killed it…I just shot…and killed it…Julia.

[Sue and Cindy enter from the foyer, Emma from the backstage entrance, Paula from upstairs, Christina and Cecilia from the lawn. They surround Julia. The lights fade.]

Tess Gallagher

Tess Gallagher's most recent collection of poetry is *Willingly* (1984). She has two previous collections of poetry and has recently begun to publish short fiction. She received Creative Writing Fellowships in 1976 and 1981.

EACH BIRD WALKING

Not while, but long after he had told me,
I thought of him, washing his mother, his
bending over the bed and taking back
the covers. There was a basin of water
and he dipped a washrag in and
out of the basin, the rag
dripping a little onto the sheet as he
turned from the bedside to the nightstand
and back, there being no place

on her body he shouldn't touch because
he had to and she helped him, moving
the little she could, lifting so he could
wipe under her arms, a dipping motion
in the hollow. Then working up from
the feet, around the ankles, over the
knees. And this last, opening
her thighs and running the rag firmly
and with the cleaning thought
up through her crotch, between the lips,
over the V of thin hairs —

as though he were a mother
who had the excuse of cleaning to touch

with love and indifference
the secret parts of her child, to graze
the sleepy sexlessness in its waiting
to find out what to do for the sake
of the body, for the sake of what only
the body can do for itself.

So his hand, softly at the place
of his birth-light. And she, eyes deepened
and closed in the dim room.
And because he told me her death as
important to his being with her,
I could love him another way. Not
of the body alone, or of its making,
but carried in the white spires of trembling
until what spirit, what breath we were
was shaken from us. Small then,
the word *holy*.

He turned her on her stomach
and washed the blades of her shoulders, the
small of her back. "That's good," she said,
"that's enough."

On our lips that morning, the tart juice
of the mothers, so strong in remembrance, no
asking, no giving, and what you said, this
being the end of our loving, so as not to hurt
the closer one to you, made me look
to see what was left of us
with our sex taken away. "Tell me," I said,
"something I can't forget." Then the story of
your mother, and when you finished
I said, "That's good, that's enough."

John Gardner

John Gardner is known for his novels, short stories, children's fairy tales, and nonfiction (*On Moral Fiction, The Art of Fiction*). His novel *October Light* won a National Book Critics Circle Award in 1976. Gardner received a Creative Writing Fellowship in 1972.

NIMRAM

Ich bin von Gott und will wieder zu Gott.
— FOR WILLIAM H. GASS

SEATED BY the window in the last row of the first-class no-smoking section, his large attaché case edged under the seat in front of him, his seatbelt snug and buckled, Benjamin Nimram drew off his dark glasses, tucked them into his inside coat-pocket, and in the same motion turned to look out at the rain on the gleaming tarmac. The dark glasses were his wife's idea, an idea he'd accepted in the way he accepted nearly all her ideas, with affection and a tuck at the corner of his mouth that signified, though his wife did not know it — or so he imagined — private amusement tinged with that faint trace of fatalistic melancholy one might catch, if one were watchful, at the periphery of all he did. Not that Nimram was a gloomy man. When he'd put behind him, at least for public appearances, that famous "Beethoven frown" — once a private joke between his wife and himself but now a thing as public as the mileage of his Rolls, since his wife had mentioned both, in an unguarded moment, to an interviewer — he'd discovered that smiling like a birthday child as he strode, tails flying, toward the light-drenched podium came as naturally to him as breathing, or at any rate as naturally as the second-nature breathing of an oboist. He had mentioned to her — more in the way of trying it out than as sober communication of a determined fact — that it made him uneasy, being recognized everywhere he went these days.

"You poor dear!" she'd said, eyes slightly widening, and he had smiled privately, realizing that now he was in for it. "We'll get a pair of those Polaroid prescription dark glasses," she'd said.

"Good idea," he'd agreed, seeing himself in them the instant he said it – the dark, heavy face, thick eyebrows, large nose, the somewhat embarrassingly expensive suit. "And a shoulder-holster, maybe," he'd thought, but had carefully shown nothing but the tuck at the corner of his mouth.

"Is something wrong?" she'd asked. She stood in the doorway, half in, half out, trowel in hand, a paper bag of some kind of chemical clamped under her arm. He'd caught her on her way out to her gardening. She was smiling brightly, head tipped and thrown toward him, back into the room. It was the look she sometimes got on the tennis court, extravagantly polite, aggressive.

"What could be wrong?" he said, tossing his arms out. "I'll pick up a pair this afternoon."

"Jerry can get them," she said. "I'll phone in ahead." Jerry was their outside man, a grinning young half-Japanese. What he did around the place – besides stand with his arms folded, or ride around the lawn on the huge green mower – had never been clear to Nimram.

"Fine," he said, "fine."

She blew him a kiss and ran out.

Poor Arline, he thought, shaking his head, slightly grinning. "I believe I was destined for this marriage," she had once told an interviewer. Though she was sometimes embarrassed almost to tears by what she read in the interviews she'd given to newspapers and magazines, she continued to give them. She saw it as part of her duty as his wife, keeping his name out there. And though she tried to be more careful, knowing how "different" things could sound in print, to say nothing of how reporters could distort if they were, as she said, "that kind" – turning trifles to tragedies, missing jokes, even suddenly attacking her for no reason (one had once called her "a musical ignoramus") – she continued to forget and speak her mind. Nimram praised her, needless to say, no matter what she said. Certainly there was never any harm in her words. Even her

cunning, when she schemed about his "image" or the I.R.S., had
the innocent openness of the Michigan fields around her father's
little place in the country, as he called it – a house sometimes
visited, long before her father had bought it, by the elder Henry
Ford.

There wasn't a great deal Arline could do for him in the world,
or anyway not a great deal he could make her feel he needed and
appreciated – aside, of course, from her elegant company at social
gatherings, for instance fund-raisers. She was "a good Michigan
girl," as she said; Republican, a member (lapsed) of the D.A.R.
Subtly – or no, not subtly, but openly, flagrantly – she had been
trained from birth for the sacred and substantial position of Good
Wife. She was a quick learner – even brilliant, he might have said
in an unguarded moment, if Nimram ever had such moments –
and she had snapped up the requisite skills of her position the way
a streetdog snaps up meat. She was not a great reader (books were
one of Nimram's passions), and music was not really her first interest in life, except, of course, when Nimram conducted it; but she
could keep a household like an old-time Viennese aristocrat; she
could "present" her husband, choosing the right restaurants,
wines, and charities, buying him not only the exactly right clothes,
as it seemed to her (and for all he knew she had unerring taste,
though sometimes her choices raised his eyebrows at first), but
also finding him the exactly right house, or, rather, Brentwood
mansion – formerly the home of a reclusive movie star – the suit-
able cars – first the Porsche, then on second thought, of course,
the Rolls – the suitably lovable fox terrier, which Arline had named
Trixie. She had every skill known to the well-to-do Midwestern
wife, including certain bedroom skills that Nimram waited with a
smile of dread for her to reveal, in her open-hearted, Michigan
way, to some yenta from *People* magazine or the L.A. *Times*. But
for all that, she had moments, he knew, when she seemed to herself
inadequate, obscurely unprepared.

"Do you like the house?" she had asked him once, with a bright
smile and an uneasiness around the eyes that made his heart go
out to her. It was only his heart that got up from the chair; the
rest of him sat solid as a rock, with a marked-up score on his knees.

"Of course I like it," he'd answered. "I love it!" When they were alone or among intimate friends his voice had, at times, a hearty bellow that could make Arline jump.

"Good!" she'd said, and had smiled more brightly, then had added, her expression unsure again, "It does seem a solid investment."

Nimram might have said, if he were someone else, "What's the difference? What's a house? I'm the greatest conductor in the world! Civilization is my house!" That, however, was the kind of thing Nimram never said to anyone, even in one of his rare but notorious rages.

Her look of uncertainty was almost anguish now, though she labored to conceal it, and so he'd laid down the score he was fiddling with, had renounced the brief flash of doubt over whether he should leave it there – defenseless on the carpet, where the dog could come in and, say, drool on it – and had swung up out of his chair and strode over to seize her in his arms and press his cheek to hers, saying, "What's this craziness? It's a beautiful house and I love it!"

There had been, apparently, an edge of uncontrol in his heartiness, or perhaps it was simply the age-old weight of the world distracting her, time and the beauty of things falling away, nothing sure, nothing strong enough to bear her up – not yet, anyway, not as quickly as that – not even the strength in her famous conductor's arms. "I'm sorry," she'd said, blinking away tears, giving her embarrassed Midwesterner laugh. "Aren't I a fool?" – biting her lips now, taking on the sins of the world.

"Come," he'd said, "we eat out." It was his standard response to all sorrows no energy of the baton could transmute; a brief arrogation of the power of God – no offense, since God had no interest in it, it seemed.

"But dinner's been – " she'd begun, drawing back from him, already of two minds.

"No no," he'd said, tyrannical. "Go get dressed. We eat out." Candlelight burning through the wine bottle, silverware shining like her dream of eternity, people across the room showing one by one and four by four their covert signs of having recognized the famous conductor, a thing they could speak of tomorrow and next week, next year, perhaps, buoy themselves up on in dreary times, the memory of that dinner miraculously blessed, as if God Himself had come to sit with them. The tuck of private amusement and sadness touched the corner of Nimram's mouth.

He was not a man who had ever given thought to whether or not his opinions of himself and his effect on the world were inflated. He was a musician simply, or not so simply; an interpreter of Mahler and Bruckner, Sibelius and Nielsen – much as his wife Arline, buying him clothes, transforming his Beethoven frown to his now just as famous bright smile, brushing her lips across his cheek as he plunged (almost hurrying) toward sleep, was the dutiful and faithful interpreter of Benjamin Nimram. His life was sufficient, a joy to him, in fact. One might have thought of it – and so Nimram himself thought of it, in certain rare moods – as one resounding success after another. He had conducted every major symphony in the world, had been granted by Toscanini's daughters the privilege of studying their father's scores, treasure-horde of the old man's secrets; he could count among his closest friends some of the greatest musicians of his time. He had so often been called a genius by critics everywhere that he had come to take it for granted that he was indeed just that – "just that" in both senses, exactly that and merely that: a fortunate accident, a man supremely lucky. Had he been born with an ear just a little less exact, a personality more easily ruffled, dexterity less precise, or some physical weakness – a heart too feeble for the demands he made of it, or arthritis, the plague of so many conductors – he would still, no doubt, have been a symphony man, but his ambition would have been checked a little, his ideas of self-fulfillment scaled down. Whatever fate had dealt him he would have learned, no doubt, to put up with, guarding his chips. But Nimram had been dealt all high cards, and he knew it. He revelled in his fortune, sprawling when he sat, his big-boned fingers splayed wide on his belly like a man who's just had dinner, his spirit as playful as a child's for all the gray at his temples, all his middle-aged bulk and weight – packed muscle, all of it – a man too much enjoying himself to have time for scorn or for fretting over whether or not he was getting his due, which, anyway, he was. He was one of the elect. He sailed through the world like a white yacht jubilant with flags.

THE RAIN fell steadily, figures and dark square tractors hurrying toward the belly of the plane and then away again, occasionally glowing under blooms of silent lightning, in the aisle behind him passengers still moving with the infinite patience of Tolstoy peasants toward their second-class seats. With a part of his mind he watched their reflections in the window and wondered idly how many of them, if any, had seen him conduct, seen anyone conduct, cared at all for the shimmering ghost he had staked his life on. None of them, so far as he could tell, had even noticed the Muzak leaking cheerfully, mindlessly, from the plane's invisible speakers. It would be turned off when the plane was safely airborne, for which he was grateful, needless to say. Yet it was touching, in a way, that the airline should offer this feeble little gesture of reassururance – *All will be well! Listen to the Muzak! All will be well!* They scarcely heard it, these children of accident, old and young, setting out across the country in the middle of the night; yet perhaps it was true that they were comforted, lulled.

Now a voice said behind him, professionally kind, "There you are. There! Shall I take these? All right?"

When he turned, the stewardess was taking the metal crutches from the young woman – girl, rather – newly planted in the seat beside him.

"Thank you," the girl was saying, reaching down to each side of her for the straps of her seatbelt.

"They'll be right up in front," the stewardess said, drawing the crutches toward her shoulder to clamp them in one arm. "If you need anything, you just sing. All right?"

"Thank you," the girl said again, nodding, drawing up the straps now, studying the buckle. She nodded one more time, smiling suddenly, seeing how the buckle worked, and closed it. She glanced briefly at Nimram, then away again. She was perhaps sixteen.

He too looked away and, with his heart jumping, considered the image of her fixed in his mind. She was so much like his wife

Arline—though of course much younger—that he was ready to believe her a lost sister. It was impossible, he knew; Arline's people were not the kind who lost things, much less the kind who had secrets, except on Christmas morning. Yet for all his certainty, some stubborn, infantile part of his brain seized on the idea with both fists and refused to let go. Her hair, like Arline's, was reddish brown, with an outer layer of yellow; hair so soft and fine it was like a brush of light. Their foreheads, noses, mouths, and chins were identical too, or so he'd thought at first. As he turned now, furtively checking, he saw that the girl's nose was straighter than Arline's—prettier, if anything—and more lightly freckled. For all that, the likeness grew stronger as he studied it.

She looked up, caught him watching her, smiled, and looked away. The blue of her eyes was much paler than the blue of Arline's, and the difference so startled him that for a moment—shifting in his seat, clearing his throat, turning to look out at the rain again— he could hardly believe he'd thought the two faces similar. He watched the girl's reflection, in the window eight inches from his face, as she reached toward the pocket on the back of the seat in front of her and drew out a magazine, or perhaps the plasticized safety card.

"I hope they know what they're doing," she said.

Her face, when he half turned to look, showed no sign of joking. Ordinarily, Nimram would have smiled and said nothing. For some reason he spoke. "This your first trip on an airplane?"

She nodded, smiling back, a smile so full of panic he almost laughed.

"Don't worry," he said, "the pilot's in front. Anything happens, he gets it first. He's very concerned about that." Nimram winked.

The girl studied him as if lost in thought, the smile on her face still there but forgotten, and it seemed to him he knew what she was thinking. She was in no condition to pick up ironies. When he'd told her the pilot was "very concerned," did he mean that the pilot was nervous? neurotic? beginning to slip? Did this big, ex- pensive-looking man in the seat beside her *know* the pilot?

"Do you know the pilot?" she asked innocently, brightening up her smile.

"A joke," he said. "Among people who fly airplanes it's the oldest joke in the world. It means don't worry."

She turned away and looked down at the plasticized card. "It's just, with the rain and everything," she said softly, "what happens if a plane gets hit by lightning?"

"I doubt that it would do any harm," he said, knowing it wasn't true. The Vienna Quartet had been killed just a year ago when their plane had been knocked down by lightning. "Anyway, we won't be going anywhere near where the lightning is. They have sophisticated weather charts, radar…anyway, most of the time we'll be high above it all. You live here in Los Angeles?"

The girl glanced at him, smiling vaguely. She hadn't heard. The Captain had broken in on the Muzak to tell them his name and the usual trivia, their projected altitude, flight time, weather, the airline's friendly advice about seatbelts. Nimram examined the girl's arm and hand on the armrest, then looked at his own and frowned. She had something wrong with her. He remembered that she'd come on with crutches, and glanced again at her face. Like her hand, it was slightly off-color, slightly puffy. Some blood disease, perhaps.

Now the stewardess was leaning down toward them, talking to both of them as if she thought they were together. Nimram studied the sharp, dark red sheen of her hair, metallic oxblood. Her face, in comparison with the girl's, was shockingly healthy. She addressed them by their names, "Mr. Nimram, Miss Curtis," a trifle that brought the melancholy tuck to Nimram's mouth, he could hardly have told you why himself – something about civility and human vulnerability, a commercially tainted civility, no doubt (he could see her quickly scanning the first-class passenger list, as per instruction, memorizing names), but civility nonetheless, the familiar old defiance of night and thunder: when they plunged into the Pacific, on the way out for the turn, or snapped off a wing on the horn of some mountain, or exploded in the air or burst into shrapnel and flame on the Mojave, they would die by name: "Mr. Nimram, Miss Curtis." Or anyway so it would be for the people in first class. "When we're airborne," the stewardess was saying, "we'll be serving complimentary drinks…." As she named them off, Miss Curtis sat frowning with concentration, as panicky as ever. She ordered a Coke; Nimram ordered wine. The stewardess smiled as if delighted and moved away.

NEITHER OF THEM noticed when the plane began to move. The girl had asked him if he flew on airplanes often, and he'd launched a full and elaborate answer – New York, Paris, Rome, Tokyo.... He beamed, gesturing as he spoke, as if flying were the greatest of his pleasures. Nothing could be farther from the truth, in fact; flying bored and annoyed him, not that he was afraid – Nimram was afraid of almost nothing, at any rate nothing he'd experienced so far, and he'd be forty-nine in June. Or rather, to be precise, he was afraid of nothing that could happen to himself, only of things that threatened others. Once he'd been hit on the Los Angeles express-way, when Arline was with him. Her head had been thrown against the dashboard and she'd been knocked unconscious. Nimram, drag-ging her from the car, cursing the police, who were nowhere to be seen, and shouting at the idiot by-standers, had found himself shak-ing like a leaf. Sometimes, lying in bed with his arm around her as she slept, Nimram, listening to the silence of the house, the very faint whine of trucks on the highway two miles away, would feel almost crushed by the weight of his fear for her, heaven bearing down on their roof like the base of a graveyard monument – though nothing was wrong, she was well, ten years younger than he was and strong as a horse from all the tennis and swimming.

In his hundreds of flights – maybe it was thousands – he'd never had once what he could honestly describe as a close call, and he'd come to believe that he probably never would have one; but he knew, as surely as a human being can know anything, that if he ever did, he probably wouldn't be afraid. Like most people, he'd heard friends speak, from time to time, about their fear of dying, and the feeling was not one he scorned or despised; but the fact remained, he was not the kind of man who had it. "Well, you're lucky," Arline had said, refusing to believe him, getting for an instant the hard look that came when she believed she was some-how being criticized. "Yes, lucky," he'd said thoughtfully. It was the single most notable fact about his life.

Abruptly, the girl, Miss Curtis, broke in on his expansive praise of airlines. "We're moving!" she exclaimed, darting her head past his shoulder in the direction of the window, no less surprised, it seemed, than she'd have been if they were sitting in a building.

Nimram joined her in looking out, watching yellow lights pass, the taxiway scored by rain-wet blue-and-white beams thrown by lights farther out. Now on the loudspeaker an invisible stewardess began explaining the use of oxygen masks and the positions of the doors, while their own stewardess, with slightly parted lips and her eyes a little widened, pointed and gestured without a sound, like an Asian dancer. The girl beside him listened as if in despair, glum as a student who's fallen hopelessly behind. Her hand on the armrest was more yellow than before.

"Don't worry," Nimram said, "you'll like it."

She was apparently too frightened to speak or turn her head.

Now the engines wound up to full power, a sound that for no real reason reminded Nimram of the opening of Brahms' First, and lights came on, surprisingly powerful, like a searchlight or the headlight of a railroad engine, smashing through the rain as if by violent will, flooding the runway below and ahead of the wing just behind him, and the plane began its quickly accelerating, furious run down the field for take-off. Like a grandfather, Nimram put his hand on the girl's. "Look," he said, showing his smile, tilting his head in the direction of the window, but she shook her head just perceptibly and shut her eyes tight. Again for an instant he was struck by the likeness, as remarkable now as it had been when he'd first seen her, and he tried to remember when Arline had squeezed her eyes shut in exactly that way. He could see her face vividly – they were outdoors somewhere, in summer, perhaps in England – but the background refused to fill in for him, remained just a sunlit, ferny green, and the memory tingling in the cellar of his mind dimmed out. The Brahms was still playing itself inside him, solemn and magnificent, aglow, like the lights of the city now fallen far beneath them, lurid in the rain. Now the plane was banking, yawing like a ship as it founders and slips over, the headlights rushing into churning spray, the unbelievably large black wing upended, suddenly white in a blast of clouded lightning, then black again, darker than before. As the plane righted itself, the pilot began speaking to the passengers again. Nimram, frowning his Beethoven frown, hardly noticed. The plane began to bounce, creaking like a carriage, still climbing to get above the weather.

"Dear God," the girl whispered.

"It's all right, it's all all right," Nimram said, and pressed her hand.

HER NAME was Anne. She was, as he'd guessed, sixteen; from Chicago; and though she did not tell him what her disease was or directly mention that she was dying, she made her situation clear enough. "It's incredible," she said. "One of my grandmothers is ninety-two, the other one's eighty-six. But I guess it doesn't matter. If you're chosen, you're chosen." A quick, embarrassed smile. "Are you in business or something?"

"More or less," he said. "You're in school?"

"High school," she said.

"You have boyfriends?"

"No."

Nimram shook his head as if in wonderment and looked quickly toward the front of the plane for some distraction. "Ah," he said, "here's the stewardess with our drinks."

The girl smiled and nodded, though the stewardess was still two seats away. "We don't seem to have gotten above the storm, do we." She was looking past him, out of the window at the towers and cloud lighting up, darkening, then lighting again. The plane was still jouncing, as if bumping things more solid than any possible air or cloud, maybe Plato's airy beasts.

"Things'll settle down in a minute," Nimram said.

Innocently, the girl asked, "Are you religious or anything?"

"Well, no — " He caught himself. "More or less," he said.

"You're more or less in business and you're more or less religious," the girl said, and smiled as if she'd caught him. "Are you a gambler, then?"

He laughed. "Is that what I look like?"

She continued to smile, but studied him, looking mainly at his black-and-gray unruly hair. "Actually, I never saw one, that I know of. Except in movies."

Nimram mused. "I guess we're pretty much all of us gamblers," he said, and at once felt embarrassment at having come on like a philosopher or, worse, a poet.

"I know," she said without distress. "Winners and losers."

He shot her a look. If she was going to go on like this she was going to be trouble. Was she speaking so freely because they were strangers? – travelers who'd never meet again? He folded and unfolded his hands slowly, in a way that would have seemed to an observer not nervous but judicious; and, frowning more severely than he knew, his graying eyebrows low, Nimram thought about bringing out the work in his attaché case.

Before he reached his decision, their stewardess was bending down toward them, helping the girl drop her tray into position. Nimram lowered his, then took the wineglass and bottle the stewardess held out. No sooner had he set down the glass than the plane hit what might have been a slanted stone wall in the middle of the sky and veered crazily upward, then laboriously steadied.

"Oh my God, dear God, my God!" the girl whispered.

"You *are* religious," Nimram said, and smiled.

She said nothing, but sat rigid, slightly cross at him, perhaps, steadying the glass on the napkin now soaked in Coke.

The pilot came on again, casual, as if amused by their predicament. "Sorry we can't give you a smoother ride, folks, but looks like Mother Nature's in a real tizzy tonight. We're taking the ship up to thirty-seven thousand, see if we can't just outfox her."

"Is that safe?" the girl asked softly.

He nodded and shrugged. "Safe as a ride in a rockingchair," he said.

They could feel the plane nosing up, climbing so sharply that for a moment even Nimram felt a touch of dismay. The bumping and creaking became less noticeable. Nimram took a deep breath and poured his wine.

Slowly, carefully, the girl raised the Coke to her lips and took a small sip, then set it down again. "I hope it's not like this in Chicago," she said.

"I'm sure it won't be." He toasted her with the wineglass – she seemed not to notice – then drew it to his mouth and drank.

HE COULDN'T tell how long he'd slept or what, if anything, he'd dreamed. The girl slept beside him, fallen toward his shoulder, the cabin around them droning quietly, as if singing to itself, below them what might have been miles of darkness, as if the planet had silently fallen out from under them, tumbling toward God knew what. Here in the dimly lit cabin, Nimram felt serene. They'd be landing at O'Hare shortly — less than two hours. Arline would be waiting in the lounge, smiling eagerly, even more pleased than usual to see him, after three long days with her parents. He'd be no less glad to see her, of course; yet just now, though he knew that that moment was rushing toward him, he felt aloof from it, suspended above time's wild drive like the note of a single flute above a poised and silent orchestra. For all he could tell, the plane itself might have been hanging motionless, as still as the pinprick stars overhead.

The cabin had grown chilly, and, carefully, making sure he didn't wake her, Nimram raised the girl's blanket toward her throat. She stirred, a muscle along her jaw twitching, but continued to sleep, her breathing deep and even. Across the aisle from them, an old woman opened her eyes and stared straight ahead, listening like someone who imagines she's heard a burglar in the kitchen, then closed them again, indifferent.

Thoughtfully, Nimram gazed at the sleeping girl. On her forehead, despite the cold, there were tiny beads of sweat. He considered brushing the hair back from her face — it looked as if it tickled — but with his hand already in the air he checked himself, then lowered the hand. She was young enough to be his daughter, he mused, pursing his lips. Thank God she wasn't. Instantly, he hated it that he'd thought such a thing. She was *some* poor devil's daughter. Then it dawned on Nimram that she was young enough, too, to be Arline's daughter, from the time before Arline and he had met. Arline was thirty-nine, the girl sixteen. The faintest trace of a prickling came to his scalp, and he felt now a different kind of chill in the cabin, as if a cloud had passed between his soul and some invisible sun. "Don't ask!" Arline would say when he drew her toward the subject of her life — that is, her love-life — before they knew each other. "I was wild," she would say, laughing,

"God!" and would touch his cheek with the back of her hand. The dark, infantile part of Nimram's mind seized on that now with the same blind obstinance as it had earlier seized on the idea that the girl was Arline's sister. Consciously, or with his brain's left lobe, perhaps, he knew the idea was nonsense. Arline's laugh had no abandoned child in it, only coy hints of old escapades — love-making on beaches or in the back seats of cars, drunken parties in the houses of friends when the parents were far away in Cleveland or Detroit, and then when she was older, affairs more serious and miserable. She had been married, briefly, to a man who had something to do with oil-rigs. About that he knew a fair amount, though with her Anglo-Saxon ideas of what was proper she hated to speak of it. In any case, the idea that the girl might be her daughter was groundless and absurd; if it remained, roaming in the dark of his mind, it remained against his will, like a rat in the basement, too canny to be poisoned or trapped. Even so, even after he'd rejected it utterly, he found that the groundless suspicion had subtly transmuted the way he saw the girl. He felt in his chest and at the pit of his stomach an echo of the anguish her parents must be feeling, a shadowy sorrow that, for all his notorious good fortune, made him feel helpless.

Strange images began to molest Nimram's thoughts, memories of no real significance, yet intense, like charged images in a dream. Memories, ideas...It was hard to say what they were. It was as if he had indeed, by a careless misstep, slipped out of time, as if the past and present had collapsed into one unbroken instant, so that he was both himself and himself at sixteen, the age of the girl asleep beside him.

He was riding on a train, late at night, through Indiana, alone. The seats were once-red plush, old and stiff, discolored almost to black. There was a round black handle, like the handle of a gear-shift, that one pulled to make the back recline. Toward the rear of the car an old man in black clothes was coughing horribly, hacking as if to throw up his lungs. The conductor, sitting in the car's only light, his black cap pulled forward to the rim of his glasses, was laboriously writing something, muttering, from time to time — never looking up from his writing toward the cougher — "God

damn you, die!" It was so vivid it made his scalp prickle, the musical thrumming of wheels on rails as distinct in Nimram's mind
as the drone of the airplane he sat in. The wheels and railjoints
picked up the muttered words, transforming them to music, a
witless, everlastingly repetitive jingle: *God damn you, die!* (click)
God damn you, die! (click)...

Sometimes he'd awakened in terror, he remembered, riding on
the train, convinced that the train had fallen off the tracks and was
hurtling through space; but when he looked out the window at
the blur of dark trees and shrubs rushing by, the ragged fields gray
as bones in the moonlight, he would be reassured – the train was
going lickety-split, but all was well. Though it seemed only an instant ago, if not happening right now, it also seemed ages ago:
he'd lived, since then, through innumerable train rides, bus rides,
plane rides – lived through two marriages and into a third, lived
through God knew how many playing jobs, conducting jobs, fund-
raising benefits, deaths of friends. He'd lived through warplane
formations over Brooklyn; explosions in the harbor, no comment
in the papers; lived through the birth and rise of Israel, had conducted the Israel Philharmonic; lived through...but that was not
the point. She was sixteen, her head hanging loose, free of the
pillow, like a flower on a weak, bent stem. All that time, the time
he'd already consumed too fast to notice he was losing it – it might
have been centuries, so it felt to him now – was time the girl would
never get.

It wasn't pity he felt, or even anger at the general injustice of
things; it was bewilderment, a kind of shock that stilled the wits. If
he were religious – he was, of course, but not in the common sense –
he might have been furious at God's mishandling of the universe, or
at very least puzzled by the disparity between real and ideal. But none
of that was what he felt. God had nothing to do with it, and the
whole question of real and ideal was academic. Nimram felt only,
looking at the girl – her skin off-color, her head unsupported yet un-
troubled by the awkwardness, tolerant as a corpse – Nimram felt
only a profound embarrassment and helplessness: helplessly fortunate and therefore unfit, unworthy, his whole life light and unprofit-
able as a puff-ball, needless as ascending smoke. He hardly knew her,

yet he felt now – knowing it was a lie but knowing also that if the girl were really his daughter it would be true – that if Nature allowed it, Mother of tizzies and silences, he would change lives with the girl beside him in an instant.

Suddenly the girl cried out sharply and opened her eyes.

"Here now! It's okay!" he said, and touched her shoulder.

She shook her head, not quite awake, disoriented. "Oh!" she said, and blushed – a kind of thickening of the yellow-gray skin. "Oh, I'm sorry!" She flashed her panicky smile. "I was having a dream."

"Everything's all right," he said, "don't worry now, everything's fine."

"It's really funny," she said, shaking her head again, so hard the soft hair flew. She drew back from him and raised her hands to her eyes. "It was the strangest dream!" she said, and lowered her hands to look out the window, squinting a little, trying to recapture what she'd seen. He saw that his first impression had been mistaken; it had not, after all, been a nightmare. "I dreamed I was in a room, a kind of moldy old cellar where there were animals of some kind, and when I tried to open the door – " She broke off and glanced around to see if anyone was listening. No one was awake. She slid her eyes toward him, wanting to go on but unsure of herself. He bent his head, waiting with interest. Hesitantly, she said, "When I tried to open the door, the doorknob came off in my hands. I started scraping at the door with my fingers and, somehow – " She scowled, trying to remember. "I don't know, somehow the door broke away and I discovered that behind the door, where the world outside should be, there was…there was this huge, like, parlor. Inside it there was every toy or doll I ever had that had been broken or lost, all in perfect condition."

"Interesting dream," he said, looking at her forehead, not her eyes; then, feeling that something more was expected, "Dreams are strange things."

"I know." She nodded, then quickly asked, "What time is it, do you know? How long before we get to Chicago?"

"They're two hours ahead of us. According to my watch – "

Before he could finish, she broke in, "Yes, that's right. I forgot."

A shudder went through her, and she asked, "Is it cold in here?"

"Freezing," he said.

"Thank God!" She looked past him, out the window, and abruptly brightened. "It's gotten nice out – anyway, I don't see any lightning." She gave her head a jerk, tossing back the hair.

"It's behind us," he said. "I see you're not afraid anymore."

"You're wrong," she said, and smiled. "But it's true, it's not as bad as it was. All the same, I'm still praying."

"Good idea," he said.

She shot a quick look at him, then smiled uncertainly, staring straight ahead. "A lot of people don't believe in praying and things," she said. "They try to make you feel stupid for doing it, like when a boy wants to play the violin instead of trumpet or drums. In our orchestra at school the whole string section's made up of girls except for one poor guy that plays viola." She paused and glanced at him, then smiled. "It's really funny how I never make sense when I talk to you."

"Sure you do."

She shrugged. "Anyway, some say there's a God and some say there isn't, and they're both so positive you wouldn't believe it. Personally, I'm not sure one way or the other, but when I'm scared I pray."

"It's like the old joke," he began.

"Do you like music?" she asked. "Classical, I mean?"

Nimram frowned. "Oh, sometimes."

"Who's your favorite composer?"

It struck him for the first time that perhaps his favorite composer was Machaut. "Beethoven?" he said.

It was apparently the right answer. "Who's your favorite conductor?"

He pretended to think about it.

"Mine's Seiji Ozawa," she said.

Nimram nodded, lips pursed. "I hear he's good."

She shook her head again to get the hair out of her eyes. "Oh well," she said. Some thought had possessed her, making her face formal, pulling the lines all downward. She folded her hands and looked at them, then abruptly, with an effort, lifted her eyes to meet his. "I guess I told you a kind of lie," she said.

He raised his eyebrows.

"I do have a boyfriend, actually." Quickly, as if for fear that he might ask the young man's name, she said, "You know how when you meet someone you want to sound more interesting than you are? Well – " She looked back at her folded hands, and he could see her forcing herself up to it. "I do this tragic act."

He sat very still, nervously prepared to grin, waiting.

She mumbled something, and when he leaned toward her she raised her voice, still without looking at him, her voice barely audible even now, and said, "I'm what they call 'terminal,' but, well, I mean, it doesn't *mean* anything, you know? It's sort of...The only time it makes me scared, or makes me cry, things like that, is when I say to myself in words, 'I'm going to...'" He saw that it was true; if she finished the sentence she would cry. She breathed very shallowly and continued, "If the airplane crashed, it wouldn't make much difference as far as I'm concerned, just make it a little sooner, but just the same when we were taking off, with the lightning and everything..." Now she did, for an instant, look up at him. "I never make any sense." Her eyes were full of tears.

"No," he said, "you make sense enough."

She was wringing her hands, smiling as if in chagrin, but smiling with pleasure too, the happiness lifting off as if defiantly above the deadweight of discomfort. "Anyway, I do have a boyfriend. He's the one that plays viola, actually. He's nice. I mean, he's wonderful. His name's Stephen." She raised both hands to wipe the tears away. "I mean, it's really funny. My life's really wonderful." She gave a laugh, then covered her face with both hands, her shoulders shaking.

He patted the side of her arm, saying nothing.

"The reason I wanted to tell you," she said when she was able to speak, "is, you've really been nice. I didn't want to – "

"That's all right," he said. "Look, that's how we all are."

"I know," she said, and suddenly laughed, crying. "That really is true, isn't it! It's just like my uncle Charley says. He lives with us. He's my mother's older brother. He says the most interesting thing about Noah's Ark is that all the animals on it were scared and stupid."

Nimram laughed.

"He really is wonderful," she said, "except that he coughs all the time. He's dying of emphysema, but mention that he ought to stop smoking his pipe, or mention that maybe he should go see a doctor, Uncle Charley goes right through the ceiling. It's really that spending money terrifies him, but he pretends it's doctors he hates. Just mention the word and he starts yelling 'False prophets! Profiteers! Pill-pushers! Snake-handlers!' He can really get loud. My father says we should tie him out front for a watchdog." She laughed again.

Nimram's ears popped. They were beginning the long descent. After a moment he said, "Actually, I haven't been strictly honest with you either. I'm not really in business."

She looked at him, waiting with what seemed to him a curiously childish eagerness.

"I'm a symphony conductor."

"Are you really?" she asked, lowering her eyebrows, studying him to see if he was lying. "What's your name?"

"Benjamin Nimram," he said.

Her eyes narrowed, and the embarrassment was back. He could see her searching her memory. "I think I've heard of you," she said.

"*Sic transit gloria mundi,*" he said, mock-morose.

She smiled and pushed her hair back. "I know what that means," she said.

The no-smoking sign came on. In the distance the earth was adazzle with lights.

IN THE LOUNGE at O'Hare he spotted his wife at once, motionless and smiling in the milling crowd—she hadn't yet seen him—her beret and coat dark red, almost black. He hurried toward her. Now she saw him and, breaking that stillness like the stillness of an old, old painting, raised her arm to wave, threw herself back into time, and came striding to meet him. He drew off and folded the dark glasses.

"Ben!" she exclaimed, and they embraced. "Honey, you look terrible!" She pulled back to look at him, then hugged him again.

"On TV it said there was a thunderstorm in L.A., one of the worst ever. I was worried sick!"

"Now now," he said, holding her a moment longer. "So how were Poppa and Momma?"

"How was the flight?" she asked. "I bet it was awful! Did the man from the kennel come for Trixie?"

He took her hand and they started, moving with long, matched strides, toward the terminal.

"Trixie's fine, the flight was fine, everything's fine," he said.

She tipped her head, mocking. "Are you drunk, Benjamin?"

They veered out, passing an old couple inching along on canes, arguing.

"I met a girl," he said.

She checked his eyes. "Pretty?" she asked – laughingly, teasingly; but part of her was watching like a hawk. And why not, of course. He'd been married twice before, and they were as different, she and himself, as day and night. Why should she have faith? He thought again of the conviction he'd momentarily felt that the girl was her daughter. Sooner or later, he knew, he would find himself asking her about it; but not now. *Scared and stupid*, he thought, remembering, and the tuck at the corner of his mouth came back. He got an image of Noah's Ark as a great, blind, dumb thing nosing carefully, full of fear, toward the smell of Ararat.

"Too young," he said. "Practically not yet of this world."

They were walking very fast, as they always did, gliding smoothly past all the others. Now and then he glanced past his shoulder, hoping to spot Anne Curtis; but it was absurd, he knew. She'd be the last of the last, chattering, he hoped, or doing her tragic act. Arline's coat flared out behind her and her face was flushed.

ALMOST AS SOON as she stepped off the plane, Anne Curtis found out from her father who it was that had befriended her. The following night, when Nimram conducted the Chicago Symphony in Mahler's Fifth, she was in the audience, in the second balcony, with her parents. They arrived late, after the Water Music, with which he had opened the program. Her father had gotten tickets only at the last minute, and it was a long drive in from La Grange. They edged into their seats while the orchestra was being rearranged, new instruments being added, the people who'd played the Handel scrunching forward and closer together.

She had never before seen a Mahler orchestra – nine French horns, wave on wave of violins and cellos, a whole long row of gleaming trumpets, brighter than welders' lights, another of trombones, two rows of basses, four harps. It was awesome, almost frightening. It filled the vast stage from wingtip to wingtip like some monstrous black creature too enormous to fly, guarding the ground with its head thrust forward – the light-drenched, empty podium. When the last of the enlarged orchestra was assembled and the newcomers had tuned, the houselights dimmed, and as if at some signal invisible to commoners, the people below her began to clap, then the people all around her. Now she too was clapping, her mother and father clapping loudly beside her, the roar of applause growing louder and deeper, drawing the conductor toward the light. He came like a panther, dignified yet jubilant, flashing his teeth in a smile, waving at the orchestra with both long arms. He shook hands with the concertmaster, bounded to the podium – light shot off his hair – turned to the audience and bowed with his arms stretched wide, then straightened, chin high, as if reveling in their pleasure and miraculous faith in him. Then he turned, threw open the score – the applause sank away – and for a moment studied it like a man reading dials and gauges of infinite complexity. He picked up his baton; they lifted their instruments. He threw back his shoulders and raised both hands till they were level with his shoulders, where he held them still, as if casting a spell on his army of musicians, all motionless as a crowd in suspended animation, the breathless dead of the whole world's history, awaiting the impossible. And then his right hand moved – nothing much, almost playful – and the trumpet call began, a kind of warning both to the auditorium, tier on tier of shadowy white faces rising in the dark, and to the still orchestra bathed in light. Now his left hand moved and the orchestra stirred, tentative at first, but presaging such an awakening as she'd never before dreamed of. Then something new began, all that wide valley of orchestra playing, calm, serene, a vast sweep of music as smooth and sharp-edged as an enormous scythe – she had never in her life heard a sound so broad, as if all of humanity, living and dead, had come together for one grand onslaught. The sound ran, gathering its strength, along the ground, building in intensity, full of doubt, even terror, but also fury, and then – amazingly, quite easily – lifted. She pressed her father's hand as Benjamin Nimram, last night, had pressed hers.

Her mother leaned toward her, tilting like a tree in high wind. "Are you sure that's him?" she asked.

"Of course it is," she said.

Sternly, the man behind them cleared his throat.

Allen Ginsberg

Allen Ginsberg's most recent collection is his *Collected Poems* (1984). He may be best known for his long poem *Howl*. He received a Creative Writing Fellowship in 1979 and earlier received a publication award for a poem included in the *American Literary Anthology*.

PLUTONIAN ODE

I

1   W HAT NEW ELEMENT before us unborn in nature? Is there a new thing under the Sun?
At last inquisitive Whitman a modern epic, detonative, Scientific theme
First penned unmindful by Doctor Seaborg with poisonous hand, named for Death's planet through the sea beyond Uranus
whose chthonic ore fathers this magma-teared Lord of Hades, Sire of avenging Furies, billionaire Hell-King worshipped once
5   with black sheep throats cut, priest's face averted from underground mysteries in a single temple at Eleusis,
Spring-green Persephone nuptialed to his inevitable Shade, Demeter mother of asphodel weeping dew,
her daughter stored in salty caverns under white snow, black hail, grey winter rain or Polar ice, immemorable seasons before
Fish flew in Heaven, before a Ram died by the starry bush, before the Bull stamped sky and earth
or Twins inscribed their memories in clay or Crab'd flood
10   washed memory from the skull, or Lion sniffed the lilac breeze in Eden —

Before the Great Year began turning its twelve signs, ere constellations wheeled for twenty-four thousand sunny years
slowly round their axis in Sagittarius, one hundred sixty-seven
thousand times returning to this night
Radioactive Nemesis were you there at the beginning black
Dumb tongueless unsmelling blast of Disillusion?
I manifest your Baptismal Word after four billion years
15   I guess your birthday in Earthling Night, I salute your dreadful presence lasting majestic as the Gods,
Sabaot, Jehova, Astapheus, Adonæus, Elohim, Iao, Ialdabaoth, Æon from Æon born ignorant in an Abyss of
Light,
Sophia's reflections glittering thoughtful galaxies, whirlpools
of starspume silver-thin as hairs of Einstein!
Father Whitman I celebrate a matter that renders Self oblivion!
Grand Subject that annihilates inky hands & pages' prayers,
old orators' inspired Immortalities,
20   I begin your chant, openmouthed exhaling into spacious sky
over silent mills at Hanford, Savannah River, Rocky
Flats, Pantex, Burlington, Albuquerque
I yell thru Washington, South Carolina, Colorado, Texas,
Iowa, New Mexico,
where nuclear reactors create a new Thing under the Sun, where
Rockwell war-plants fabricate this death stuff trigger in
nitrogen baths,
Hanger-Silas Mason assembles the terrified weapon secret by
ten thousands, & where Manzano Mountain boasts to
store
its dreadful decay through two hundred forty millenia while
our Galaxy spirals around its nebulous core.
25   I enter your secret places with my mind, I speak with your
presence, I roar your Lion Roar with mortal mouth.
One microgram inspired to one lung, ten pounds of heavy
metal dust adrift slow motion over grey Alps
the breadth of the planet, how long before your radiance
speeds blight and death to sentient beings?

Enter my body or not I carol my spirit inside you, Unap-
  proachable Weight,
O heavy heavy Element awakened I vocalize your conscious-
  ness to six worlds
30 I chant your absolute Vanity. Yeah monster of Anger birthed
  in fear O most
Ignorant matter ever created unnatural to Earth! Delusion
  of metal empires!
Destroyer of lying Scientists! Devourer of covetous Generals,
  Incinerator of Armies & Melter of Wars!
Judgment of judgments, Divine Wind over vengeful nations,
  Molester of Presidents, Death-Scandal of Capital politics! Ah civilizations stupidly industrious!
Canker-Hex on multitudes learned or illiterate! Manufactured Spectre of human reason! O solidified imago of
  practitioners in Black Arts
35 I dare your Reality, I challenge your very being! I publish
  your cause and effect!
I turn the Wheel of Mind on your three hundred tons! Your
  name enters mankind's ear! I embody your ultimate
  powers!
My oratory advances on your vaunted Mystery! This breath
  dispels your braggart fears! I sing your form at last
behind your concrete & iron walls inside your fortress of rubber & translucent silicon shields in filtered cabinets and
  baths of lathe oil,
My voice resounds through robot glove boxes & ingot cans
  and echoes in electric vaults inert of atmosphere,
40 I enter with spirit out loud into your fuel rod drums underground on soundless thrones and beds of lead
O density! This weightless anthem trumpets transcendent
  through hidden chambers and breaks through iron
  doors into the Infernal Room!
Over your dreadful vibration this measured harmony floats
  audible, these jubilant tones are honey and milk and
  wine-sweet water

Poured on the stone block floor, these syllables are barley
groats I scatter on the Reactor's core,
I call your name with hollow vowels, I psalm your Fate close
by, my breath near deathless ever at your side
45   to Spell your destiny, I set this verse prophetic on your mau-
soleum walls to seal you up Eternally with Diamond
Truth! O doomed Plutonium.

I I

The Bard surveys Plutonian history from midnight lit with
Mercury Vapor streetlamps till in dawn's early light
he contemplates a tranquil politic spaced out between Nations' thought-forms proliferating bureaucratic
& horrific arm'd, Satanic industries projected sudden with
Five Hundred Billion Dollar Strength
around the world same time this text is set in Boulder, Colorado before front range of Rocky Mountains
50   twelve miles north of Rocky Flats Nuclear Facility in United
States on North America, Western Hemisphere
of planet Earth six months and fourteen days around our Solar System in a Spiral Galaxy
the local year after Dominion of the last God nineteen hundred seventy-eight
Completed as yellow hazed dawn clouds brighten East, Den-
ver city white below
Blue sky transparent rising empty deep & spacious to a morning star high over the balcony
55   above some autos sat with wheels to curb downhill from
Flatiron's jagged pine ridge,
sunlit mountain meadows sloped to rust-red sandstone cliffs
above brick townhouse roofs
as sparrows waked whistling through Marine Street's summer green leafed trees.

I I I

This ode to you O Poets and Orators to come, you father
    Whitman as I join your side, you Congress and Ameri-
    can people,
you present meditators, spiritual friends & teachers, you O
    Master of the Diamond Arts,
60   Take this wheel of syllables in hand, these vowels and conso-
    sonants to breath's end
take this inhalation of black poison to your heart, breathe out
    this blessing from your breast on our creation
forests cities oceans deserts rocky flats and mountains in the
    Ten Directions pacify with this exhalation,
enrich this Plutonian Ode to explode its empty thunder
    through earthen thought-worlds
Magnetize this howl with heartless compassion, destroy this
    mountain of Plutonium with ordinary mind and body
    speech,
65   thus empower this Mind-guard spirit gone out, gone out,
    gone beyond, gone beyond me, Wake space, so Ah!

Verse

2   *Walt Whitman*

3   *sea: Pluto, past planets Uranus and Neptune. Dr. Glen Seaborg, "Dis-*
    coverer of Plutonium."

4   *Pluto was father to Eumenides, the Furies who return to avenge mind-*
    less damage done in passion, aggression, ignorance, etc. Pluto was also
    Lord of Wealth.

6   *Demeter: Pluto's mother-in-law, the Earth fertility goddess whose daughter*
    Persephone was stolen for marriage by underworld lord Pluto and kept in
    his caverns a half year at a time, released to her mother each spring.
    Demeter gave wheat to man at Eleusis, site of her temple, one place in
    ancient world where Pluto was also worshipped with ceremonies indi-
    cated above.

7   *W. C. Williams wrote of Asphodel "that greeny flower" as the blossom of*
    Hades.

8   *Fish, Ram, Bull, Twins, Crab, Lion: Ages of Pisces, Aries, Taurus, Gemini, Cancer, Leo. 2000 years each age.*

11   *Platonic, or Babylonian or Sidereal "Great Year" = 24,000 years = half life of Plutonium radioactivity. This fact, pointed out to me by Gregory Corso, inspired this Poem.*

12   *The 24,000-year span of the Great Year = 167,000 cycles = 4 Billion Years, supposed Age of Earth.*

13   *Ref.: Six senses including mind.*

16   *Jehova to Ialdabaoth: Archons of successive Æons born of Sophia's thought, according to Ophitic & Barbelo-Gnostic myths.*

20-23 *Plutonium Factories, whose location by state and whose function in Bomb-making are here described.*

24   *240,000 years the supposed time till Plutonium becomes physically inert.*

26-27 *Ten pounds of Plutonium scattered throughout the earth is calculated sufficient to kill 4 Billion people.*

29   *Six worlds of Gods, Warrior Demons, Humans, Hungry Ghosts, Animals, & Hell Beings held together in the delusion of time by pride, anger & ignorance: a Buddhist concept.*

33   *Divine Wind = kamikaze, typhoon, wind of Gods.*

36   *300 tons of Plutonium, estimate circa 1978 of the amount produced for American bombs.*

37   *"I sing your form" etc. "The Reactor hath hid himself thro envy. I behold him. But you cannot behold him till he be revealed in his System." Blake, Jerusalem, Chapter II Plate 43 1.9-10.*

43   *Traditional libation to Hades poured at Temple of Eleusis, and by Odysseus at the Necromanteion at Acheron.*

45   *Diamond: ref. to Buddhist doctrine of Sunyata, i.e. existence as simultaneously void and solid, empty and real, all-penetrating egoless (empty void) nature symbolized by adamantine Vajra or Diamond Sceptre.*

48   *Estimated World Military Budget, 116 Billion U.S. share, Oct. 1978.*

61-63 *Four characteristics of Buddha-nature activity: to pacify, enrich, magnetize & destroy.*

65   *Americanese approximation & paraphrase of Sanskrit Prajnaparamita (Highest Perfect Wisdom) Mantra: Gate Gate Paragate Parasamgate Bodhi Svaha.*

Louise Glück

Louise Glück's poem, "Horse," will be included in her fall 1985 collection, *The Triumph of Achilles*. Her earlier books include *House on Marshland* and *Descending Figure*. She received a Discovery Award in 1970 and a Creative Writing Fellowship in 1979.

HORSE

WHAT DOES the horse give you
that I cannot give you?

I watch you when you are alone,
when you ride into the field behind the dairy,
your hands buried in the mare's
dark mane.

Then I know what lies behind your silence:
scorn, hatred of me, of marriage. Still,
you want me to touch you; you cry out
as brides cry, but when I look at you I see
there are no children in your body.
Then what is there?

Nothing, I think. Only haste
to die before I die.

In a dream, I watched you ride the horse
over the dry fields and then
dismount: you two walked together;
in the dark, you had no shadows.

But I felt them coming toward me
since at night they go anywhere,
they are their own masters.

Look at me. You think I don't understand?
What is the animal
if not passage out of this life?

John Hawkes

John Hawkes is the author of several novels and collections
of short stories, including *Beetle Leg*, *The Lime Twig*, *The
Passion Artist*, and, most recently, *Humors of Blood and Skin:
A John Hawkes Reader*. He received a Literary Study Group
grant in 1968.

THE TRAVELER

EARLY ONE MORNING in a town famous for
the growing of some grape, I arose from my bed in the inn and
stepped outside alone to the automobile. I smelled the odor of
flowers thirsting early for the sun; deep green fields stretched to
either side of the road, wet and silent; it was the cold dawn of the
traveler and I wished suddenly for a platter of home-cooked saus-
age. The car was covered with the same white dew as the grass,
and when I opened the door I smelled the damp leather, the still
cold oil and the gasoline that had been standing the night long.
Soon the hot day would be upon us; the dust of driving would
whirl us into villages, every hour or two whirl chickens and small
children across the roads like weeds.

Down the road came a young bent-backed girl. On her shoulders she carried a yoke from either end of which hung a milk can,
and over her shoulders she wore a shawl. Her legs were bare and
scratched by the thistle. Slowly she came into the inn yard and approached me, each step loudly sloshing the milk.

"Your name, Fräulein?"

"Just Milkmaid," she said.

"Well, Milkmaid, how many cows have you milked this morning?"

"Five, Mein Herr," she said. Her arms were pimpled with a
curious raw color as if they had been sunburned the day before
but now were cold. The girl tugged at her shawl, trying to hide

the hump of her spine below the yoke. She seemed to know that I, Justus Kümmerlich, would miss nothing. She took the lid from one of her buckets – a steam rose from the white milk lying flat now inside – and offered me a ladleful small and thick.

"But it is still warm," I exclaimed.

"Yes," she laughed, "I have only now stripped it from them." And she made a milking motion with her hands and peered up at me.

I put the wood to my lips and quickly drank down the milk still raw with the warmth of the cows that gave suck to this community. I paid her and she walked again to the road, herself sloshing like a cow. Long and carefully I wiped my mouth.

Then, having drunk of the rich countryside, I climbed behind the wheel of my car and started the engine. I leaned from the door: "Auf Wiedersehen, Milkmaid!" I put my foot on the accelerator, once, twice, and the engine rocked full throttle in several explosions of cylinders and exhaust. Smoke filled the yard. I raced the engine again and took hold of the hand brake; the pressure of the automobile filled the dashboard; vibrations possessed the automobile in all its libertine mechanization, noise, and saliency.

"Wait!" At first I hardly heard the cry, "Wait, wait!" But from the inn ran my wife, calling loudly the word shaped in vapor, twisting her ankles with every step, and one could see she felt the possibility of being left behind, left all alone, so driven was she to run like a wasp across this strange and empty yard. I imagined how she must have been wakened from her country sleep and how she must have started, frightened at the roar of the racing engine.

"What, Sesemi," allowing the engine to cool down and idle, "no hat?" But she did not smile and did not stop her trembling until I had silenced the machine.

SO WE JOURNEYED, bearing always south, bearing down upon the spike-helmeted policemen of small villages, coming abreast of flocks of geese by the road, driving toward some church spire in the distance, racing down our rich continent all that summer and settling ourselves to sleep each night in the spring-weakened hollows of familiar beds which, no matter how old we grow, tell us

always of mother and father and sick child as we roll from side to
side through the years.

"Justus, do you know what day this is?"

"No," I replied and kept my eyes to the road so flat now against
the contour of the sea.

"They sent little Mauschel out of the house...."

"No riddles, Sesemi. No riddles."

The sun was hot on the roof of the automobile and I sat with
my chin lifted. Always I drove with my head raised slightly and
looked clearly and relentlessly at the space ahead and now and then
swabbed my neck, leaving the handkerchief to soak, so to speak,
around my collar. That day the countryside was sunswept and a
pale blue as if at any moment the earth itself might turn to water.

"Don't you recall it, Justus? Don't you recall the wreath?" Sesemi
peered out of the window into the blue stratum of air spread over
the sand. She was remembering, of course, and seemed to be washing her little eyes in that blue air, cleansing her sight if only to enjoy the scratching progress of the impurity across the conjunctiva.
What memories she retained: only the unpleasant ones, the specks
of gloom, the grains in the eye which, months later, she would tell
me about. But the eyes of certain people are never without a
redness inside the lids.

"I do not remember. Perhaps this is not a special day after all,
Sesemi."

"It was evening, Justus."

"Then perhaps it was not a special evening, Sesemi."

"Oh, yes. How lonely your brother would be now, except for
Metze and Mauschel. And you and me, Justus."

"Don't taunt me, Sesemi. Please."

Late that afternoon we approached a small city and I steered the
automobile quickly as I could through the outskirts to the center
of this traveler's resting place until I found the bank and parked
in front of it. A group of children collected immediately around
my automobile and began to touch the hood, the fenders, the
spokes in the wheels.

There are banks all over the world and I am always at home in
a bank. Nothing else is needed when one brushes off his coat and

makes his appearance before the faceless tellers of these institutions. The clerk did not ask to see my credentials, sensing at once that his bank with its gold clock was my hostel, that some of my assets, a stranger's assets, were vaulted there waiting only upon my demand and my signature — Justus Kümmerlich. I noted that the pen trembled when he thrust it, his fingers pinching the wet point, through the grille.

"Thank you," I said shortly and raised my eyes.

There was a hair on the pen point. I handed it back to the clerk, indicating the dirt, and lit a cigar. I could not hurry bank business. I looked around the room — the same, all the same, this very bastion in Zurich, Paris, Milan, even small Tiergarten, retaining faithfully all one's fortunes, the scruples of one's piety and reserve.

"A traveler must be cautious, I imagine," came the sudden whisper.

"I beg pardon?"

"Cautious with money, Mein Herr. I imagine one does well to carry little." He dropped the pen, then reappeared, attempting to wipe dry that face and quiet those round eyes. "Traveling, sir, I should think one would take only the barest amount...thieves, chambermaids, accidents. Nicht wahr?"

I began to write. The round worried face hovered there behind the mesh.

"If one is ordained to have it, one's money is not stolen, my friend. If there is money in your pocket, it will stay. If money is your domesticity, you will have only to be a good housekeeper. When traveling, my friend, it is simple: one has merely to know how to pin one's pocketbook inside the pillow." I laughed and pushed the pen and the check into those reaching fingers.

He murmured something and then, smiling, sucking his breath, began to count with a terrible aimless dexterity, an inhuman possessiveness, confident but suffering while my money passed through his hands.

"Mein Herr," he whispered, "don't leave these bills in your hotel room."

I took the packet and counted it quickly myself. The grillework closed without a sound.

I reached the automobile and wrenched open the door. "Mein Herr, Mein Herr," begged the children, "take us with you!" Against the hot leather seat I lay back my head and smiled though the eyes were shut. "Well, Sesemi. The Riviera?"

I PAID the hotel manager in advance. I stared into his small French eyes carefully and signed my name on his register. I guessed immediately that there was no sand in his shoes and that he drank a good deal of wine.

"But the linen," staring at him again, "what of the linen?"

"Herr Kümmerlich, smooth and white, of course! Perfectly white!"

The room was small. It contained a white bed and a few white mats placed on the empty table and on the arms of the chair, a room facing the ocean and filled with that tomb odor of habitations built by the sea. Each time I entered there was the sensation of a mild loneliness, a realization that it was not one's own.

In the beginning I thought that if we tired of going to the beach, we might sun ourselves on the porch completely encircling our floor of the hotel. But those who walked the porch at night spoiled it for the day. It was not long before I moved my chair so that it blocked our own screened doors, which opened upon the rotting and down-sloping porch. The first night the sea was loud; we could hear it green and barbarous, having emptied itself of humans there below. The sun sank like a woman into a hot bath; it became dark and the night was suddenly singing with mosquitoes and violins.

Sesemi was at last done with her kneeling at the bedside and climbed in beside me. We lay in the dark. Someone, perhaps a child, had fastened two large starfish to the screens of our porch door and now I saw them, silhouetted in dead sea fashion, between the blue night outside and the blackness within, all around us. From the next room came a little voice:

"Mamma, a drink of water, bitte."

We lay still. The starfish rustled against the screen in a slight wind. The sea was beginning now to turn to foam, the hopeless separation of day and night, against all shores.

"Mama. A drink of water, bitte."

"Sesemi," I said in the dark, "if the child will not be quiet and go to sleep, you must fetch some water."

"Ja, Justus."

My eyes would not close. Even an older man — I was pleased to count myself among them — watches the stars when he lies down in a strange place, watches them in their cold heaven as he wonders what he may find on the beach when next the sun rises and the sea grows calm. I reached out and reassured myself of the light switch, relaxed my arms straight by my sides, thought of the meal I should order at dawn, and subsided into that state of alertness which for those who have found the middle of life is called sleep.

But I woke and the violins, not the insects, were still. Some equatorial disturbance was reflected now in the sea, which mounted steadily upon the scales of the shore, that sea which drowned the midnight suicides. I lifted my head quickly. There were two in embrace. Together they leaned heedlessly into our screened doors as if they thought the room empty, the two become a single creature that rolled its back and haunches into the mesh, scraped its four feet now and then on the porch wood. Their single body moved, scratched the wire, intent upon the revealing intro-spection of the embrace, immobile, swept by the black sea breezes.

"Pfui! Pfui!" I cried, clutching at the top of my pajamas. And they were gone, drifting down the porch.

I got out of bed and trembled in the cold. Deftly, overcome with conscience, I pulled the billfold from my linen coat and opened my valise.

"Justus. What are you doing?"

"The pins," I hissed over my shoulder, "the pins!"

I DID NOT eat heavily the next morning. But with the ringing of the gong and the screeching of a pack of gulls that early took flight from the roof of the hotel, Sesemi and I appeared among the first breakfasters and met, as we met morning and morning again, those old ladies who sat one to a table drinking their black coffee. It was said in the hotel that we Germans would not miss a meal, and that we even sat in the midst of the deaf ladies that we might eat the sooner. The old ladies were all grandmothers who had survived their young. All of them wore violet shawls over the quick irregular protrusions that were their backs and shoulder blades. They stayed in the dining room a precise time, each of them; and then, before the sun was fully risen, they retreated up to their drawn rooms to wait through the long day for sundown. They preferred the cool, they sought the shade like snails, and feared what they called the stroke.

Whenever we entered the dining room Sesemi helped one of them to sit; whenever we left the dining room Sesemi helped one of them to exit. Every morning the hotel manager came among the tables and spoke to each old woman and finally to myself, urging his guests to enjoy some special luxury, but knowing all too well the fruitlessness of his invitation. The dining room was a quiet place; the old women hardly tinkled spoon to cup until, in French, one of them would say, "Ladies, ladies, here comes the sun!" And, putting down their napkins they would faintly stir, then flee.

And a moment later the beach would be turned to fire, scattered over with the burning bathers and their umbrellas, bathers who were as eager to lie in the violet rays as the ladies were to escape them. The young ate no breakfast but went directly from their beds to the beach as if their youthful bodies and anonymous lively figures needed no food, except the particles of sunshine, to exist upon. The Germans were good at volley ball. The others, the French, rarely played the game, but paired off, man and woman, woman and man, to lie on their bright blankets and hold hands, inert about the beach like couples of black and slender seals.

The sun was always upon its dial, sending down to the beach intangible rays of heat and fomenting over this area its dangerous diffusion of light. The world came to us behind shut eyes. A silent bombardment descended upon the women with dark glasses while old gentlemen stuck out their legs as for treatment, expecting the sun to excite those shrunken tendons. Feet ran close to our heads on the sand. The catchers of starfish came dangerously near and a small boy stepped on my arm at midmorning. The immensity of the sun was challenging, all the biology of myself, Justus, my lungs and liver, my blood-pumping system, cried out to meet the sun, to withstand the rising temperature, to survive the effects, the dehydration, of such a sun. We saw the child who had called for water in the darkness; well might it thirst.

When I went down to the water, Sesemi, sitting upon a towel, waved good-bye and admonished me to return if the seas were too cold or if I felt cramps. Women have no place in the water. What is the sea if not for the washing of dead relatives and for the swimming of fish and men? On this trip, only a few steps, I left behind my wife, my housecoat, the muffler, the partially smoked cigar that marked me for this world, and then, feeling the sands go wet, braced myself for that plunge into the anonymous black.

When I began walking upon that nearer undersurface which can never breathe the air upon which the less heroic sea creatures move, I saw the thirsty child standing knee-deep and not far off, watching me. The child did not wave or smile but merely watched as if its parents had perhaps told it something about Herr Kümmerlich. But no, as I splashed forward, I realized that the child was speculating, trying to calculate the moment when I should leave my feet and trust myself to ride upon the waves. I shut my eyes and heard it calling suddenly for its papa to come and see.

I was an excellent floater. I could drift farther from shore than anyone, buoyed and perfectly calm, flat on my back, so unsinkable was my body, classic and yet round with age as my father's. Floating is a better test of character than swimming – creatures that float are indestructible and children beware of them. Their parents have only admiration for him who moves effortlessly, purposefully, out to sea.

"That is Herr Kümmerlich out there."

"What? That far?"

"Ja. Herr Kümmerlich. And, see, not a splash."

Now I was floating, perfectly proportioned, helmeted in my old bathing cap and rocking steadily. What a swim it was, what sport! The water carried me fathoms high and I lay on the surface, the plane, from which the winds started and across which grew the salt in its nautical gardens. I was the master and the ship. Now and then my breast went under, I rolled for a long while in the hollow of a swell. My feet cut the water like a killer shark's fins, I breathed deep – Justus Kümmerlich – in the world of less-than-blood temperature. The knees float, the head floats, the scrotum is awash; here is a man upon the sea, a rationalist thriving upon the great green spermary of the earth!

I might never have returned. The sea is made of male elements and I was vigorously contented there on the crest of it all. But at that instant there came suddenly the cutting of two sharp arms and the beating of a swimmer's legs. He made straight for me and at the last moment lifted his mouth to exclaim: "Mein Herr, Frau Kümmerlich is worried. She would be pleased if you returned to shore," and he shot by, racing, his head buried again in the foam of his blind channel. He was carrying on his back his little thin thirsty son, the boy sitting upright as on a dolphin and uncon-cerned with the violence of his father's strokes.

Sesemi was waiting on the dry sand with the towel. It was a noon sun, straight above us and near to the earth. I exposed myself to it and the thousand molecules of salt crystallized on my fresh-ened skin. My hair was suddenly dry as straw. I heard her saying, "Justus, Justus," but I never moved and heard nothing but the swishing on the sun's tails. After all the peace of the ocean, now there was none; there was only the immoderate heat and a sudden blackness that fell upon me in the form of a great dead gull filled with fish. And so I stayed in the sun too long, and so I burned.

For three days I lay in our room occupying the bed alone, and blistered. A thick warm water swelled under the skin of my red body, my temperature would drop suddenly, chilled, and nausea would come in a storm. I knew the twilight of the sunburn, the sheet stuck to me like a crab. In the dead of night I would hear the speechless methodical striking of my compatriots' fists into the gasping sides of the volley ball. All memory, the entire line of my family, was destroyed in the roaring of the sea and the roaring of the sun. What horror when the bed turned and rocked gently out on the thick swells.

At last I woke. Like a gangrenous general waking from a stupor in his hot, fly-filled field tent, I peered through the sticky substance of eyeball and eyelid and saw the gray of the late afternoon, the gray of the dying window blinds tightly drawn. The room was disheveled and torn as if their attendance upon me had been a violent thing. But now they too were serene.

Sesemi and the child were huddled together in the corner in the half-turned chair. They were watching me and smiling. Wearily and happily they were hugging each other – little Frau Kümmerlich, her hair undone, was hugging the child about the waist. They came to the bed together; Sesemi held his hand.

"Justus," she said, and looked into the diffused parts of my eyes. "Justus," she whispered, "it has been a long while."

Then I was able to think of them and my lips slid open long enough for me to say, "Yes, Sesemi. Yes, it has."

"O die Fröhlichkeit!" she whispered, dropping her head to the tepid, sun-smelling sheet. The boy picked up the pan and went out the door, as habit had taught him, to empty it.

When I was able to travel, when I was able once more to hum the *Lorelei*, and we quit the town, I stopped the automobile before a butcher's shop and ordered the throat cut and the lamb packed whole with ice and rock salt in a wooden box.

"The whole lamb," I explained to Sesemi, "is for my brother. For Lebrecht! You see, Sesemi, I am the father after all."

We started home.

Maxine Hong Kingston

Maxine Hong Kingston is the author of *China Men* and *The Woman Warrior: Memories of a Girlhood Among Ghosts*, which was selected by the National Book Critics Circle as the best work of nonfiction published in 1976. She was awarded a Creative Writing Fellowship in 1980.

from CHINA MEN

GRADING PAPERS night after night for years, BaBa became susceptible to the stories men told, which were not fabulations like the fairy tales and ghost stories told by women. The Gold Mountain Sojourners were talking about plausible events less than a century old. Heroes were sitting right there in the room and telling what creatures they met on the road, what customs the non-Chinese follow, what topsy-turvy land formations and weather determine the crops on the other side of the world, which they had seen with their own eyes. Nuggets cobbled the streets in California, the loose stones to be had for the stooping over and picking them up. Four Sojourners whom somebody had actually met in Hong Kong had returned from the Gold Mountain in 1850 with three thousand or four thousand American gold dollars each. These four men verified that gold rocks knobbed the rivers; the very dirt was atwinkle with gold dust. In their hunger the men forgot that the gold streets had not been there when they'd gone to look for themselves.

One night of a full moon, BaBa neglected to grade papers, and joined the talking men and listening women. His oldest brother, Dai Bak, who had already traveled to Cuba and back, told how fish the size of long squash fell with the rain. "In Cuba the sky rains fish — live, edible fish. Fish *this* big fell on the roofs and sidewalks. Their tails and fins were flipping. Thick gray fish, little orange and yellow ones, all different species of fish. I caught a rainbow fish in my frying pan. We had to shovel them off the roofs before the sun rotted them."

"Isn't Havana a seaport?" BaBa asked. "Isn't Cuba an island? Couldn't it have happened that a tornado sucked the seas up into the air, and water fell back down like rain on the land, fish and seaweed and all?"

"No. We were inland, and it wasn't salt water but fresh water sprinkling in raindrops. In fact, they were freshwater trout that fell. And it wasn't storming. I saw fish fall. It rains fish in Cuba." Everyone believed Dai Bak, since he was older than BaBa.

Most of the men had already been to the Gold Mountain and did not ask as at the beginning of going-out-on-the-road, "Does it rain, then, on the other side of the world?"

"I saw plains covered with cattle from horizon to horizon," said Grandfather. "The cowboys herd thousands of head of cattle, not one cowboy leading one cow on a rope like here."

"On the Gold Mountain, a man eats enough meat at one meal to feed a family for a month," said Great Grandfather. "Yes, slabs of meat." The hungrier the family got, the bigger the stories, the more real the meat and the gold.

Grandfather also said, "The Gold Mountain is lonely. You could get sick and almost die, and nobody come to visit. When you're well, you climb out of your basement again, and nobody has missed you." "Idiot," shouted Grandmother. "What do you know? Don't listen to the idiot. Crazy man. Only an idiot would bring up a bad luck story like that tonight." They acted as if he hadn't said it.

Great Grandfather said, "In Hawai'i the papayas are so big, the children scoop out the seeds and carve faces and light candles inside the shell. The candles grow on trees. You can make black ink from the nuts of that same tree."

"Don't sign contracts," he said. "Go as free working men. Not 'coolies.'" He undid his shirt and showed a white scar that was almost lost in his wrinkles. "We're men, not boy apprentices."

"America — a peaceful country, a free country." America. The Gold Mountain. The Beautiful Nation.

The night grew late. The men talking story, lighting chains of cigarettes, and drinking wine, did not need to sleep in order to have dreams. "Let me show you. Let me show you. My turn. My turn." Even the ones who had only explored the world as far as Canton and Hong Kong had stories. Second Uncle, Ngee Bak, dressed in his Western suit, grabbed an old man's cane and strutted straight through the house. "My name is John Bullyboy," he said, imitating a foreign walk and talk, stiff-legged and arrogant, big nostrils in the air, cane swishing about and hitting chinamen and dogs. He did not swerve for shit in his path. Those playing blindmen bumped into the English demon and knocked him over. The women scolded, "Do we have to remind you that you have to work in the morning? You're making so much noise, you're waking the babies." But the men talked on, and the women went to bed selfrighteous and angry; *they* would rise early to feed the chickens and the children; *they* were not childish like men. But the women couldn't sleep for the rumbling laughter, and returned, not to be left out. Grandmother brought out the gold that Great Great Grandfather, Great Grandfather, Grandfather, and the uncles had earned. Hardly diluted by alloys, it gave off red glints in the lantern light. The family took turns hefting the gold, which was heavier than it looked; its density was a miracle in the hand. A chain lowering into the palm coiled and folded on its links like a gold snake. Grandmother boiled gold and they drank the water for strength. Gold blood ran in their veins. How could they not go to the Gold Mountain again, which belonged to them, which they had invented and discovered?

Suddenly a knocking pounded through the house. Someone with a powerful hand was at the front gate in the middle of the night. Talk stopped. Everyone reached for a weapon – a cleaver, a hammer, a scythe. They blew out lights and listened for breathing and footsteps. A lookout shouted down from the coign door, "It's Kau Goong." Great Uncle.

"Kau Goong's come home." They threw open doors. The children were up now too. "Huh!" In strode Kau Goong, Grandmother's brother, an incarnation of a story hero, returning during a night of stories, a six-foot-tall white gorilla with long hair and white eyebrows that pointed upward like an owl's, his mouth jutting like an ape's, saying "Huh!" "Huh! Here I am," he roared. "I've come back." He threw down his bags. "Help yourselves! Ho!" His sister's relatives scrambled for the gifts. Nobody asked where he had won these prizes. He threw off his coat and unbuckled pistols and silver knives. While the family emptied the bags, he cleaned his guns, twirled the cylinders, blew and sighted through the bullet chambers and bores. In better times, he had walked unarmed up to rich people and taken their money. He was the biggest man in the known world, and there was no law.

"It just so happened," said Ah Po, "that when you were on your journey, pirates boarded a passenger boat going upriver and one going downriver, and sacked them both. I'm glad you're safe." Ransoms had been collected and paid.

"Dangerous times," said Kau Goong. He shook his head. "Sixty dollars for an old lady." "Yes, sixty dollars for an old lady." This was a family saying, meaning nobody was safe from kidnappers.

The family divided up used shoes, a coat, a blanket, and some lunches. "These old shoes hardly replace all the loot the bandits took from us," said Ah Po. "You'll have to look harder for those raiders. The last time they came here, I peeked from my hiding place up on the roof, and at that very moment, the full moon shone on a bandit's face. It was a Mah from Duck Doo. Let's raid their village and take our stuff back. Revenge."

Too few boats were plying the rivers. Kau Goong had boarded them as far as the ocean and also far inland, and had found no money, jewels, or silks. "Is this all?" said Ah Po.

"We need to go-out-on-the-road again," Kau Goong roared. "We need to go to the Gold Mountain." And since the Chinese word for "need" and "want" and "will" is one and the same word, he was also saying, "We want to go-out-on-the-road again. We will go to the Gold Mountain."

"Every man who leaves must reach the Gold Mountain, and every man must come home to Han Mountain," said Grandmother and Mother, unable to stop the emigration, and hoping that saying something would make it so. The men reassured them that, of course, they were Sojourners only, that they meant to come back, not settle in America with new wives. "Didn't I return last time?

And the time before that?" they said; "I'm a Gold Mountain So-journer, only a tourist," and kept other possibilities secret from women.

"One last time out-on-the-road," said the oldest men.

No infant cried out, no fireball flashed a warning, no careless eater dropped a dish or a chopstick, no sick neighbor knocked asking for medicine, no deer or rooster called in the moonlight, no cloud passed over the full moon. Crickets continued chirping. Nothing unusual happened; all remained in continuance. So, omens favorable, one of the grandfathers said, "Write a list of the men going-out-on-the-road."

BaBa set down the date, which was in 1924, and listed: Grand-father, Second Grandfather, Third Grandfather, Fourth Grand-father, Great Uncle, First Uncle, Second Uncle, and Third Uncle. After Third Uncle's name, he wrote his own name. He wanted to taste the rain fish; he wanted to pocket some gold. He wanted to say good-bye to the students. "You'll have to find a new teacher; I'm going to the Gold Mountain." He would quit school in the middle of a lesson.

"I'll get a legal visa," he said. Words of anguish came up from Ah Po, "But you're only a boy."

The travelers teased him. "Hoo! So he thinks he can walk about the West posing as a scholar." "He'll saunter up to the Immigration Demon and say, 'I'm an academician. Hand over my visa.'" "They'll clap him in jail for lying." "How are you going to prove that you're a scholar? Open up your skull and show them your brains?" "Just because he's skinny and too weak for physical labor, he thinks the white demons will say he's obviously a scholar. But they can't tell a teacher's body from a laborer's body."

"I have a diploma."

"Huh. He thinks they make laws to search out scholars to teach them and rule them. Listen, stupid, nobody gets to be classified 'Scholar.' You can't speak English, you're illiterate, no scholar, no visa. 'Coolie.' Simple test."

A kinder uncle reminded him of a father's advice to his son. "'Son, books can't be turned into food when you're hungry, nor into clothes when you're cold.'"

At the request of the women, he wrote lists of things to bring back from the Gold Mountain: Dunhill lighters, Rolex wristwatches, Seth Thomas clocks, Parker pens, Singer sewing machines, glass window panes, davenports, highboys, pianos.

"You'll make a lot of money," said MaMa. "You'll come home rich. You'll fly. You'll show them."

The next day the families unburied their documents – visas, passports, re-entry permits, American birth certificates, American citizenship papers – and distributed them. BaBa and Sahm Bak, Third Uncle, beginners, let it out that they were interested in purchasing papers and that they were willing to be adopted by Gold Mountain Sojourners who were legal citizens of the United States of America. These Americans had declared the birth of a new son for every year they had been visiting in China and thereby made "slots" for many "paper sons." When a Sojourner retired from going-out-on-the-road or died, he made another slot. Somebody took his place. The last owner of papers taught their buyer the details about the house, the farm, the neighborhood, the family that were nominally his now. A Test Book accompanied the papers; the Sojourners who had traveled on that set of papers had recorded the questions the Immigration Demons had asked, and how they had answered. The men preparing to go wandered in the fields and among the mud huts and great houses of the village, chanting these facts to a beat, rhymed them, quizzed one another. They ate sturgeon for mental prowess. They paid big fees to memory experts, and it was like in the old days when the Jesuit priest Matteo Ricci taught how to study for the Imperial Examinations, which were no more. BaBa read Test Books to their new owners, who repeated the words to memorize another man's life, a consistent life, an American life.

BaBa would go with two sets of papers: bought ones and his own, which were legal and should get him into the Gold Mountain according to American law. But his own papers were untried, whereas the fake set had accompanied its owners back and forth many times. These bought papers had a surname which was the same as our own last name – unusual luck: he would be able to keep the family name. He would carry his diplomas, and if they did not work, he would produce the fake papers.

Our family calculated money for passage. They mortgaged a field and also borrowed fifteen hundred dollars from the neighbor in the front house and another fifteen hundred dollars from the neighbor in the back house. (This three thousand dollars must have been in Chinese money.) They promised high interest, and it was also understood that our family, including the descendants, even after the monetary repayment of the debt, would show gratitude to those families, wherever their descendants, forever.

Husbands and wives exchanged stories to frighten one another. The men told about a husband who smeared his cheating wife with honey and tied her naked on an ant hill. The women told how there was once a queen, who, jealous of the king's next wife, had this other woman's arms and legs cut off and her eyes, tongue, and ears cut out. She shoved her through the hole of the outhouse, then showed her to the king, who looked down and said, "What's that?" "It's the human pig," said the queen. The wives, of course, agreed with the American antimiscegenation laws; the men would have to come home, and also they would have to be faithful, preferably celibate.

The villagers unfolded their maps of the known world, which differed: turtles and elephants supported the continents, which were islands on their backs; in other cartographies, the continents were mountains with China the middle mountain, Han Mountain or Tang Mountain or the Wah Republic, a Gold Mountain to its west on some maps and to its east on others. Yet the explorers who had plotted routes to avoid sea monsters and those who had gone in the directions the yarrow fell had found gold as surely as the ones with more scientific worlds. They had met one another as planned in Paris or Johannesburg or San Francisco.

"Bali," said a very great grandfather, pointing at the fabulous island where the holy monkeys live. He had seen the monkeys dance. Hou Yin the Monkey God lives on Bali. A generation of great grandfathers had gone there and brought back wives. Others had remained and turned into monkeys.

"Not me," said First Uncle, Dai Bak. "No big cities in Bali. The money is in the big cities now. I'm going to San Francisco."

"Chicago," said Second Uncle, Ngee Bak. "Right in the middle of North America."

"Canada," said Third Uncle, Sahm Bak. "I hear it's easier to get into Canada."

"I'm going as a worker if I can't go as a teacher," BaBa said. His brothers laughed at him. Those frail hands lifting sledgehammers? "Don't go," said Ah Po. "You're never coming back." And then she wept, having spoken his life.

The band of Gold Mountain travelers walked to the ocean. Almost a troop themselves, they were not challenged by bandits, rebels, government or warlord armies, or by demons, to whom China belonged now. At the waterfront, the oldest men dickered in demon language for ships, "How much? Dollars? No, too much." BaBa was glad that he was the youngest and had go-betweens.

BaBa never told us about sailing on a ship. He did not say whether he went as a carpenter or crewman or passenger from Canton or Macao or Hong Kong. Did masts and riggings, sails, smokestacks, and bridges block the sky, and at night did the ship's lights wash out the stars? Or could he stand on the deck and again see the sky without anything in the way? He would have had suitcases full of dried food. He would have brought seeds of every kind of vegetable.

The ship docked in Cuba, where the surf foamed like the petticoats of the dancing ladies. This part of the journey was legal. For money, BaBa rolled cigarettes and cigars ("Mexican cigarettes") and worked in the sugarcane fields. He did not see any rain of fish, but promises would be kept on the Gold Mountain mainland.

I tell everyone he made a legal trip from Cuba to New York. But there were fathers who had to hide inside crates to travel to Florida or New Orleans. Or they went in barrels and boxes all the way up the coast to New York harbor. BaBa may have been in charge of addressing those crates, marking them "Fragile" in Chinese and English and Spanish. Yes, he may have helped another father who was inside a box.

I THINK this is the journey you don't tell me:

The father's friends nailed him inside a crate with no conspicuous air holes. Light leaked through the slats that he himself had fitted together, and the bright streaks jumped and winked as the friends hammered the lid shut above his head. Then he felt himself being lifted as in a palanquin and carried to a darker place. Nothing happened for hours so that he began to lose his bearings — whether or not he was in a deep part of the ship where horns and anchor chains could not be heard, whether or not there had already been a pulling away from land, a plunging into the ocean, and this was steady speed. The father sat against a corner and stretched each limb the diagonal of the box, which was a yard by a yard by a yard. He had padded the bottom with his bedding and clothes. He had stuffed dried food, a jar of water, and a chamber pot in a bag. The box contained everything. He felt caught.

Various futures raced through his mind: walking the plank, drowning, growing old in jail, being thrown overboard in chains, flogged to tell where others were hiding, hung by the neck, returned to China — all things that happened to caught chinamen.

Suddenly — a disturbance — a giant's heart came to life; the ship shook and throbbed. A pulse had started up, and his box vibrated with it. He thought he could hear men running and calling. He must be near the engine room or a deck, near people.

The father's thoughts reached out as if stretching in four directions — skyward, seaward, back toward land, and forward to the new country. Oh, he did yearn for the open sea. The nerves in his chest and legs jumped with impatience. In the future he had to walk on deck the entire voyage, sleep on it, eat there.

He ought to have brought a knife to cut holes in the wood, or at least to carve more lines into the grain. He wanted to look out and see if his box had dropped overboard and was floating atop water, a transparency that ought not to be able to bear weight could have been immersed and this wooden air bubble hanging at a middle depth, or falling through the whale waters. People said that a Dragon King ruled an underwater city in the Yellow River; what larger oceanic unknown — tortoises twenty feet across, openmouthed fish like the marine monster that swallowed the sutras — swam alongside or beneath him. What eels, sharks, jellies, rays glided a board's-width away? He heard the gruff voices of water lizards calling for the night rain. He must not be afraid; it was sea turtles and water lizards that had formed a bridge for King Mu of Chou.

Because of fear, he did not eat nor did he feel hungry. His bowels felt loose and bladder full, but he squeezed shut ass and sphincter against using the chamber pot. He slept and woke and slept again, and time seemed long and forever. Rocking and dozing, he felt the ocean's variety – the peaked waves that must have looked like pines; the rolling waves, round like shrubs, the occasional icy mountain; and for stretches, lulling grasslands.

He heard voices, his family talking about gems, gold, cobbles, food. They were describing meat, just as they had his last evenings home. "They eat it raw." "All you can eat." The voices must have been the sounds of the ocean given sense by his memory. They were discussing a new world. "Skyscrapers tall as mountains." He would fly an æroplane above the skyscrapers tall as mountains. "They know how to do things there; they're very good at organization and machinery. They have machines that can do anything." "They'll invent robots to do all the work, even answer the door." "All the people are fat." "They're honest. If they say they'll do something, they do it. A handshake is enough." "They arrive for appointments at the very moment they say they will." "They wrap everything – food, flowers, clothes. You can use the paper over again. Free paper bags." "And westward, there are wild horses. You can eat them or ride them." It alarmed him when the strange talk did not cease at his concentration. He was awake, not dozing, and heard mouth noises, sighs, swallows, the clicking and clucking of tongues. There were also seas when the waves clinked like gold coins, and the father's palm remembered the peculiar heaviness of gold. "Americans are careless; you can get rich picking over what they drop." "Americans are forgetful from one day to the next." "They play games, sports; grown men play ball like children." "All you have to do is stay alert; play a little less than they do, use your memory, and you'll become a millionaire." "They have swimming pools, elevators, lawns, vacuum cleaners, books with hard covers, X-rays." The villagers had to make up words for the wonders. "Something new happens every day, not the same boring farming."

The sea invented words too. He heard a new language, which might have been English, the water's many tongues speaking and speaking. Though he could not make out words, the whispers sounded personal, intimate, talking him over, sometimes disapproving, sometimes in praise of his bravery.

"It's me. It's me." A solid voice. Concrete words. "I'm opening the box." It was the smuggler, who squeaked the nails out and lifted the lid. He helped the father climb out of the box with firm and generous hands. "You're safe to come out and walk," he said. The size of the room outside the box seemed immense and the man enormous. He brought fresh food from the dining room and fresh water and he talked to the father.

Suddenly they heard a march of footsteps, the leather heels of white demons. Coming steadily toward them. The two men gave each other a look, parted, and ran between the hallways of cargo, ducked behind crates. The door clanked open, shut, and the father heard the footsteps nearing. He made out the sounds of two people pacing, as if searching for a stowaway. Crouched like a rabbit, he felt his heart thud against his own thigh. He heard talking and fervently wished to know whether they were discussing stowaways. He looked for other places to dart, but the crates, lashed with rope, towered above him in straight stacks. He was in a wedge with an opening like a cracked door. The cargo room was small after all, a mere closet, and he could not step from aisle to aisle without being seen; his footsteps would echo on the metal floor. If only there were portholes to jump through or tarpaulins to hide under.

The white demons' voices continued. He heard them speak their whispery language whose sentences went up at the end as if always questioning, sibilant questions, quiet, quiet voices. The demons had but to walk this far and see into the wedge. His friend, the smuggler, could say, "I came to check the ropes," or "The captain ordered me to take inventory." Or "I'm looking for stowaways, and I found one," and deliver him up. But there were no explanations for him, a stowaway chinaman. He would not be able to talk convincingly; he would have to fight. He hardly breathed, became aware of inadequate shallow breaths through his nose.

Then, so close to his face he could reach out and touch it, he saw a white trouser leg turn this way and that. He had never seen anything so white, the crease so sharp. A shark's tooth. A silver blade. He would not get out of this by his own actions but by luck. Then, blessedness, the trouser leg turned once more and walked away.

He had not been caught. The demons had not looked down. After a time, the two hiders called to each other and came out hysterical with relief. Oh, they had the luck of rich men. The trousers had practically brushed his face.

"It's time to go back in your box," said the smuggler. A moment before, the father had thought it would be a joy to be back in, but as the lid shut on him again, reluctance almost overwhelmed him. He did not visit outside of the box again. He rode on, coming to claim the Gold Mountain, his own country.

The smuggler came occasionally and knocked a code on the wood, and the stowaway father signaled back. Thus he knew that he had not been forgotten, that he had been visited. This exchange of greetings kept him from falling into the trance that overtakes animals about to die.

At last the smuggler let him out; the ship had docked at a pier in New York. He motioned the father up hatches, across empty decks, around corners to an unguarded gangway. He would not have to swim past patrol boats in the dark. "Come. Come. Hurry," the smuggler guided him. He staggered along on cramped legs; the new air dizzied him. As they were saying good-bye, the smuggler said, "Look," and pointed into the harbor. The father was thrilled enough to see sky and skyscrapers. "There." A gray and green giantess stood on the gray water; her clothes, though seeming to swirl, were stiff in the wind and the moving sea. She was a statue and she carried fire and a book. "Is she a goddess of theirs?" the father asked. "No," said the smuggler, "they don't have goddesses. She's a symbol of an idea." He was glad to hear that the Americans saw the idea of Liberty so real that they made a statue of it.

The father walked off the ship and onto the Gold Mountain. He disciplined his legs to step confidently, as if they belonged where they walked. He felt the concrete through his shoes. The noise and size of New York did not confuse him; he followed a map that his kinsmen had drawn so clearly that each landmark to Chinatown seemed to be waiting to welcome him. He went to the Extending Virtue Club, where people from his own village gave him a bed in a basement; it could have been a grocery shelf or an ironing table or the floor under a store counter. To lie stretched out on any part of the Gold Mountain was a pleasure to him.

OF COURSE, my father could not have come that way. He came a legal way, something like this:

Arriving in San Francisco Bay, the legal father was detained for an indefinite time at the Immigration Station on Angel Island, almost within swimming distance of San Francisco. In a wooden house, a white demon physically examined him, poked him in the ass and genitals, looked in his mouth, pulled his eyelids with a hook. This was not the way a father ought to have been greeted. A cough tickled his chest and throat, but he held it down. The doctor demon pointed to a door, which he entered to find men and boys crowded together from floor to ceiling in bunkbeds and on benches; they stood against the walls and at the windows. These must be the hundred China Men who could enter America, he thought. But the quota was one hundred a year, not one hundred per day, and here were packed more than one hundred, nearer two hundred or three. A few people made room for him to set down his suitcases. "A newcomer. Another newcomer," they called out. A welcome party made its way to him. "I'm the president of the Self-Governing Association," one of them was telling him in a dialect almost like his. "The most important rule we have here is that we guard one another's chances for immigration." He also asked for dues; the father gave a few dimes toward buying newspapers and phonograph records, an invention that he had never heard before. "Now you're eligible to vote," said the president, who then said that he had won his office by having been on the island the longest, three and a half years. The legal father's heart sank, and rose again; there must be something wrong with this man, not a good man, a criminal to be jailed for so long. "Do you want to spend money on a rubber ball? Vote Yes or No." The legal father voted No. How odd it would be to say to these men, "Play ball. Go ahead. Play with it," as if they were boys and could play.

Even the boys wouldn't play. Who can be that lighthearted? He wasn't really going to stay here for more than a day or two, was he? He made his way across the room. Some of the men were gambling, others exercising, cutting one another's hair, staring at their feet or folded hands or the floor. He saw two men handcuffed to each other. Readers chanted San Francisco newspapers, *Young China* and *Chinese World*. The legal father, who was skillful and lucky, joined a game and won forty silver dollars, and gave away one for the rubber ball. He learned who was being deported and who was serving a year's sentence before deportation.

A bell went off like a ship's alarm, but it was a dinner bell. The father followed the others to a dining hall. About ten women were coming out. They were the first women he had seen since China, and they already belonged to husbands. He did not know that he had come to a country with no women. The husbands and wives talked quickly as the guards pushed them past one another. The father saw the man ahead of him hold hands with a woman for a moment and – he saw it – pass her a note. She dropped it. She knelt and, fixing her shoe with one hand, snatched the piece of paper with the other. A big white matron grabbed her arm and took the paper. Though these people were all strangers, the father joined the men who surrounded the matron. They wrested the paper from her and tore it up. The legal father ate some of the shreds. That was the last time the men's and women's mealtimes overlapped. There seemed to be no other immediate consequences; perhaps denial of entry would be the punishment.

The China Men who worked in the kitchen brought food cooked and served in buckets. "Poison," the prisoners grumbled. "A couple of years ago," said the president of the Self-Governing Association, "the demons tried to starve us to death. They were taking the food money for themselves. If it weren't for us rioting, you newcomers wouldn't be eating so much today. We faced bayonets for this food." The legal father wasn't sure he would've wanted any more of the slop they were eating.

The men spent the long days rehearsing what they would say to the Immigration Demon. The forgetful men fingered their risky notes. Those who came back after being examined told what questions they had been asked. "I had to describe all the streets in my village." "They'll ask, 'Do you have any money?' and 'Do you have a job?'" "They've been asking those questions all this week," the cooks and janitors confirmed. "What's the right answer?" asked the legal fathers. "Well, last week they liked 'No job' because it proves you were an aristocrat. And they liked 'No money' because you showed a willingness to work. But this week, they like 'Yes job' and 'Yes money' because you wouldn't be taking jobs away from white workers." The men groaned, "Some help." The demons did not treat people of any other race the way they did Chinese. The few Japanese left in a day or two. It was because their emperor was strong.

Footsteps walked across the ceiling, and bedsprings squeaked above their heads. So there were more of them locked on the second floor. "The women are up there," the father was told. Diabolical, inauspicious beginning – to be trodden over by women. "Living under women's legs," said the superstitious old-fashioned men from the backward villages. "Climbed over by women." It was bad luck even to walk under women's pants on clotheslines. No doubt the demons had deliberately planned this humiliation. The legal father decided that for a start in the new country, he would rid himself of Chinese superstitions; this curse would not count.

He read the walls, which were covered with poems. Those who could write protested this jailing, this wooden house (*wood* rhyming with *house*), the unfair laws, the emperor too weak to help them. They wrote about the fog and being lonely and afraid. The poets had come to a part of the world not made for honor, where "a hero cannot use his bravery." One poet was ready to ride his horse to do mighty American deeds but instead here he sat corraled, "this wooden house my coffin." The poets must have stayed long to carve the words so well. The demons were not going to free him, a scholar, then. Some were not poems exactly but statements. "This island is not angelic." "It's not true about the gold." One man blamed "the Mexican Exclusion Laws" for his imprisonment. The writers were anonymous; no official demon could trace them and penalize them. Some signed surname and village, but they were still disguised; there were many of that name from that village, many men named Lee from Toi Shan, many a Hong of Sun Woi, and many a Three District Man and Four District No Such Man. There were dates of long stays.

Night fell quickly; at about four o'clock the fog poured down the San Francisco hillsides, covered the bay, and clouded the windows. Soon the city was gone, held fast by black sea and sky. The fog horns mourned. San Francisco might have been a figment of Gold Mountain dreams.

The legal father heard cries and thumps from someone locked in a separate shed. Words came out of the fog, the wind whipping a voice around the Island. "Let me land. Let me out. Let me land. I want to come home."

In the middle of one night when he was the only man awake, the legal father took out his Four Valuable Things, and using spit and maybe tears to mix the ink, he wrote a poem on the wall, just a few words to observe his stay. He wrote about wanting freedom. He did not sign his name; he would find himself a new American name when he landed. If the U.S. government found out his thoughts on freedom, it might not let him land. The next morning the readers sang the new poem for the others to hear. "Who wrote this wonderful poem during the night?" they asked, but the father modestly did not say.

For one another's entertainment, the men rehearsed and staged skits, puppet shows, and heroic parts of operas. They juggled fruit, bottles, and the new rubber ball. The father, who was traveling with the adventures of Yüeh Fei, the Patriot, in six volumes, read aloud the part where Yüeh Fei's mother carved on his back four words: FIRST – PROTECT MY NATION. He held up for all to see the illustrations of warriors in battle. He also carried the poems of Li Po, the best poet, the Heavenly Poet, the Great White Light, Venus. The father sang about a sentry stopping Li Po from entering a city. Li Po was drunk as usual and riding a mule. He refused to give his name to the sentry, but wrote a daring poem that he was a man from whose mouth the emperor had wiped the drool; the emperor's favorite wife had held his inkslab. The impressed sentry granted him entrance. This poem heartened the men; they laughed and clapped at Li Po's cleverness and the sentry's recognition of him and poetry.

"What is a poem exactly?" asked an illiterate man, a Gold Mountain Sojourner who had spent twenty years in America and was on his way back to his family. "Let me give it a try," he said. "A short poem: 'On the Gold Mountain, I met black men black like coal.' Is that a poem?" The literate men were delighted. "Marvelous," they said. "Of course, it's a poem." "A simile. A simile. Yes, a poem." The legal father liked it so much, he remembered it forever.

The legal father learned many people's thoughts because he wrote their letters. They told their wives and mothers how wonderful they found the Gold Mountain. "The first place I came to was The Island of Immortals," they told him to write. "The foreigners clapped at our civilized magnificence when we walked off the ship in our brocades. A fine welcome. They call us 'Celestials.'" They were eating well; soon they would be sending money. Yes, a magical country. They were happy, not at all frightened. The Beautiful Nation was glorious, exactly the way they had heard it would be. "I'll be seeing you in no time." "Today we ate duck with buns and plum sauce," which was true on days when the China Men in San Francisco sent gifts.

Every day at intervals men were called out one by one. The legal father kept himself looking presentable. He wore his Western suit and shined shoes, constantly ready.

One morning the barracks awoke to find a man had hanged himself. He had done it from a railing. At first he looked as if he had been tortured, his legs cut off. He had tied his legs at the knees like an actor or beggar playing a man with no legs, and hung himself by pushing over his chair. His body had elongated from hanging all night. The men looked through his papers and found X's across them. When new arrivals looked for beds, nobody told them that a dead, hung man had slept in that one.

Also, the rumor went, a woman upstairs had killed herself by sharpening a chopstick and shoving it through her ear. Her husband had sent for her, and she did not understand why he did not come to take her home.

At last came the legal father's turn to be interrogated. He combed his hair again. He said his good-byes. Inside the interrogation room were several white demons in formal wear; the legal father gauged by the width of lapels and toes that his own suit was not quite stylish. Standing beside the table was a Chinese-looking soldier in American uniform and a demon soldier in the same uniform. This Chinese American was the interpreter. The legal father sat opposite the interrogators, who asked his name, his village, where he was born, his birth date – easy questions.

"Can you read and write?" the white demon asked in English and the Chinese American asked in Cantonese.

"Yes," said the legal father.

But the secretary demon was already writing No since he obviously couldn't, needing a translator.

"When did you cut off your pigtail?" asked the translator.

"In 1911," said the legal father. It was a safe answer, the year he would have picked anyway, not too early before the Republic nor too late, not too revolutionary nor too reactionary. Most people had cut their hair in 1911. He might have cut it for fashion as much as for revolution.

"Do you have relatives who are American citizens?"

The janitor, a China Man, who just then entered the room with dustpan and broom, nodded.

"Yes."

"Who?"

"My grandfather is an American. My father is an American. So I'm an American, also my three older brothers and three uncles – all Americans."

Then came the trap questions about how many pigs did they own in 1919, whether the pig house was made out of bricks or straw, how many steps on the back stoop, how far to the outhouse, how to get to the market from the farm, what were the addresses of the places his grandfather and father and brothers and uncles had lived in America. The interrogators liked asking questions with numbers for answers. Numbers seemed true to them. "How many times did your grandfather return to the United States?" "Twice." "Twice?" "Yes, twice. He was here once and returned twice. He was here three times altogether. He spent half his life in America and half in China." They looked into his eyes for lies.

Even the Chinese American looked into his eyes, and they repeated his answers, as if doubting them. He squelched an urge to change the answers, elaborate on them. "Do you have any money?" "Yes." "How much?" He wondered if they would charge him higher fees the more money he reported. He decided to tell the truth; lying added traps. Whether or not he spoke the truth didn't matter anyway; demons were capricious. It was up to luck now.

They matched his answers to the ones his relatives and fellow villagers gave. He watched the hands with yellow hair on their backs turn the copies of his grandfather's and father's papers.

They told him to go back to the jail, where he waited for more weeks. The next time he was called to be examined – *searched* the Chinese word – they asked again, "What American relatives do you have?"

"My grandfather and father," he said again, "and also my three brothers and three uncles."

"Your grandfather's papers are illegal," the Chinese American translated. "And your father is also an illegal alien." One by one the demons outlawed his relatives and ancestors, including a Gold Rush grandfather, who had paid a bag of gold dust to an American Citizenship Judge for papers. "There are no such things as Citizenship Judges," said the Immigration Demon and put an X across the paper that had been in the family for seventy-five years. He moved on to ask more trap questions, the directions the neighbors' houses faced and the number of water buffaloes in 1920, and sent him back to the barracks.

He waited again. He was examined again, and since he had an accurate memory, he told them the same number of pigs as the last two times, the same number of water buffaloes (one), the same year of cutting his queue, and at last they said, "You may enter the United States of America." He had passed the American examination; he had won America. He was not sure on what basis they let him in – his diploma, his American lineage (which may have turned out to be good after all), his ability to withstand jailing, his honesty, or the skill of his deceits.

This legal father then worked his way across the continent to New York, the center of America.

Galway Kinnell

Galway Kinnell won the Pulitzer Prize for his *Selected Poems* (1982). "The Seekonk Woods" will appear in his forthcoming collection, *The Past*. He was awarded Creative Writing Fellowships in 1970, 1977 and 1984.

THE SEEKONK WOODS

WHEN FIRST I walked here I hobbled
along ties set too close together
for a boy to step naturally on each.
When I grew older, I thought, my stride
would reach every other and thereafter
I would walk in time with the way
toward the meeting place of rails
in that yellow Lobachevskian haze up ahead.
Right about here we put down our pennies, dark
on shined steel, where they trembled, fell still,
and waited for the locomotive rattling its berserk
wheel-rods into perfect circles out of Attleboro
to crush them into bright wafers, the way a fork
might mash into view the inner light of a carrot
in a stew. In this late March sunshine,
crossing the trees at the angle the bow makes
when the violinist effleurages the C
three octaves above middle C out of the chanterelle,
the old vertical birthwood remembers
its ascent lines, shrunken by half, exactly
back down, each tree's on its fallen last summer.
Back then, dryads lived in these oaks;
these rocks were altars, which often asked
blood offerings – but this one, once, bone, too,

the time Billy Wallace tripped and broke out
his front teeth. Fitted with gold replicas,
he asked, speaking more brightly, "What good
is a golden mouth when there's only grass
to eat?" Though it was true Nebuchadnezzar
spent seven years down on all fours eating
vetch and alfalfa, ruminating the mouth-feel
of "bloom" and "wither," earth's first catechism,
until he was healed, nevertheless we knew
if you held a grass blade between both thumbs
and blew hard you could blurt its last shrieks
out of it – like those beseeching leaves oaks
didn't drop last winter just now scratched out
on a least breeze, let-me-die-let-me-die.
Maybe Billy, lured by bones' memory,
comes back, sometimes, too, to the Seekonk Woods,
to stand in the past and just look at it.
Here he might kneel, studying this clump of grass,
a god inspecting a sneeze. Or he might stray
into the now-untrafficked whistling-lanes
of the mourning doves, who used to call and call
into the future, and give a start, as though,
this very minute, by awful coincidence,
they reached it. And at last traipse off
down the tracks, with stumbling, arrhythmic gait,
as wanderers must do, once it hits them,
this over-the-unknown route, too, ends up
right where time wants. On this spot
I skinned the muskrat. I buried the rat.
The musk breezed away. Of the fur
I made a hat, which as soon as put on
began to rot off, and even now stinks
so sharply my scalp crawls. In circles,
of course, keeping to the skull. Though
one day this scrap of damp skin
will crawl all the way off, and the whole organism
follow. But which way? To effuse with musk?

Or rot with rat? Oh no, we don't choose,
there's a law: *As one supremes,*
so one croaks – forever muskrat! When,
a quarter-turn after the sun, the half-moon
too goes down and one finds oneself
in the night's night, then somewhere
thereabouts in the dark must be death.
Knowledge beforehand of the end is surely
existence's most spectacular feat – and yet right here,
on this ordinary afternoon, in these humblest woods,
with a name meaning "black goose" in Wampanoag,
or in modern Seekonkese, "slob blowing fat nose,"
this unlikely event happens again – a creature
straggling along the tracks foreknows it.
Then too long to touch every tie, my stride
is now just too short to reach every other;
and so I am to be still the wanderer,
in velocity if not in direction, the hobble
of too much replaced by the common limp
of too little. But I almost got there.
I almost stepped according to the liturgical,
sleeping gods' snores you can hear singing up
from former times inside the ties. I almost
set foot in that border zone, where what follows
blows back, shimmering everything, making
walking like sleepwalking, railroad tracks
a lane among poplars on a spring morning,
where a man, limping but blissful, dazedly
makes his way homeward, his lips, which kissing
taught to bunch up like that, blowing
from a night so overfilled with affection
it still hasn't completely finished passing
these few bent strands of hollowed-out air,
haunted by future, into a tune on the tracks.
I think I'm about to be shocked awake.
As I was in childhood, when I battered myself
back to my senses against a closed door,

or woke up hanging out an upstairs window.
Somnambulism was my attempt to slip
under cover of nightmare across no father's land
and put my arms around a phantasm. If only
I had found a way to enter his hard time
served at labor by day, by night in solitary,
and put my arms around him in reality,
I might not now be remaking him
in memory still; anti-alchemizing bass kettle's
golden reverberations again and again back down
to hair, flesh, blood, bone, the base metals.
I want to crawl face down in the fields
and graze on the wild strawberries, my clothes
stained pink, even for seven years,
if I must, if they exist. I want to lie out
on my back under the thousand stars and think
my way up among them, through them,
and a little distance past them, and attain
a moment of nearly absolute ignorance,
if I can, if human mentality lets us.
I have always intended to live forever,
but, even more, to live now. The moment
I have done one or the other, I here swear,
I will come back from the living and enter
death everlasting: consciousness defeated.
But I will not offer, no, I'll never
burn my words. Wishful phrases! The once-
poplars creosoted asleep under the tracks
have stopped snoring. What does that mean?
The bow saws at G. A leaf rattles on its tree.
The rails may never meet, O fellow Euclideans,
for you, for me. So what if we groan?
That's our noise. Laughter is our stuttering
in a language we can't speak yet. Behind,
the world made of wishes goes dark. Ahead,
if not tomorrow then never, shines only what is.

Etheridge Knight

Etheridge Knight's books are *Poems from Prison, Belly Song and Other Poems* and *Born of a Woman*. He received the 1985 Shelley Award from the Poetry Society of America. Knight was awarded a Creative Writing Fellowship in 1972.

THE BONES OF MY FATHER

1

THERE ARE no dry bones
here in this valley. The skull
of my father grins
at the Mississippi moon
from the bottom
of the Tallahatchie,
the bones of my father
are buried in the mud
of these creeks and brooks that twist
and flow their secrets to the sea.
But the wind sings to me
here the sun speaks to me
of the dry bones of my father.

2

There are no dry bones
in the northern valleys, in the Harlem alleys
young / black / men with knees bent
nod on the stoops of the tenements
and dream
of the dry bones of my father.

And young white longhairs who flee
their homes, and bend their minds
and sing their songs of brotherhood
and no more wars are searching for
my father's bones.

3

There are no dry bones here.
We hide from the sun.
No more do we take the long straight strides.
Our steps have been shaped by the cages
that kept us. We glide sideways
like crabs across the sand.
We perch on green lilies, we search
beneath white rocks...
THERE ARE NO DRY BONES HERE

The skull of my father
grins at the Mississippi moon
from the bottom
of the Tallahatchie.

Connecticut – February 21, 1971

Stanley Kunitz

Stanley Kunitz received the Pulitzer Prize in 1959 for his *Selected Poems: 1928-1958*. His new collection, in which "The Image Maker" appears, is called *Next-to-Last Things*. He was awarded a Senior Fellowship in 1985.

THE IMAGE-MAKER

A WIND passed over my mind,
insidious and cold.
It is a thought, I thought,
but it was only its shadow.
Words came,
or the breath of my sisters,
with a black rustle of wings.
They came with a summons
that followed a blessing.
I could not believe
I too would be punished.
Perhaps it is time to go,
to slip alone, as at a birth,
out of this glowing house
where all my children danced.
Seductive Night! I have stood
at my casement the longest hour,
watching the acid wafer
of the moon slowly dissolving
in a scud of cloud, and heard
the farthest hidden stars
calling my name.
I listen, but I avert my ears

from Meister Eckhart's warning:
All things must be forsaken.
God scorns
to show Himself among images.

Philip Levine

Philip Levine's collections of poetry have won the Lenore Marshall Award and The American Book Award, and he was co-winner of a National Book Critics Circle Award. His most recent collection is his *Selected Poems* (1984). He received Creative Writing Fellowships in 1970, 1976 and 1981.

NEW SEASON

M Y SON and I go walking in the garden.
It is April 12, Friday, 1974.
Teddy points to the slender trunk
of the plum and recalls the digging
last fall through three feet
of hard pan and opens his palms
in the brute light of noon, the heels
glazed with callus, the long fingers
thicker than mine and studded with
silver rings. My mother is 70 today.
He flicks two snails off a leaf
and smashes them underfoot
on the red brick path. Saturday,
my wife stood here, her cheek cut
by a scar of dirt, dirt on her bare
shoulders, on the brown belly,
damp and sour in the creases
of her elbows. She held up a parsnip
squat, misshapen, a tooth pulled
from the earth, and laughed
her great white laugh. Teddy talks
of the wars of the young, Larry V.
and Ricky's brother in the movies,
on Belmont, at McDonald's,

ready to fight for nothing, hard,
redded or on air, 'low riders,
grease, what'd you say about my mama!'
Home late, one in the back seat,
his fingers broken, eyes welling
with pain, the eyes and jawbones
swollen and rough. 70 today, the woman
who took my hand and walked me
past the corridor of willows
to the dark pond where the one swan
drifted. I start to tell him
and stop, the story of my 15th spring.
That a sailor had thrown a black baby
off the Belle Isle Bridge was
the first lie we heard, and the city
was at war for real. We would waken
the next morning to find Sherman tanks
at the curb and soldiers camped
on the lawns. Damato said he was
'goin downtown bury a hatchet
in a nigger's head.' Women
took coffee and milk to the soldiers
and it was one long block party
till the trucks and tanks loaded up
and stumbled off. No one saw
Damato for a week, and when I did
he was slow, head down, his right arm
blooming in a great white bandage.
He said nothing. On mornings I rise
early, I watch my son in the bathroom,
shirtless, thick-armed and hard,
working with brush and comb
at his full blond head that suddenly
curled like mine and won't
come straight. 7 years passed
before Della Daubien told me
how three white girls from the shop

sat on her on the Woodward Streetcar
so the gangs couldn't find her
and pull her off like they did
the black janitor and beat
an eye blind. She would never
forget, she said, and her old face
glows before me in shame
and terror. Tonight, after dinner,
after the long, halting call
to my mother, I'll come out here
to the yard rinsed in moonlight
that blurs it all. She will not
become the small openings
in my brain again through which the wind
rages, though she was the ocean
that ebbed in my blood, the storm clouds
that battered my lungs, though I hide
in the crotch of the orange tree
and weep where the future grows
like a scar, she will not come again
in the brilliant day. My cat Nellie,
15 now, follows me, safe
in the dark from mockingbird
and jay, her fur frost tipped
in the pure air, and together we hear
the wounding of the rose, the willow
on fire — to the dark pond
where the one swan drifted, the woman
is 70 now — the willow is burning,
the rhododendrons shrivel
like paper under water, all
the small secret mouths are feeding
on the green heart of the plum.

W. S. Merwin

W. S. Merwin is a distinguished translator and prose writer
as well as a poet. His list of awards includes a Pulitzer Prize,
a Bollingen Prize and a P.E.N. Translation Prize. His Creative
Writing Fellowships were awarded in 1969 and 1977.

THE SOUND OF THE LIGHT

I HEAR sheep running on the path of broken limestone
through brown curled leaves fallen early from walnut limbs
at the end of a summer how light the bony
flutter of their passage I can
hear their coughing their calling and wheezing even the warm
greased wool rubbing on the worn walls I hear them
passing passing in the hollow lane and there is still time

the shuffle of black shoes of women climbing
stone ledges to church keeps flowing up the dazzling hill
around the grassy rustle of voices
on the far side of a slatted shutter
and the small waves go on whispering on the shingle
in the heat of an hour without wind it is Sunday
none of the sentences begins or ends there is time

again the unbroken rumble of trucks and the hiss
of brakes roll upward out of the avenue
I forget what season they are exploding through
what year the drill on the sidewalk is smashing
it is the year in which you are sitting there as you are
in the morning speaking to me and I hear
you through the burning day and I touch you
to be sure and there is time there is still time

Mary Oliver

Mary Oliver won a Pulitzer Prize for her collection *American Primitive*. She was awarded a Creative Writing Fellowship in 1972.

HUMPBACKS

*

THERE IS, all around us,
this country
of original fire.

You know what I mean.

The sky, after all, stops at nothing, so something
        has to be holding
our bodies
in its rich and timeless stables or else
we would fly away.

*

Off Stellwagen
off the Cape,
the humpbacks rise. Carrying their tonnage
        of barnacles and joy
they leap through the water, they nuzzle back under it
like children
at play.

*

They sing, too.
And not for any reason
you can't imagine.

*

Three of them
rise to the surface near the bow of the boat,
then dive
deeply, their huge scarred flukes
tipped to the air.

We wait, not knowing
just where it will happen; suddenly
they smash through the surface, someone begins
shouting for joy and you realize
it is yourself as they surge
upward and you see for the first time
how huge they are, as they breach,
and dive, and breach again
through the shining blue flowers
of the split water and you see them
for some unbelievable
part of a moment against the sky —
like nothing you've ever imagined —
like the myth of the fifth morning galloping
out of darkness, pouring
heavenward, spinning; then

*

they crash back under those black silks
and we all fall back
together into that wet fire, you
know what I mean.

*

I know a captain who has seen them
playing with seaweed, swimming
through the green islands, tossing
the slippery branches into the air.

I know a whale that will come to the boat whenever
she can, and nudge it gently along the bow
with her long flipper.

I know several lives worth living.

*

Listen, whatever it is you try
to do with your life, nothing will ever dazzle you
like the dreams of your body,

its spirit
longing to fly while the dead-weight bones

toss their dark mane and hurry
back into the fields of glittering fire

where everything,
even the great whale,
throbs with song.

Cynthia Ozick

Cynthia Oznick has garnered many prizes and awards for her fiction and criticism, including O'Henry Awards for her short fiction, the American Academy of Arts Award for Literature, and a Mildred and Harold Strauss Living Award. She received a Work-in-Progress grant from the N.E.A. in 1968.

from TRUST

AND UPON Holiness cannot build, Worldliness is founded. Now when Holiness essays introspection and ends with self-deception, it gives birth to Worldliness. That moment when Holiness, with whatsoever good will, enters the museum hall — in the guise, oh, of the quaint artifact, grail shown under glass, for instance, or miracle-working saint's toe-bone displayed as remarkable (for new reasons, in a newer sense) — in that moment exactly Holiness dies, and in that moment exactly Worldliness inhales its expirations and lives.

— These aphorisms (for all their windiness I don't hesitate to call them that, for they were less than parables and more than mere turns of phrase) were Enoch's long ago, when my mother attempted to compensate me for the inaccessibility of Puritanism with its opposite, cosmopolitanism, which (I have already mentioned it) she liked to term the recoupment of Europe. And she equated Enoch with Europe, and carried me to France the very year the war ended, together with the refugee from Holland whom she had taken on as my governess, and stood with us at the border of Germany, a place where too many roads met, each infested with a line of abandoned tanks like enormous vermin — and there, while I writhed and vomited close by one of those great dusty tractor-wheels, full in the sight of a handful of unamazed Cockney infantrymen (afterward my mother learned that the country cow whose milk I had been given to drink had a disease), the Dutchwoman said, "I shall not go across there." And my mother complained, "But I'm married to a Jew, and I don't mind going across." We did not go across, but wandered southward instead, pleasure-seekers among the displaced, hence more displaced than anyone – "I feel like a survivor," my mother said now and again, "I don't mean from the war of course," while the Dutchwoman reached out for me with strong freckled arms and, fiercely and privately, trusting I would not betray her, whispered, "a survivor from the age of governesses!" – before Hitler she had been a medical student at the University of Leyden. ("Yet she didn't even ask whether the milk was pasteurized!" my mother fumed. "She could have asked to have them boil it at least! I don't approve of refugees, they have no sense of responsibility.") So I was sick against a tank, and in the pit of that sickness, while the pad of dust on the tank's steel belt swam spasmodically under my rain of filth, I heard my mother rail against the unsanitary survivors of a war not yet three months dissolved into history.

For some reason – perhaps it was the laughter of the soldiers, guiding and advising me: "Puke on, darlin', lots of muck on the Jerry barstid, 'ere naow 'aven't yuh missed a bit of its bluddy foot?" – my mother felt compelled to explain herself: *she* was a survivor, she made out, not of bomb and blaze – one could always get over a *war*, and if one didn't one was dead anyway and it didn't matter – in short she had survived not mere catastrophe but a whole set of wrong ideas. She had outlasted her moment and outlived her time. All the ideals of her girlhood had betrayed her by unpredictably diminishing; "see," she said, and pointed down one of those many roads at a one-legged giant who had hobbled out of the horizon, "that is what has become of the social consciousness of my generation." The Dutchwoman frowned so horribly at this that I had another fit of retching. "I don't pay you thirty-five dollars a week to poison my child," my mother promptly admonished her, but she did not have her mind on it; the maimed fellow had come into view and all of us – my mother, the Dutch governess, the three Cockney infantrymen, and I – looked on in fearful admiration as he swung himself forward on a staff the thickness of a young tree. He was burly and dark, and, for that place and season, not at all haggard; he thrust a paper at the soldiers and propelled himself over the border. "'E'd got a pass from up back," said one of the Cockneys. "Big for an I-talian," replied the second. "They'd ought to get back where they cyme from, them blowkes," observed the third, and then turned back to me with a whistle: "'Aven't yuh myde a job of't, girlie! It's all the shype of the Mediterr-y-nian Owshin yuh've give up!"

And it was a kind of map I had spewed over the hem of the German tank – a map made of vomit, with viscous seas and amorphous continents, a Mediterranean of bad milk in the heart of this known and yellowish world – not simply known but precisely known, exactly and profoundly known (although land and lake were joined and parted indistinguishably by a lava of wakened dust), known, memorized, and understood, unmistakably and perilously known by its terrific stink. My mother covered her face in disgust – "God knows what was wrong with that damned cow," she mumbled, half stifled, into her glove, "it's like her to be sick and make a stench," and pulled me back to the car. Although she was not fond of me, the Dutchwoman, who during the final eruption had been obliged to support my head, took my hand almost kindly. The map had begun to drip off the tread, hung with nuggets of mud. And then Africa succumbed, and then the shadow of Asia, and then the vague Americas, and lastly Europe gave way, split open by sudden rivers; the yellow Mediterranean of milk overran them all, sucking up mass after mass and sending out those reeking fetid familiar airs, so that even the hardy Cockneys swore and moved away. "It is not her fault," my governess quietly snarled; she had her foot on the clutch. "It is the stink of Europe." One of the soldiers pressed his nose in a music-hall gesture: the button on his sleeve caught the sunlight and danced it up and down: his arm snapped up with a start. The bit of wire that marked the border was all at once murmuring with tremor. "What is it?" my mother cried hoarsely – "Did you hear?" "The bluddy devil!" screeched the soldier, letting go his nose. It came at us again just then – a sting of noise grave and quick. The Dutchwoman had started the motor and was slowly turning us, creeping off the gravel into the edges of a blighted field, silent; our wheels grew muffled in grass. The echo of the discharge lay embedded in the morning light as punctiliously as a surgeon's gash. "Is it backfire?" said my mother. "What *is* it?" She fretted at her fingernail as the car righted itself in the road, and looked out behind her through a small side window: "There it is again!" she exclaimed; the precise little roar stuttered in the sky; the knobs on the dashboard chattered. "Ah, they've gone over," she said, "look." I looked, and in a queer detachment of motion seemed to see the three Cockneys dangling like marionettes or hanged men over Germany; beneath the three arcs of their simultaneous leaps the border-wire dimly strummed. They struck the ground a second afterward like felled game, all in a crouch; we watched them spring erect. "I think," said my mother in surprise, "it was a shot. It must have been a shot," she repeated, craning backward. The Dutchwoman did not stir. My mother swung open the door of the car and jumped decisively out. I followed her – suddenly I felt immensely better, not sick at all. The three infantrymen were running down one of those roads that fingered out like a candelabrum on the other side of the border. "They're chasing someone," my mother shouted excitedly. "Can you see him? It's that man without the leg." "No," said my governess from inside the car – resolutely her eyes shunned Germany; she kept her speckled hands on the wheel and would not move – "they are not chasing him. He has shot himself." But we saw him then, and the soldiers flying toward him, whipping dust but never coming nearer, as in a dream; he had gone far, that giant, farther than it appeared, for it took half a mile to diminish him, and when the soldiers had run themselves into midgets, still racing and yet no nearer, his big shadowy head continued to loom, and his staff seemed no less a leafless tree – it was as though they pursued the irreducible moon, or a god. He was fixed in the middle of the road, and the legless thigh rocked fitfully, kicking. "She's crazy," my mother sneered, "I see him now, I can see his stick in the air" – it swept the sky and seemed to writhe from his grasp and slipped like a straw to the ground, and the giant, with the shudder of cut-down tower or sail of ship, sank after it.

The three soldiers carried him back, each one bearing a single member. From the border-wire where we waited it was a strange triangle – first they took the head and the two arms, then they tried one of the arms, the good leg and the head, and after that the leg, the head, and the stump. But it was no use, the fellow was too heavy and big, they could not divide his weight properly in this fashion; the man who had the head was always at a disadvantage. At last they each took one of the three good limbs, and let the two shorter appendages, the stump and the head, hang down out of the way, with equal freedom and equal unimportance; and in this manner they struggled back to their station at the border.

"Ah," my mother muttered resentfully, "I didn't come to Europe for *this*." The body lay where the soldiers had heaped it; one was shouting into a walkie-talkie, and the two others stood sweating and sighing, fumbling with their trousers, rubbing their damp palms on their damp shirts. "On the far side of the line," the shouter shouted, "in the groin, the cryzy blowke. In the groin, darlin', I said groin," he went on yelling, "not spine, *groin*." We got back into the car and the Dutchwoman drove as though whipping a horse; we cantered into the white sun of noon. "You've dirtied your blouse," said my mother, picking at my collar – "that putrid smell." She opened her nostrils over the yellow stain, but her nose in meditation was as alien to me as the look of my own vomit. I did not feel responsible. "Leave her be," said my governess in her brutal accent, "when you are so near Germany there are worse things to smell." My mother frowned warily – "What?" "Corpses," said the Dutchwoman, kicking the flanks of the gas pedal. "Well, well," said my mother, "you people like to turn every stink into a moral issue. Can't you go any faster, Anneke?" she demanded, unlocking her brows, although the landscape flew. "The way you step on that pedal you'd think you were a corpse yourself."

But it was, in a way, corpses which had brought us to that place at that unlikely time, it was on account of corpses that we were there at all: corpses and Enoch, who had been appointed an adviser to corpses, an amicus curiæ with respect to corpses, a judge, jury, witness, committeeman, representative, and confidant of corpses. He had no office, but went wandering from boundary to boundary sorting out corpses, collecting new sources of more corpses, over-

seeing and administering armies of corpses. Some he yielded to
their claimants for burial, and some he had dug up and reburied
for no plain reason, and some he let lie where they had been
thrown: he was a liaison between the dead and the living, and
between the dead and the dead, and between the soon-dead and
the too-soon dead. And he was a liaison among the dead of all the
nations. "In Europe" (in one hotel room after another his ironic
growl would wake me between nightmares) "there is only one
united country, only one with unanimous voters, a single party,
an uncontradicted ideology, an egalitarian unhierarchical church,
an awesome police-power..." "Go to sleep, Enoch," I would hear
my mother's whine, reprimanding out of the dark. "The country
of the dead," he gave out at last, and gave in, and fell asleep and
snored, gravely, like a hawk over carrion – until, in the morning
(for he hated to get up), "Wake up, Enoch" – this from my mother
– and then, "Wormy, wormy, wormy, early in the mourning our
curse shall rise to Thee" – this from Enoch, hymn-singing.

For at that time my mother still went everywhere with her husband. Sometimes we would all travel in a body – Enoch, my
mother, the Dutchwoman, and I in the lead-car, and two cars full
of Enoch's assistants following after – but more often I would be
left behind with my governess to play on some littered and sorrow-
ful beach, where I would amuse myself by searching for shells – not
seashells: for the Dutchwoman had taught me how to dig after
empty cartridges nesting just below the wet sand, like clams, at
the margin of the water.

"Can't they explode?" my mother objected, handling my collection of shells at the end of a day's harvest. "If she happened to
drop one? She shouldn't be allowed to keep them."

"They are empty and harmless," remarked my governess without
interest.

"But there might be a good one mixed in with the others," my
mother said, tying a veil over her hat; she was preparing to take a
night train with Enoch to a city in the north, where a fresh ship-
ment of corpses waited.

"They are all of them already exploded," repeated the Dutchwoman. "They have been used," she observed almost angrily.

"Oh, but you really can't be sure!" my mother reproved. It seemed she was angry too, and not at the cartridges. She sheathed her forefinger with one of them, tapping it like a thimble. "How can you be sure?"

"Because there has been a war, madam; there has been shooting," said the Dutchwoman.

"As though she owned the war!" my mother announced to the ceiling. "What a nuisance you are, Anneke – you aren't the only one who has had to take hardships, you know."

"Yes," said the Dutchwoman tonelessly, "we were told that in America the sugar was rationed. How bitter your tea must have tasted."

My mother pretended to laugh; her mouth drew wrathfully back. "You don't like Americans, Anneke."

"I don't like *you*, madam."

"I pay you for your duties, not for your approval." But my mother's mirth had turned inexplicably genuine: she was amused, up to a point, by aggressiveness in servants. – "After all," she used to say, "if they go *too* far one can always fire them."

The Dutchwoman was careful not to go too far; she valued her position, since she had so little to do. While I ran about in the foam, she would doze on the mossy rocks, and did not care what I did, or whom I found for a playmate. A little country boy, whose hair had been shaved off altogether and whose red scalp shook out scales, gave me the ringworm; patches round as pennies emerged on my hands and on my chin, and my armpits itched intolerably. But the Dutchwoman declared that I had touched poison-ivy leaves against her warning, and I never contradicted her to my mother. Often she took me to eat in dim restaurants black with flies where there were no tablecloths or menus, and the food was so unfamiliar that I felt ill at the sight of it – brown and green sauces under which chunks of white fat lay folded in a bath of grease. All the while my mother believed that we dined on the boulevard, and made alarmed noises over the restaurant bills my governess used mysteriously to produce. But still the Dutchwoman was careful, very careful. "If you say one word," she would threaten me, "Mrs. Vand will send me away, and you will be left alone. Soon you will lose your way in the roads, and they will mistake you for a refugee child, they will put you in a camp for refugee children. Then you will contract a disease among all the sick little Jewesses. Afterward they will send you far away to Palestine where you will die in the desert of thirst."

"But I'm not Jewish," I protested. "And I'm not afraid of being thirsty, Anneke; I hate milk anyhow since it made me sick."

"Milk! You'll beg for water the way you begged for fake Coca-Cola on the boulevard today. Or else," she went on menacingly, "you will be shot before the Wailing Wall by a firing-squad from Arabia. Why not, since your father is Jewish?"

"Enoch isn't my father!" I cried, exuberant with relief. "He hasn't even been married to my mother very long – that makes him only my stepfather, you see, Anneke?"

The Dutchwoman chortled scornfully. "Did you think I'm so stupid not to understand that? But still you do not know who your real father is. What makes you sure *he* isn't a Jew? Do you think they will spare you when they find out that? No, I warn you, confide to your mother how you rubbed Jean François' contagion and off you go to Palestine."

Thereafter I could be relied on absolutely.

"She's loyal to you," my mother stated firmly, in frequent recognition of my governess' success with me. "The child is devoted, although she seems so cold. But she's cold even to me, without showing half so much loyalty, so what am I to expect? If not for that, I should have dismissed you long ago. I'll be frank with you, I can't bear a surly temperament. Of course you're not paid to like me, I don't say that. But at least you ought to conceal your bigotry."

"Bigotry?" the Dutchwoman sneered innocently. "I do not know that word."

"Don't you? It comes of being so conceited. It's a good thing you didn't finish at that medical school. You would have made a very bad doctor. You would have cared more for your own prestige than for anything," my mother noted with the acuteness of complacency.

"I had already chosen my field," the Dutchwoman said abruptly. "It was chemical research – I should not have liked to practice. But then haven't I told you how the German soldiers were billeted in our laboratories? They closed the school, and it did not matter what I liked." She shrugged and eyed my mother's pocketbook. "When is madam coming back?"

"Not for a week at least. It depends on the size of the job my husband finds up there. We're going to Normandy for some sort of ceremony afterward. It's to commemorate the invasion. You know it will all be as boring as the grave, full of speeches in atrocious English by foreign generals, but *c'est la guerre*, it can't be helped."

"The war has made many new positions," the Dutchwoman remarked quietly.

"You mean in relief work? Enoch is not in relief work. Unless you count burial as relief. I suppose it is, for the dead."

"No, I was thinking of my own position," said the Dutchwoman, looking first at me and then again at the pocketbook.

"My husband regards his corpses as displaced persons. He's very sympathetic toward them. His aim, you know, is to have the murderer lie down with the murdered. It's a kind of prophetic view. But in almost every case it can't be done. All the murderers are still alive, it seems."

"Mr. Vand is full of sayings," the Dutchwoman said slyly.

"He's a clever man," my mother agreed. "I just wish he'd exert himself a little with the child. I brought her out here expressly for that, but he won't take the trouble."

"Perhaps he is too busy," said the Dutchwoman accommodatingly.

"He holds a very high post," my mother persisted. "He is devoted to his work."

"Yes," the Dutchwoman affirmed in a very soft voice, smiling fixedly, "grave-digging nowadays leaves time for nothing else."

"That doesn't sit right with me, Anneke, you are too arrogant," my mother warned.

"But it is all meant in good faith, madam. The Americans have bureaucratized even grave-digging. It will be done much faster by the Americans. Your husband will see to it."

"My husband has great administrative capacity," my mother petulantly defended herself. "He has a kind of political genius. In fact," she concluded proudly, "he's often mistaken for a European on that account."

"What a shame," observed the Dutchwoman, slyer now than before, "that his present job is not political."

"There is no job today that is not political," my mother said. "It's only the dead who can afford to have no politics."

"That is another of Mr. Vand's sayings, isn't it? He is so clever it is a shame really," my governess repeated, "that he has no political influence. Perhaps that is why he is thought to be a European."

My mother blazed. "He has influence enough."

"He would do nothing for my brother. My brother was deported for underground activities. He has three children and speaks seven languages. Now he is an orderly in a hospital in Amsterdam. Mr. Vand would do nothing for him."

"There are already too many interpreters."

"Last month there was a position open. I heard Mr. Vand speak of it to you. But it came to nothing."

"Perhaps your brother did not qualify."

"No," said the Dutchwoman, "he did not qualify. They would take only an American. So many of the refugees are Polish, and the American did not know Polish. In spite of it they chose him."

"You don't understand, Anneke," my mother protested. "My husband's organization is merely an arm of the Government. It isn't in his hands to make policy."

"Of course," the Dutchwoman concurred, still steadily smiling. "That is precisely what I said. He has no political importance whatever."

"You cannot belittle Enoch Vand," my mother retorted. "Perhaps you should measure his importance by the number of people he has it in his power to dismiss. I have some importance myself in that respect. Be careful, Anneke, or I'll decide to show my importance in a way you would not like."

I looked up from my shells in alarm, but my mother's speech did not appear to have frightened my governess. "Certainly," she resumed amicably, "nowadays you Americans decide everything. But the child would not like you to send me away. It would not be good for the child."

"Nevertheless," said my mother, but there was no real menace in her voice any more. She opened her pocketbook and took out a wallet. "Do you want your wages now or when I come back?"

"Now," said Anneke without hesitation.

"You had better get rid of those shells."

"Yes, madam."

"See that you obey your governess," my mother admonished me. – Outdoors the chauffeur's horn called. – "Goodbye."

I did not answer. "Goodbye," said the Dutchwoman generously, pushing me forward to be kissed.

My mother bent to me quickly; I saw her tense stretched nostrils. She steamed with toilet-water. "My husband will be Ambassador some day," she stated, and went out without rancor to her car.

The Dutchwoman was counting bills and folding them one by one into a little purse. "That will be a great jump from the burial committee. Here," she said, and threw me a five-franc piece.

"Anneke, I want to keep my shells."

She was at once serious. "I'll show you where to find more," she offered promptly, "if you promise to stay in the room by yourself tonight."

"You know I'm not supposed to be left alone," I reminded her.

"If I swear not to tell Mrs. Vand?"

She gave me another coin, light and smooth as a wafer, and we shook hands on the bargain.

In the evening she went away wearing a blue dress and a yellow band in her hair, and did not come back until morning.

"Were you afraid?"

"No," I said bravely, "but there were noises."

"When you sleep there are no noises. Tonight you must be sure to sleep."

"Are you going away again?"

"I have to spend the night with a friend. Come," she urged, "I know a new place near the sea wall where there are cartridges."

But I had a dream, and saw a thing with ochre eyes and a brass tail which ended in a dagger; monster-like it leaped through the window and rattled its metal forelock on the metal bedpost: and

I screamed in my sleep and woke the concierge's husband, although he was somewhat deaf.

All the keys trembled on his great steel ring, and his teeth were ridged with gold, and his tongue churned the spittle in the forest of his lip-hairs. But I understood nothing. And so the concierge came down the corridor in her coffee-smelling robe, rubbing her glasses with the vigor of suspicion; and very slowly and loudly, as though I were the one who was deaf, she questioned me. "Où est Madame Vand?" "Elle est partie pour le nord," I said in the French I had learned from the children on the beach. "Et ta soeur?" "Je n'ai pas de soeur." "Ah! Une gouvernante!" "Oui," I replied. "Où est-ce qu'elle est?" "Je ne sais pas." "Est-ce que ta gouvernante est sortie de la maison?" "Oui." At this information the concierge assessed her husband's considerable mustache with a look of disgust. "Ah, nous y violà!" she shrieked. "Quand est-ce qu'elle va venir?" "Je ne sais pas," I said again; "la nuit passée elle est venue à…à six heures du matin." "C'est ça!" mumbled the husband, "pas de chance," as though it were all up to his wife, and while the key-ring dangled and jangled from the crook of his knuckle they went on conferring sibilantly. Finally the concierge prodded my pillow with her fat squat fingers; it was the motion of a judge with his gavel. "Qu'est-ce que ton père fait?" she demanded with a terrifying solemnity; and because I did not know the word for stepfather, I answered as though Enoch were really what she thought him: "Mon père est fonctionnaire," I said in the phrase I had often heard Anneke use on the boulevard. "Américain," the concierge conceded in triumph, and waggled the tassel of her belt at her husband: "Le grand malheur! Alors, de quoi te plains-tu?" And I saw from the swagger of their departing backs that they were satisfied: Monsieur Vand was good for the rent-money; an abandoned child had not been left on their hands after all.

The Dutchwoman returned with the daylight; I had not slept the whole night. She went to the window and stood veiled by the early glimmer, pulling at the ribbon which had raveled in her hair; and while she leaned, her elbows on the sill and her fingers working invisible as submarines in the short tough snarls, it seemed she listened, as for footsteps; but only the faint knocking of a chain, and then the rocking of a quick bicycle on cobblestones came up to us from the street. I lay amazed: there were long creases in her dress, and long creases in her cheek carved by the wrinkles of some alien bedsheet: the side of her face was grooved like the belly of a beach against which the tide has repeatedly shouldered, and the red dawn lit into bright shallow scars the fluted skin. She was, for the moment, qualified by some private act or notion – an ugliness new in the world had mounted her and reigned in the ruts of her flesh and in the swift sly receding clangor of the bicycle and in the secret morning.

She began to hum, rolling down her stockings. – "Anneke?" I ventured.

"Are you awake?" She looked over crossly. "Go back to sleep. It's too early."

"The concierge was here, Anneke."

"What?"

"The concierge – "

"In the middle of the night? What did you tell her?"

"I said you would come back in the morning."

"Now you have done it! Listen, if your mother should find out – "

"Oh, I won't tell her, I promise!"

"The concierge will tell her. Now I am finished."

"Ah, no, Anneke," I moaned under her fierce palms loosened from their lair; they hung against my face, broad and retributive and racy with an oiled nighttime odor and the distinguishable smells, like fog and ash, of her hair; and in the warm pale hearts, sentencing and consigning me, of the palms of her hands I seemed to see those deserts of Palestine, warm and pale, hot and white, laden with drifted sand like salt.

In the afternoon, although the sun poured honey, we did not go down to the sea. It was my penalty. The Dutchwoman took up my box of shells and flung it into an iron barrel, filled half with kitchen refuse and half with rain-water, that loomed in the yard behind the concierge's rooms, busy with flies; innumerable foul splashes of rust leaped up and scattered their thousand wings into the dread colonial airs ("irretrievable, irretrievable," roared the gypped black carousing flies) – "If you had cherished each one like the separate gems of a treasure I should do the same," she announced with the bitter strength of justice: "I do only what your mother wishes." And now everything must be explained to the concierge (how mild my punishment compared to that!), who was snooper, intruder, prevaricator, twister, telltale – everything must be set out straight. "The foolish child," the Dutchwoman took up, "she had a bad dream. What a pity, the very hour I was called away."

The concierge made a noncommittal sound against her upper palate. From the porch of the house the far waves flickered.

"On such short notice it was impossible to get a nurse...the doctor had to ask me for the night – "

"Exactly what is the matter with your friend?" inquired the concierge with dry civility.

"A serious disease, poor thing."

"*Quel dommage!*" The concierge neatly bit off a hangnail. "Will she live?"

"With God's help," the Dutchwoman said piously.

"Let us pray the disease is not of a contagious nature," remarked the concierge, outdoing my governess in solicitous religiosity by crossing herself briefly; but her voice seemed oddly cool.

I thought I would placate them both by a show of concern equal to their own. "Anneke," I gave out penitently, "does your friend have the ringworm?" – remembering the torments of poor Jean François.

"No, it is something else."

"Does her head itch?" I pursued nevertheless.

The concierge howled. "*Voilà!*" She slapped her shinbone as though in the presence of a stupendous joke. "You have the right idea, but the wrong end," she went on boisterously cackling, and took her hilarity into the house.

"Sssstupid alleycat!" hissed the Dutchwoman after her. "Rotting eye of a fisssh!" And when she turned to glare at me, her mouth was wild and wishful as though it had tasted quarry.

Some days afterward Enoch and two of his assistants arrived quietly in a mild brown car. "Your mother stopped in Paris on the way down," he told me. "Her car's smashed up – she had an accident. The chauffeur was injured, and she's gone to see about the insurance."

"And Mrs Vand?" said my governess with a disapproval faintly discernible. "Madam is all right?"

My stepfather looked surprised. "Of course she's all right. She's coming the rest of the way by train. – Meanwhile I have some paperwork to take care of. I may as well do it here as anywhere, since it's on the way."

"On the way where?" I wondered.

"Zürich. We're due there day after tomorrow."

"Is my mother going too?"

"It's up to her," he said, and threw me one of his rare amused visionary smiles: "Do I ever know what she'll do? Not until it's too late, you can bet on that."

The men retired to my mother's room, where the concierge had set up half a dozen card tables; and all afternoon the two assistants, light-haired bashful earnest young men, drew meticulous marks on yellow form-sheets, while Enoch, reclining elbow-deep in mimeographed documents as thick as Russian novels, disputed with them in a clatter of alien syllables.

"What language is that?" I asked the Dutchwoman.

"Don't eavesdrop," she chided me, although she was plainly listening herself: the windows were open and the dark and serious voices of the men fell to the garden. We lay in the shade of the eaves on a strip of blue canvas. The Dutchwoman took off her sunglasses – she had been peering into an old stained American picture-weekly in which my sandals had been wrapped. "It is Czech and Rumanian and Polish and Hungarian and German."

"Do they know all those languages?" I marveled.

"They are reading lists of names. – Where are you going?" she broke off. "You are not to bother Mr. Vand!" She snatched after me, but I left her pinching air and faintly calling, and when I gained the threshold of my mother's chamber her cries had grown too dim to matter, or too indifferent.

"Well, come in," said Enoch, absorbed and aloof.

"We heard you in the garden," I began.

The two young men lifted their fountain pens curiously, watching Enoch.

"What are those names?"

Enoch did not reply.

I tried again. "Whose names are you looking at?"

"Everybody's," said the first assistant.

"Europe's," said the second assistant.

"Nobody's," said Enoch. "They are all dead."

"I saw a man shoot himself," I readily offered, "once when I was throwing up. He had only one leg."

Enoch tamely viewed me. "That's better than none."

"But he died," I countered, as though that were some sort of argument. "In the road. Anneke saw it too."

"Well, it's what your mother brought you for," he broke out in his businesslike way, folding and unfolding a leaf spotted with black numbers; under the little table his impatient feet turned caustically outward. "In America everybody has two legs. She wanted you to be enriched," he said, clinging to the last word disconsolately; I wondered if it were a bit of mimicry.

In any case it reminded me of my pocket. Smugly I felt in there. "Anneke gave me ten francs," I boasted. "I still have three. I bought Coca-Cola."

"As a state of being childhood has nothing to recommend it," Enoch murmured, and lifted, without assurance of comfort, one of those great volumes crowded with death.

"Well, it's temporary," one of his assistants gave out just then.

The air seemed discommoded. Enoch seized the moment. "That depends." His big brown head fell forward on his page like a statue tumbling down. His hair had already begun to grow sparsely: it made him look like a Julius Cæsar bare of laurel. He creaked around to face his young men as though discovering a pair of intruders — "Go on," he ordered, and set them to work again by the elevation of a single finger.

"Lev Ben-zion Preiserowicz," intoned the first assistant.

"Auschwitz," answered the other.

"Wladzia Bazanowska."

"Belsen."

"Schmul Noach Pincus."

"Buchenwald," came the echo, slow as a thorn.

"Velvel Kupperschmid."

"Dachau," the voice fell like an axe.

"Wolfgang Edmund Landau-Weber."

"Buchenwald," the reader yawned.

"Roza Itte Gottfried."

"Belsen," said Enoch's young assistant, picking at his teeth with an ivory thumbnail.

They went on in this manner unremittingly; I was soon bored. It was like what I imagined prayer to be, full of attack and ebb, flow and useless drain, foolish because clearly nobody heard, neither deaf heaven nor the dry-lipped deafer communicants; it was in short a sad redundant madrigal, droned out for its own sad sake, and all those queer repugnant foreign names, cluttering the air without mercy, seemed pointless, pushy, offensive, aggressive, thrusting themselves unreasonably up for notice: I thought of the flies spraying out from their barrel of filth, whipping wing-noises as savage as the noises of these wingless graceless names. "Itsaak Lazar Chemsky," said the first young man, smoothing his creamy mustard hair, tugging now and then at his constricting too-hot tasteful tie: and "Rivka Czainer," he said, and "Mottel Yarmolinski, Chaya Tscherniknow, Dvora-gittel Langbeiner," he said, "Pesha Teitelbaum, Janek Kedlacki, Sholem Shlomo Pinsky, Yoneh Hillel Yarmuk," he said, and the sun slunk lower into the room while the concierge came and went with coffee cups; and he said "Maishe Lipsky, Dovid Ginsberg, Kalman Dubnitz," and still the list was not exhausted; and the other had his list, but it was even more soporific, the same sounds again and again and again, Dachau, Belsen, Auschwitz, Buchenwald, the order varying, Auschwitz, Buchenwald, Belsen, Dachau, now and then an alteration in the tick and swing, Belsen, Maidenek, Auschwitz, Chelmo, Dachau, Treblinka, Buchenwald, Mauthausen, Sovibar — tollings like the chorus of some unidentifiable opera of which I could remember the music but not the import — and all the while Enoch sat spitting on his thumb and crackling the hides of those book-thick blotty documents, heaped like masonry, through which he drove his indefatigable pen.

After a time I broke through their chant and counterpoint. "If they are all dead why do you keep their names?"

"To have a record," said the first assistant.

"To arrange for the funerals," said the second assistant.

"For no reason in the world," said Enoch, and peeled from his shoulders a finely rolled shrug. He blinked at me portentously. "Smoke leaves no records and cinders don't have funerals." It was one of those futuristic or apocalyptic statements which were his habit; his tone diagrammed a moon-surface, pitted and piteous, burning incomprehensibly into eternity. It was a reminder of his perpetual dialogue, of his idolatry even: he was always addressing some image or apparition or muse, perhaps Clio, perhaps some crazed Goddess of the Twentieth Century whom he had given up appeasing, and could only malign.

The others detected his calumny, and, without recognizing it as a sort of worship, supposed it to be the ill-temper of an admirable eccentricity. It made them shy of him, yet imitative. They were grave and diffident youths, yet not without the sing-song of fancy: they gazed at me full of secret teasing. And they wrinkled their papers with an obliging and casual horror, plainly believing that Enoch apostrophized, if not themselves, then merely Death: and all in the manner of a man possessed of scorn. But Enoch was forty then, immured in careerism and beyond romanticizing death. He did not think (as they did): Lethe. For him it was instead (a thing for them impossible), briskly, brutally: slaughter. He was well past Lethe, and well past Nepenthe, and far past the Styx or Paradise. He took it all as simple butchery, and a demeaning waste of time to poetize. What he put down in those immense ledgers was, I suppose, notations on his creed: perhaps he thought of himself as a scholar-saint, Duns Scotus or maybe Maimonides, feeding data to his goddess as others swing censers or take ashen thumbprints on their brows – he gave her what he could. She might have been, as I have said, History; or, what is more probable, the grim-faced nymph Geopolitica, wearing a girdle of human skin and sandals sinewed and thonged by the sighs of dead philosophers. She might even have been Charity, although that is less plausible. Still, who-ever she was, he vilified her roundly; his imprecations were sly but to the point. He cursed her for the smoke and the cinders and the corpses, and pleaded for the Evil Inclination and the Angel of Death jointly to carry her off; but she remained. I wonder how he saw her, whether all gold and Greek and comely, or hideously whorled and coiled with intellect. Howsoever it was, he was himself her cultist, he had succumbed, she owned him absolutely. She had achieved terror, power, majesty, the throne and crown and sceptre and sway and seat of his mind – seizures, above all, of genius. Perhaps he conceived of it all as the old wearisome affair called getting ahead, or making a career, or driving on, or reaching for the topmost rung – whichever phrase the moment favored – and did not meditate on those fabled pursuits, Argonauts after golden fleece, Israelites after Zion, which were like his own. He pursued: the others knew that he pursued, and imagined (as surely my mother imagined) it was promotion, a better classification, more men under him, something reckonable and recognized, that made him pant – in short, the future. And he could not confess for the sake of whom or what he dug down deep in those awesome volumes, sifting their name-burdened and number-laden leaves as soil is spaded and weighted in search of sunken graves and bones time-turned to stone – he could not say or tell. That apparition (image? vision?), succubus barnacled to his brain, was a cunning mist there in my mother's room where Enoch leaned brooding among the paper remnants of the damned: the lists and questionnaires, the numbers and their nemeses; every table spread with the worms' feast; the room a registry and bursary for smoke and cinders. Over it all his goddess hung. If she wore a pair of bucklers for her breasts, they gleamed for him and shimmered sound like struck cymbals; if slow vein-blood drooped like pendants from her gored ears, they seemed to him jewels more gradual than pearls – she formed herself out of the slaughter; the scarves and winds of smoke met to make her hair, the cinders clustered to make her thighs; she was war, death, blood, and spilled the severed limbs of infants from her giant channel in perpetual misbirths; she came up enlightened from that slaughter like a swimmer from the towering water-wall with his glorified face; she came up an angel from that slaughter and the fire-whitened cinders of those names. She came up Europa.

Europa: so my mother was right. She had desired for me the re-coupment of Europe, by which she plainly meant conversion; and she had borne me purposefully and hopefully to the scorched plain, all the while swearing to castles and cathedrals, and seizing like a missionary on those improbable doctrines of hers, those feudal sentimentalities of tapestry and cloister, rubric and falcon, shrine and knight's tomb, as though she imagined spells lay in-choate in that old stained soil. She had brought me to see the spires of those places, quick as scimitars, and minarets like over-turned goblets, and the domes, windows, and pillars of those exhausted groves; also icons rubbed beyond belief; and moats flushed with mold; and long vaporous seacoasts; and portraits of shallow-necked ancient ladies with small ringed hands; and, by the hundreds, mild madonnas suckling. We were bare and blank, by comparison, at home; we were all steel. So she brought me to those points of germination, in fact to her idea of civilization, as savage as anyone's: and she promised from this fountain of the world (she called it life, she called it Europe) all spectacle, domin-ion, energy, and honor. And all the while she never smelled death there.

Enoch and Europe: she saw them as one, and in Enoch saw plainly a capacity for spectacle, dominion, energy and honor – and more, a kind of command without speculation, an unbrooding place-oblivion that breathed Europe as though Europe were a gas more natural to him than any air. And all the while she never thought what that gas might be; she saw him dizzied by it, driven by it, claimed and owned by it; and all the while she never thought what that gas might be, dreamed it as some sort of nimbus to praise him, or film to gild or tissue to adorn him, or lens (cloth-of-gold, wing of butterfly) through which he glimpsed rare and secret refractions of the Europe she desired, secret and brilliant incarnations of her illusions. And all the while she never smelled death there, or thought what that gas might be.

But it was deathcamp gas, no nimbus, that plagued his head and drifted round his outstretched arm and nuzzled in the folds of his trouser-cuffs and swarmed from his nostrils to touch those un-shrouded tattooed carcasses of his, moving in freight cars over the gassed and blighted continent.

So my mother was both right and wrong: right because, through a romantic but useful perspicacity, she had penetrated the cloud of power that brightly ringed her husband, and guessed how Europe had mastered him; and wrong, at the same time deeply wrong in thinking it was *her* Europe to which he was committed and had given himself over, her Europe of spectacle, dominion, energy and honor, a Europe misted by fame and awe. And all that while my mother did not smell the deathcamp gas. She wondered that Enoch was not a stranger in those places and among those deeds; but she could not smell the deathcamp gas welling from his eyes. She saw him overwhelmed, and thought it was by ambition; she saw him dedicated, and thought it was to his advancement; she saw him absorbed, and thought it was in his career in government. But she did not see the goddess: that Europa who had engulfed him with her pity and her treasons and her murderous griefs, and her thighs of cinders and her hair of smoke, and her long, long fraud of age on age, and her death-choked womb.

It was not merely that the goddess in her dark shapes was invisible, for my mother was used to the invisible; she entertained ariels of her own, and could readily exchange one magic for another, and would have celebrated distress and decay and eery hopelessness (even trading in spectacle, dominion, energy, and honor) if only someone had taken the trouble to point out their withered elegances: she was not blunt to beauty's divers opportunities. It was not, then, that my mother, with all her cunning and all her inspiration, was incapable of seeing or imagining who or what had him in thrall — what violent figure, what vast preoccupation, what preying *belle dame sans merci* (she was bold enough for these and anything). It was precisely his thralldom that escaped her. No goddess eluded Allegra Vand; she failed rather to catch hold of Enoch himself. She did not suspect the priest and cultist in him: how then could she picture icons round his halls? She did not guess that he worshipped because she did not think him accessible to the devotional impulse. About Enoch she was quite stupid; she was quite mistaken; she blundered into ironies. To amuse himself, he compounded them. She could not take him in, as she had taken in William entire, turning exact assessment into a devouring. Did she wish to re-father me? (Ah, that stark and persistent notion of hers.) Very well; he made bad-mannered noises and hoped the while I would always emulate his example. And did she wish him to strike in me Europe's lovely note? He clangored his lists of the murdered. Did she wish him to be for me what William was not? He obliged her by being profane. – It was clear that she had carried me from the disaffected William to fling me at a misconceived Enoch: from Homo Puritanus, as she supposed it, to Secular Man. And, mocking her error, he went at his secularity with the fanaticism of a preacher bursting into homilies. Then began the grand burlesque of those burgeoning aphorisms: "What Holiness would not undertake," he avowed, damning and deriding William for his finicky lawyerish hesitations concerning my moral education, "Worldliness shall" – and my mother watched in pleased innocence as he thumbed his breast with gusto. And then, rapidly following, he would bellow all those other maxims on the subject which I have already recorded: Upon what Holiness cannot build, When Holiness essays introspection, That moment when Holiness with whatsoever good will...and further confessions of Homo Profanus, Worldliness Incarnate, Cosmopolitanism Idealized, the Adam of Europe fallen into Paradise. But still my mother did not hear the brittle mirth in those saws and convolutions. And all the while freight-trains scratching on bomb-twisted tracks howled out of the east with a cargo of tattooed corpses for Enoch the Secular Man; and racing from border to border he said aloud to his wife (who thought it very clever of him), "The house of death hath many mansions"; and in the privacy of his intellect he lit centuries and burned history to hallow his intemperate goddess. My mother was deaf to his ironies and did not dream she traveled with a man anointed. In short, she missed the whole sense of his character.

It was the reason they got on.

Grace Paley

Grace Paley's most recent collection of stories is *Later the Same Day*, which follows her earlier collections *Enormous Changes at the Last Minute* and *The Little Disturbances of Man*. Ms. Paley received a Work-in-Progress grant in 1967.

FAITH IN A TREE

JUST WHEN I most needed important conversation, a sniff of the man-wide world, that is, at least one brainy companion who could translate my friendly language into his tongue of undying carnal love, I was forced to lounge in our neighborhood park, surrounded by children.

All the children were there. Among the trees, in the arms of statues, toes in the grass, they hopped in and out of dog shit and dug tunnels into mole holes. Wherever the children ran, their mothers stopped to talk.

What a place in democratic time! One God, who was King of the Jews, who unravels the stars to this day with little hydrogren explosions, He can look down from His Holy Headquarters and see us all: heads of girl, ponytails riding the springtime luck, short black bobs, and an occasional eminence of golden wedding rings. He sees south into Brooklyn how Prospect Park lies in its sand-rooted trees among Japanese gardens and police, and beyond us north to dangerous Central Park. Far north, the deer-eyed eland and kudu survive, grazing the open pits of the Bronx Zoo.

But me, the creation of His soft second thought, I am sitting on the twelve-foot-high, strong, long arm of a sycamore, my feet swinging, and I can only see Kitty, a co-worker in the mother trade – a topnotch craftsman. She is below, leaning on my tree, rumpled in a black cotton skirt made of shroud remnants at about fourteen cents a yard. Another colleague, Anne Kraat, is close by on a hard park bench, gloomy, beautiful, waiting for her luck to change.

Although I can't see them, I know that on the other side of the dry pool, the thick snout of the fountain spout, hurrying along the circumference of the parched sun-struck circle (in which, when Henry James could see, he saw lilies floating), Mrs. Hyme Caraway pokes her terrible seedlings, Gowan, Michael, and Christopher, astride an English bike, a French tricycle, and a Danish tractor. Beside her, talking all the time in fear of no response, Mrs. Steamy Lewis, mother of Matthew, Mark, and Lucy, tells of happy happy life in a thatched hotel on a Greek island where total historical recall is indigenous. Lucy limps along at her skirt in muddy cashmere. Mrs. Steamy Lewis really swings within the seconds of her latitude and swears she will have six, but Mr. Steamy Lewis is not expected to live.

I can easily see Mrs. Junius Finn, my up-the-block neighbor and evening stoop companion, a broad barge, like a lady, moving slow — a couple of redheaded cabooses dragged by clothesline at her stern; on her fat upper deck, Wiltwyck,* a pale three-year-old roaring captain with smoky eyes, shoves his wet thumb into the wind. "Hurry! Hurry!" he howls. Mrs. Finn goes puff puffing toward the opinionated playground, that sandy harbor.

Along the same channel, but near enough now to spatter with spite, tilting delicately like a boy's sailboat, Lynn Ballard floats past my unconcern to drop light anchor, a large mauve handbag, over the green bench slats. She sighs and looks up to see what (if anything) the heavens are telling. In this way, once a week, toes in, head high and in three-quarter turn, arms at her side, graceful as a seal's flippers, she rests, quiet and expensive. She never grabs another mother's kid when he falls and cries. Her particular Michael on his little red bike rides round and round the sandbox, while she dreams of private midnight.

"Like a model," hollers Mrs. Junius Finn over Lynn Ballard's head.

---

* Wiltwyck is named for the school of his brother Junior, where Junior, who was bad and getting worse, is still bad, but is getting better (as man is *perfectible*).

I'm too close to the subject to remark. I sniff, however, and accidentally take sweetness into my lungs. Because it's the month of May.

Kitty and I are nothing like Lynn Ballard. You will see Kitty's darling face, as I tell her, slowly, but me – quick – what am I? Not bad if you're a basement shopper. On my face are a dozen messages, easy to read, strictly for friends, Bargains Galore! I admit it now.

However, the most ordinary life is illuminated by a great event like fame. Once I was famous. From the meaning of that glow, the modest hardhearted me is descended.

Once, all the New York papers that had the machinery to do so carried a rotogravure picture of me in a stewardess's arms. I was, it is now thought, the third commercial air-flight baby passenger in the entire world. This picture is at the Home now, mounted on laundry cardboard. My mother fixed it with glass to assail eternity. The caption says: One of Our Youngest. Little Faith Decided to Visit Gramma. Here She Is, Gently Cuddled in the Arms of Stewardess Jeannie Carter.

Why would anyone send a little baby anywhere alone? What was my mother trying to prove? That I was independent? That she wasn't the sort to hang on? That in the sensible, socialist, Zionist world of the future, she wouldn't cry at my wedding? "You're an American child. Free. Independent." Now what does that mean? I have always required a man to be dependent on, even when it appeared that I had one already. I own two small boys whose dependence on me takes up my lumpen time and my bourgeois feelings. I'm not the least bit ashamed to say that I tie their shoes and I have wiped their backsides well beyond the recommendations of my friends, Ellen and George Hellesbraun, who are psychiatric social workers and appalled. I kiss those kids forty times a day. I punch them just like a father should. When I have a date and come home late at night, I wake them with a couple of good hard shakes to complain about the miserable entertainment. When I'm not furiously exhausted from my low-level job and that bedraggled soot-slimy house, I praise God for them. One Sunday morning, my neighbor, Mrs. Raftery, called the cops because it was 3 a.m. and I was vengefully singing a praising song.

Since I have already mentioned singing, I have to tell you; it is not Sunday. For that reason, all the blue-eyed, boy-faced policemen in the park are worried. They can see that lots of our vitamin-enlarged kids are planning to lug their guitar cases around all day long. They're scared that one of them may strum and sing a mountain melody or that several, a gang, will gather to raise their voices in medieval counterpoint.

Question: Does the world know, does the average freed-man realize that, except for a few hours on Sunday afternoon, the playing of fretted instruments is banned by municipal decree? Absolutely forbidden is the song of the flute and oboe.

Answer (explanation): This *is* a great ballswinger of a city on the constant cement-mixing remake, battering and shattering, and a high note out of a wild clarinet could be the decibel to break a citizen's eardrum. But what if you were a city-loving planner leaning on your drawing board? Tears would drop to the delicate drafting sheets.

Well, you won't be pulled in for whistling and here come the whistlers – the young Saturday fathers, open-shirted and ambitious. By and large they are trying to get somewhere and have to go to a lot of parties. They are sleepy but pretend to great energy for the sake of their two-year-old sons (little boys need a recollection of Energy as a male resource). They carry miniature footballs though the season's changing. Then the older fathers trot in, just a few minutes slower, their faces scraped to a clean smile, every one of them wearing a fine gray head and eager eyes, his breath caught, his hand held by the baby daughter of a third intelligent marriage.

One of them, passing my tree, stubs his toe on Kitty's sandal. He shades his eyes to look up at me against my sun. That is Alex O. Steele, who was a man organizing tenant strikes on Ocean Parkway when I was a Coney Island Girl Scout against my mother's socialist will. He says, "Hey, Faith, how's the world? Heard anything from Ricardo?"

I answer him in lecture form:

Alex Steele. Sasha. Yes. I have heard from Ricardo. Ricardo even at the present moment when I am trying to talk with you in a civilized way, Ricardo has rolled his dove-gray brain into a glob of spit in order to fly secretly into my ear right off the poop deck of Foamline's World Tour Cruiseship *Eastern Sunset*. He is stretched out in my head, exhausted before dawn from falling in love with an *Eastern Sunset* lady passenger on the first leg of her many-masted journey round the nighttimes of the world. He is *this minute* saying to me,

"Arcturus Rise, Orion Fall..."

"Cock-proud son of a bitch," I mutter.

"Ugh," he says, blinking.

"How are the boys?" I make him say.

"Well, he really wants to know how the boys are," I reply.

"No, I don't," he says. "Please don't answer. Just make sure they don't get killed crossing the street. That's your job."

"WHAT?" says Alex Steele. "Speak clearly, Faith, you're garbling like you used to."

"I'm joking. Forget it. But I did hear from him the other day." Out of the pocket of my stretch denims I drag a mashed letter with the exotic stamp of a new under-developed nation. It is a large stamp with two smiling lions on a field of barbed wire. The letter says: "I am not well. I hope I never see another rain forest. I am sick. Are you working? Have you seen Ed Snead? He owes me $180. Don't badger him about it if he looks broke. Otherwise send me some to Guerra Verde c/o Dotty Wasserman. Am living here with her. She's on a Children's Mission. Wonderful girl. Reminds me of you ten years ago. She acts on her principles. I *need* the money."

"That is Ricardo. Isn't it, Alex? I mean, there's no signature."

"Dotty Wasserman!" Alex says. "So that's where she is... a funny plain girl. Faith, let's have lunch some time. I work up in the East Fifties. How're your folks? I hear they put themselves into a Home. They're young for that. Listen, I'm the executive director of Incurables, Inc., a fund-raising organization. We do wonderful things, Faith. The speed of life-extending developments...By the way, what do you think of this little curly Sharon of mine?"

"Oh, Alex, how old is she? She's darling, she's a little golden baby, I love her. She's a peach."

"Of course! *She's* a peach, you like anyone better'n you like us," says my son Richard, who is jealous – because he came first and was deprived at two and one half by his baby brother of my single-hearted love, my friend Ellie Hellesbraun says. Of course, that's a convenient professional lie, a cheap hindsight, as Richard, my oldest son, is brilliant, and I knew it from the beginning. When he was a baby all alone with me, and Ricardo his daddy was off exploring some deep creepy jungle, we often took the ferry to Staten Island. Then we sometimes took the ferry to Hoboken. We walked bridges, just he and I, I said to him, Richie, see the choo choos on the barges, Richie, see the strong fast tugboat, see the merchant ships with their tall cranes, see the *United States* sail away for a week and a day, see the Hudson River with its white current. Oh, it isn't really the Hudson River, I told him, it's the North River; it isn't really a river, it's an estuary, part of the sea, I told him, though he was only two. I could tell him scientific things like that, because I considered him absolutely brilliant. See how beautiful the ice is on the river, see the stony palisades, I said, I hugged him, my pussycat, I said, see the interesting world.

So he really has no kicks coming, he's just peevish.

"We're really a problem to you, Faith, we keep you not free," Richard says. "Anyway, it's true you're crazy about anyone but us."

It's true I do like the other kids. I am not too cool to say Alex's Sharon really is a peach. But you, you stupid kid, Richard! Who could match me for pride or you for brilliance? Which one of the smart third-grade kids in a class of learned Jews, Presbyterians, and bohemians? You are one of the two smartest and the other one is Chinese – Arnold Lee, who does make Richard look a little simple, I admit it. But did you ever hear of a child who, when asked to write a sentence for the word "who" (they were up to the hard *wh*'s), wrote and then magnificently, with Oriental lisp, read the following: "Friend, tell me WHO among the Shanghai merchants does the largest trade?"*

"That's a typical yak yak out of you, Faith," says Richard.

"Now Richard, listen to me, Arnold's an interesting boy; you

---

* The teacher, Marilyn Gewirtz, the only real person in this story, a child admirer, told me this.

wouldn't meet a kid like him anywhere but here or Hong Kong. So use some of these advantages I've given you. I could be living in the country, which I love, but I know how hard that is on children – I stay here in this creepy slum. I dwell in soot and slime just so you can meet kids like Arnold Lee and live on this wonderful block with all the Irish and Puerto Ricans, although God knows why there aren't any Negro children for you to play with…"

"Who needs it?" he says, just to tease me. "All those guys got knives anyway. But you don't care if I get killed much, do you?"

How can you answer that boy?

"You don't," says Mrs. Junius Finn, glad to say a few words. "You don't have to answer them. God didn't give out tongues for that. You answer too much, Faith Asbury, and it shows. Nobody fresher than Richard."

"Mrs. Finn," I scream in order to be heard, for she's some distance away and doesn't pay attention the way I do, "what's so terrible about fresh. EVIL is bad. WICKED is bad. ROBBING, MURDER, and PUTTING HEROIN IN YOUR BLOOD is bad."

"Blah blah," she says, deaf to passion. "Blah to you."

Despite no education, Mrs. Finn always is more in charge of word meanings than I am. She is especially in charge of Good and Bad. My language limitations here are real. My vocabulary is adequate for writing notes and keeping journals but absolutely useless for an active moral life. If I really knew this language, there would sure be in my head, as there is in Webster's or the *Dictionary of American Slang*, that unreducible verb designed to tell a person like me what to do next.

Mrs. Finn knows my problems because I do not keep them to myself. And I am reminded of them particularly at this moment, for I see her roughly the size of life, held up at the playground by Wyllie, who has rolled off the high ruddy deck of her chest to admire all the English bikes filed in the park bike stand. Of course that is what Junior is upstate for: love that forced possession. At first his father laced him on his behind, cutting the exquisite design known to generations of daddies who labored at home before the rise of industrialism and group therapy. Then Mr. Finn remembered his childhood, that it was Adam's Fall not Junior that was responsible. Now the Finns never see a ten-speed Italian racer without family sighs for Junior, who is still not home as there were about 176 bikes he loved.

Something is wrong with the following tenants: Mrs. Finn, Mrs. Raftery, Ginnie, and me. Everyone else in our building is on the way up through the affluent society, putting five to ten years into low rent before moving to Jersey or Bridgeport. But our four family units, as people are now called, are doomed to stand culturally still as this society moves on its caterpillar treads from ordinary affluent to absolute empire. All this in mind, I name names and dates. "Mrs. Finn, darling, look at my Richard, the time Junior took his Schwinn and how Richard hid in the coal in the basement thinking of a way to commit suicide," but she coolly answers, "Faith, you're not a bit fair, for Junior give it right back when he found out it was Richard's."

O.K.

Kitty says, "Faith, you'll fall out of the tree, calm yourself." She looks up, rolling her eyes to show direction, and I see a handsome man in narrow pants whom we remember from other Saturdays. He has gone to sit beside Lynn Ballard. He speaks softly to her left ear while she maintains her profile. He has never spoken to her Michael. He is a famous actor trying to persuade her to play opposite him in a new production of *She*. That's what Kitty, my kind friend, says.

I am above that kindness. I often see through the appearance of things right to the apparition itself. It's obvious that he's a weekend queer, talking her into the possibilities of a neighborhood threesome. When her nose quivers and she agrees, he will easily get his really true love, the magnificent manager of the supermarket, who has been longing for her at the check-out counter. What they will do then, I haven't the vaguest idea. I am the child of puritans and I'm only halfway here.

"Don't even think like that," says Kitty. No. She can see a contract in his pocket.

There is no one like Kitty Skazka. Unlike other people who have similar flaws that doom, she is tolerant and loving. I wish Kitty could live forever, bearing daughters and sons to open the heart of man. Meanwhile, mortal, pregnant, she has three green-eyed daughters and they aren't that great. Of course, Kitty thinks they are. And they are no worse than the average gifted, sensitive child of a wholehearted mother and half-a-dozen transient fathers.

Her youngest girl is Antonia, who has no respect for grownups. Kitty has always liked her to have no respect; so in this, she is quite satisfactory to Kitty.

At some right moment on this Saturday afternoon, Antonia decided to talk to Tonto, my second son. He lay on his belly in the grass, his bare heels exposed to the eye of flitting angels, and he worked at a game that included certain ants and other bugs as players.

"Tonto," she asked, "what are you playing, can I?"

"No, it's my game, no girls," Tonto said.

"Are you the boss of the world?" Antonia asked politely.

"Yes," said Tonto.

He thinks, he really believes, he is. To which I must say, Righto! you *are* the boss of the world, Anthony, you are prince of the day-care center for the deprived children of working mothers, you are the Lord of the West Side loading zone whenever it rains on Sundays. I have seen you, creepy chief of the dark forest of four ginkgo trees. The Boss! If you would only look up, Anthony, and boss me what to do, I would immediately slide down this scabby bark, ripping my new stretch slacks, and do it.

"Give me a nickel, Faith," he ordered at once.

"Give him a nickel, Kitty," I said.

"Nickels, nickels, nickels, whatever happened to pennies?" Anna Kraat asked.

"Anna, you're rich. You're against us," I whispered, but loud enough to be heard by Mrs. Junius Finn, still stopped at the mouth of the playground.

"Don't blame the rich for everything," she warned. She herself, despite the personal facts of her economic position, is disgusted with the neurotic rise of the working class.

Lynn Ballard bent her proud and shameless head.

Kitty sighed, shifted her yardage, and began to shorten the hem of the enormous skirt she was wearing. "Here's a nickel, love," she said.

"Oh boy! Love!" said Anna Kraat.

Antonia walked in a wide circle around the sycamore tree and put her arm on Kitty, who sewed, the sun just barely over her left shoulder – a perfect light. At that very moment, a representational artist passed. I think it was Edward Roster. He stopped and kneeled, peering at the scene. He squared them off with a film-maker's viewfinder and said, "Ah, what a picture!" then left.

"Number one!" I announced to Kitty, which he was, the very first of the squint-eyed speculators who come by to size up the stock. Pretty soon, depending on age and intention, they would move in groups along the paths or separately take notes in the shadows of the statues.

"The trick," said Anna, downgrading the world, "is to know the speculators from the investors..."

"I will never live like that. Not I," Kitty said softly.

"Balls!" I shouted, as two men strolled past us, leaning toward one another. They were not fairies, they were Jack Resnick and Tom Weed, music lovers inclining toward their transistor, which was playing the "Chromatic Fantasy." They paid no attention to us because of their relation to this great music. However, Anna heard them say, "Jack, do you hear what I hear?" "Damnit yes, the over-romanticizing and the under-Baching, I can't believe it."

Well, I must say when darkness covers the earth and great darkness the people, I will think of you: two men with smart ears. I don't believe civilization can do a lot more than educate a person's senses. If it's truth and honor you want to refine, I think the Jews have some insight. Make no images, imitate no God. After all, in His field, the graphic arts, He is pre-eminent. Then let that One who made the tan deserts and the blue Van Allen belt and the green mountains of New England be in charge of Beauty, which He obviously understands, and let man, who was full of forgiveness at Jerusalem, and full of survival at Troy, let man be in charge of Good.

"Faith, will you quit with your all-the-time philosophies," says Richard, my first- and disapproving-born. Into our midst, he'd galloped, riding an all-day rage. Brand-new ball bearings, roller skates, heavy enough for his big feet, hung round his neck.

I decided not to give in to Richard by responding. I digressed and was free: A cross-eyed man with a red beard became president of the Parent-Teachers Association. He appointed a committee of fun-loving ladies who met in the lunchroom and touched up the coffee with little gurgles of brandy. He had many clever notions about how to deal with the money shortage in the public schools. One of his great plots was to promote the idea of the integrated school in such a way that private-school people would think their kids were missing the real thing. And at 5 a.m., the envious hour, the very pit of the morning of middle age, they would think of all the public-school children deeply involved in the urban tragedy, something their children might never know. He suggested that one month of public-school attendance might become part of the private-school curriculum, as natural and progressive an experience as a visit to the boiler room in first grade. Funds could be split 50-50 or 30-70 or 40-60 with the Board of Education. If the plan failed, still the projected effort would certainly enhance the prestige of the public school.

Actually something did stir. Delegations of private progressive-school parents attacked the Board of Ed. for what became known as the Shut-out, and finally even the parents-and-teachers associations of the classical schools (whose peculiar concern always had been educating the child's head) began to consider the value of exposing children who had read about the horror at Ilium to ordinary street fights, so they could understand the *Iliad* better. Public School (in Manhattan) would become a minor like typing, required but secondary.

Mr. Terry Koln, full of initiative, energy, and light-heartedness, was re-elected by unanimous vote and sent on to the United Parents and Federated Teachers Organization as special council member, where in a tiny office all his own he grew marijuana on the windowsills, swearing it was deflowered marigolds.

He was the joy of our P.T.A. But it was soon discovered that he had no children, and Kitty and I have to meet him now surreptitiously in bars.

"Oh," said Richard, his meanness undeflected by this jolly digression:

"The ladies of the P.T.A.
wear baggies in their blouses
they talk on telephones all day
and never clean their houses."

He really wrote that, my Richard. I thought it was awfully good, rhyme and meter and all, and I brought it to his teacher. I took the afternoon off to bring it to her. "Are you joking, Mrs. Asbury?" she asked.

Looking into her kind teaching eyes, I remembered schools and what it might be like certain afternoons and I replied, "May I have my Richard, please, he has a dental appointment. His teeth are just like his father's. Rotten."

"Do take care of them, Mrs. Asbury."

"God, yes, it's the least," I said, taking his hand.

"Faith," said Richard, who had not gone away. "*Why* did you take me to the dentist that afternoon?"

"I thought you wanted to get out of there."

"Why? Why? Why?" asked Richard, stamping his feet and shouting. I didn't answer. I closed my eyes to make him disappear.

"Why not?" asked Phillip Mazzano, who was standing there looking up at me when I opened my eyes.

"Where's Richard?" I asked.

"This is Phillip," Kitty called up to me. "You know Phillip, that I told you about?"

"Yes?"

"Phillip," she said.

"Oh," I said and left the arm of the sycamore with as delicate a jump as can be made by a person afraid of falling, twisting an ankle, and being out of work for a week.

"I don't mind school," said Richard, shouting from behind the tree. "It's better than listening to her whine."

He really talks like that.

Phillip looked puzzled. "How old are you, sonny?"

"Nine."

"Do nine-year-olds talk like that? I think I have a boy who's nine."

"Yes," said Kitty. "Your Johnny's nine, David's eleven, and Mike's fourteen."

"Ah," said Phillip, sighing; he looked up into the tree I'd flopped from – and there was Judy, Anna's kid, using my nice warm branch. "God," said Phillip, "more!"

Silence followed and embarrassment, because we outnumbered him, though clearly, we tenderly liked him.

"How is everything, Kitty?" he said, kneeling to tousle her hair. "How's everything, my old honey girl? Another one?" He tapped Kitty's tummy lightly with an index finger. "God!" he said, standing up. "Say, Kitty, I saw Jerry in Newark day before yesterday. Just like that. He was standing in a square scratching his head."

"Jerry?" Kitty asked in a high loving squeak. "Oh, I know. Newark all week... Why were you there?"

"Me? I had to see someone, a guy named Vincent Hall, a man in my field."

"What's your field?" I asked.

"Daisies," he said. "I happen to be in the field of daisies."

What an answer! How often does one meet in this black place, a man, woman, or child who can think up a pastoral reply like that?

For that reason I looked at him. He had dark offended eyes deep in shadow, with a narrow rim of whiteness under the eyes, the result, I invented, of lots of late carousing nights, followed by eye-wrinkling examinations of mortalness. All this had marked him lightly with sobriety, the first enhancing manifest of ravage.

Even Richard is stunned by this uncynical openhearted notation of feeling. Forty bare seconds then, while Jack Resnick puts his transistor into the hollow of an English elm, takes a tattered score of *The Messiah* out of his rucksack, and writes a short Elizabethan melody in among the long chorus holds to go with the last singing sentence of my ode to Phillip.

"Nice day," said Anna.

"Please, Faith," said Richard. "Please. You see that guy over there?" He pointed to a fat boy seated among adults on a park bench not far from listening Lynn Ballard. "He has a skate key and he won't lend it to me. He stinks. It's your fault you lost the skate key, Faith. You know you did. You never put anything away."

"Ask him again, Richard."

"You ask him, Faith. You're a grownup."

"I will not. You want the skate key, you ask him. You have to go after your own things in this life. I'm not going to be around forever."

Richard gave me a gloomy, lip-curling look. No. It was worse than that. It was a baleful, foreboding look; a look which as far as our far-in-the-future relations were concerned could be named ill-auguring.

"You never do me a favor, do you?" he said.

"*I'll* go with you, Richard." Phillip grabbed his hand. "We'll talk to that kid. He probably hasn't got a friend in the world. I'm not kidding you, boy, it's hard to be a fat kid." He rapped his belly, where, I imagine, certain memories were stored.

Then he took Richard's hand and they went off, man and boy, to tangle.

"Kitty! Richard just hands him his skate, his hand, and just goes off with him...That's not like my Richard."

"Children sense how good he is," said Kitty.

"He's good?"

"He's really not *so* good. Oh, he's good. He's considerate. You know what kind he is, Faith. But if you don't really want him to be good, he will be. And he's very strong. Physically. Someday I'll tell you about him. Not now. He has a special meaning to me."

Actually everyone has a special meaning to Kitty, even me, a dictionary of particular generalities, even Anna and all our children.

Kitty sewed as she spoke. She looked like a delegate to a Conference of Youth from the People's Republic of Ubmonsk from Lower Tartaria. A single dark braid hung down her back. She wore a round-necked white blouse with capped sleeves made of softened muslin, woven for aged bridesbeds. I have always listened carefully to my friend Kitty's recommendations, for she has made one mistake after another. Her experience is invaluable.

Kitty's kids have kept an eye on her from their dear tiniest times. They listened to her reasons, but the two eldest, without meaning any disrespect, had made different plans for their lives. Children are all for John Dewey. Lisa and Nina have never believed that

Kitty's life really worked. They slapped Antonia for scratching the enameled kitchen table. When Kitty caught them, she said, "Antonia's a baby. Come on now girls, what's a table?"

"What's a *table?*" said Lisa. "What a nut! She wants to know what a table is."

"Well, Faith," said Richard, "*he* got the key for me."

Richard and Phillip were holding hands, which made Richard look like a little boy with a daddy. I could cry when I think that I always treat Richard as though he's about forty-seven.

Phillip felt remarkable to have extracted that key. "He's quite a kid, Faith, your boy. I wish that my Johnny in Chicago was as great as Richard here. Is Johnny really nine, Kitty?"

"You bet," she said.

He kept his puzzled face for some anticipated eventuality and folded down to cross-legged comfort, leaning familiarly on Nina and Lisa's backs. "How are you two fairy queens?" he asked and tugged at their long hair gently. He peeked over their shoulders. They were reading Classic Comics, *Ivanhoe* and *Robin Hood.*

"I hate to read," said Antonia.

"Me too," hollered Tonto.

"Antonia, I wish *you'd* read more," said Phillip. "Antonia, little beauty. These two little ones. Forest babies. Little sunny brown creatures. I think *you* would say, Kitty, that they understand their bodies?"

"Oh, yes, I would," said Kitty, who believed all that.

Although I'm very shy, I tend to persevere, so I said, "You're pretty sunny and brown yourself. How do you make out? What are you? An actor or a French teacher, or something?"

"French..." Kitty smiled. "He could teach Sanskrit if he wanted to. Or Filipino or Cambodian."

"Cambodge..." Phillip said. He said this softly as though the wars in Indochina might be the next subject for discussion.

"French teacher?" asked Anna Kraat, who had been silent, grieved by spring, for one hour and forty minutes. "Judy," she yelled into the crossed branches of the sycamore. "Judy...French..."

"So?" said Judy. "What's so great? Je m'appelle Judy Solomon. Ma père s'appelle Pierre Solomon. How's that, folks?"

"Mon père," said Anna. "I told you that before."

"Who cares?" said Judy, who didn't care.

"She's lost two fathers," said Anna, "within three years."

Tonto stood up to scratch his belly and back, which were itchy with wet grass. "Mostly nobody has fathers, Anna," he said.

"Is that true, little boy?" asked Phillip.

"Oh yes," Tonto said. "My father is in the Equator. They never even had fathers," pointing to Kitty's daughters. "Judy has two fathers, Peter and Dr. Kraat. Dr. Kraat takes care of you if you're crazy."

"Maybe I'll be your father."

Tonto looked at me. I was too rosy. "Oh no," he said. "Not right now. My father's name is Ricardo. He's a famous explorer. Like an explorer, I mean. He went in the Equator to make contacts. I have two books by him."

"Do you like him?"

"He's all right."

"Do you miss him?"

"He's very fresh when he's home."

"That's enough of that!" I said. It's stupid to let a kid talk badly about his father in front of another man. Men really have too much on their minds without that.

"He's quite a boy," said Phillip. "You and your brother are real boys." He turned to me. "What do I do? Well, I make a living. Here. Chicago. Wherever I am. I'm not in financial trouble. I figured it all out ten years ago. But what I really am, really…" he said, driven to lying confidence because he thought he ought to try that life anyway. "What I truly am is a comedian."

"That's a joke, that's the first joke you've said."

"But that's what I want to be…a comedian."

"But you're not funny."

"But I am. You don't know me yet. I want to be one. I've been a teacher and I've worked for the State Department. And now what I want to be's a comedian. People have changed professions before."

"You can't be a comedian," said Anna, "unless you're funny."

He took a good look at Anna. Anna's character is terrible, but she's beautiful. It took her husbands about two years apiece to see how bad she was, but it takes the average passer, answerer, or asker about thirty seconds to see how beautiful she is. You can't warn men. As for Kitty and me, well, we love her because she's beautiful.

"Anna's all right," said Richard.

"Be quiet," said Phillip. "Say, Anna, are you interested in the French tongue, the French people, French history, or French civilization?"

"No," said Anna.

"Oh," he said, disappointed.

"I'm not interested in anything," said Anna.

"Say!" said Phillip, getting absolutely red with excitement, blushing from his earlobes down into his shirt, making me think as I watched the blood descend from his brains that I would like to be the one who was holding his balls very gently, to be exactly present so to speak when all the thumping got there.

Since it was clearly Anna, not I, who would be in that affectionate position, I thought I'd better climb the tree again just for the oxygen or I'd surely suffer the same sudden descent of blood. That's the way nature does things, swishing those quarts and quarts to wherever they're needed for power and action.

Luckily, a banging of pots and pans came out of the playground and a short parade appeared – four or five grownups, a few years behind me in the mommy-and-daddy business, pushing little go-carts with babies in them, a couple of three-year-olds hanging on. They were the main bangers and clangers. The grownups carried three posters. The first showed a prime-living, prime-earning, well-dressed man about thirty-five years old next to a small girl. A question was asked: WOULD YOU BURN A CHILD? In the next poster he placed a burning cigarette on the child's arm. The cool answer was given: WHEN NECESSARY. The third poster carried no words, only a napalmed Vietnamese baby, seared, scarred, with twisted hands.

We were very quiet. Kitty put her head down into the dark skirt of her lap. I trembled. I said, Oh! Anna said to Phillip, "They'll only turn people against them," and turned against them herself at once.

"You people will have to go," said Douglas, our neighborhood cop. He had actually arrived a few minutes earlier to tell Kitty to beg Jerry not to sell grass at this end of the park. But he was ready. "You just have to go," he said. "No parades in the park."

Kitty lifted her head and with sweet bossiness said, "Hey Doug, leave them alone. They're O.K."

Tonto said, "I know that girl, she goes to Greenwich House. You're in the fours," he told her.

Doug said, "Listen Tonto, there's a war on. You'll be a soldier too someday. I know you're no sissy like some kids around here. You'll fight for your country."

"Ha ha," said Mrs. Junius Finn, "that'll be the day. Oh, say, can you see?"

The paraders made a little meeting just outside our discussion. They had to decide what next. The four grownups held the tongues of the children's bells until that decision could be made. They were a group of that kind of person.

"What they're doing is treason," said Douglas. He had decided to explain and educate. "Signs on sticks aren't allowed. In case of riot. It's for their own protection too. They might turn against each other." He was afraid that no one would find the real perpetrator if that should happen.

"But Officer, I know these people. They're decent citizens of this community," said Phillip, though he didn't live in the borough, city, or state, let alone vote in it.

Doug looked at him thoroughly. "Mister, I could take you in for interference." He pulled his cop voice out of his healthy diaphragm.

"Come on…" said Kitty.

"You too," he said fiercely. "Disperse," he said, "disperse, disperse."

Behind his back, the meeting had been neatly dispersed for about three minutes. He ran after them, but they continued on the park's circumference, their posters on the carriage handles, very solemn, making friends and enemies.

"They look pretty legal to me," I hollered after Doug's blue back.

Tonto fastened himself to my leg and stuck his thumb in his mouth.

Richard shouted, "Ha! Ha!" and punched me. He also began to grind his teeth, which would lead, I knew, to great expense. "Oh, that's funny, Faith," he said. He cried, he stamped his feet dangerously, in skates. "I hate you. I hate your stupid friends. Why didn't they just stand up to that stupid cop and say fuck you. They should of just stood up and hit him." He ripped his skates off, twisting his bad ankle. "Gimme that chalk box, Lisa, just give it to me."

In a fury of tears and disgust, he wrote on the near blacktop in pink flamingo chalk – in letters fifteen feet high, so the entire Saturday walking world could see – WOULD YOU BURN A CHILD? and under it, a little taller, the red reply, WHEN NECESSARY.

And I think that is exactly when events turned me around, changing my hairdo, my job uptown, my style of living and telling. Then I met women and men in different lines of work, whose minds were made up and directed out of that sexy playground by my children's heartfelt brains, I thought more and more and every day about the world.

Marge Piercy

Marge Piercy is the author of several novels, several collections of poetry, essays, reviews and a play. Her most recent book of poetry is *My Mother's Body* (1985). She received a Creative Writing Fellowship in Poetry in 1978.

IF THEY COME IN THE NIGHT

LONG AGO on a night of danger and vigil
a friend said, *Why are you happy?*
He explained (we lay together
on a hard cold floor) what prison
meant because he had done
time, and I talked of the death
of friends. *Why are you happy
then* he asked, close to
angry.

I said, I like my life. If I
have to give it back, if they
take it from me, let me only
not feel I wasted any, let me
not feel I forgot to love anyone
I meant to love, that I forgot
to give what I held in my hands,
that I forgot to do some little
piece of the work that wanted
to come through.

Sun and moonshine, starshine,
the muted gray light off the waters
of the bay at night, the white

light of the fog stealing in,
the first spears of the morning,
how beautiful touching a face
I love. We all lose
everything. We lose
ourselves. We are lost.

Only what we manage to do
lasts, what love sculps from us;
but what I count, my rubies, my
children, are those moments
wide open when I know clearly
who I am, who you are, what we
do, a marigold, an oakleaf, a meteor,
with all my senses hungry and filled
at once like a pitcher with light.

Kenneth Rexroth

Kenneth Rexroth's varied work includes a novel, many collections of translations, seven collections of poetry and a play. He won the Copernicus Award for Lifetime Achievement from the Academy of American Poets. His Creative Writing Fellowship was awarded in 1977.

ON FLOWER WREATH HILL

for Yasuyo Morita

I

An aging pilgrim on a
Darkening path walks through the
Fallen and falling leaves, through
A forest grown over the
Hilltop tumulus of a
Long dead princess, as the
Moonlight grows and the daylight
Fades and the Western Hills turn
Dim in the distance and the
Lights come on, pale green
In the streets of the hazy city.

II

Who was this princess under
This mound overgrown with trees
Now almost bare of leaves?
Only the pine and cypress
Are still green. Scattered through the
Dusk are orange wild kaki on
Bare branches. Darkness, an owl
Answers the temple bell. The
Sun has passed the crossroads of

Heaven.
   There are more leaves on
The ground than grew on the trees.
I can no longer see the
Path; I find my way without
Stumbling; my heavy heart has
Gone this way before. Until
Life goes out memory will
Not vanish, but grow stronger
Night by night.
    Aching nostalgia –
In the darkness every moment
Grows longer and longer, and
I feel as timeless as the
Two thousand year old cypress.

   III

The full moon rises over
Blue Mount Hiei as the orange
Twilight gives way to dusk.
Kamo River is full with
The first rains of Autumn, the
Water crowded with colored
Leaves, red maple, yellow gingko,
On dark water, like Chinese
Old brocade. The Autumn haze
Deepens until only the
Lights of the city remain.

   IV

No leaf stirs. I am alone
In the midst of a hundred
Empty mountains. Cicadas,
Locusts, katydids, crickets,
Have fallen still, one after

Another. Even the wind
Bells hang motionless. In the
Blue dusk, widely spaced snowflakes
Fall in perfect verticals.
Yet, under my cabin porch,
The thin, clear Autumn water
Rustles softly like fine silk.

V

This world of ours, before we
Can know its fleeting sorrows,
We enter it through tears.
Do the reverberations
Of the evening bell of
The mountain temple ever
Totally die away?
Memory echoes and reechoes
Always reinforcing itself.
No wave motion ever dies.
The white waves of the wake of
The boat that rows away into
The dawn, spread and lap on the
Sands of the shores of all the world.

VI

Clustered in the forest around
The royal tumulus are
Tumbled and shattered gravestones
Of people no one left in
The world remembers. For the
New Year the newer ones have all been cleaned
And straightened and each has
Flowers or at least a spray
Of bamboo and pine.
It is a great pleasure to

Walk through fallen leaves, but
Remember, you are alive,
As they were two months ago.

VII

Night shuts down the misty mountains
With fine rain. The seventh day
Of my seventieth year,
Seven-Seven-Ten, my own
Tanabata, and my own
Great Purification. Who
Crosses in midwinter from
Altair to Vega, from the
Eagle to the Swan, under the earth,
Against the sun? Orion,
My guardian king, stands on
Kegonkyoyama.
So many of these ancient
Tombs are the graves of heroes
Who died young. The combinations
Of the world are unstable
By nature. Take it easy.
Nirvana.
Change rules the world forever.
And man but a little while.

VIII

Oborozuki,
Drowned Moon,
The half moon is drowned in mist
Its hazy light gleams on leaves
Drenched with warm mist. The world
Is alive tonight. I am
Immersed in living protoplasm,
That stretches away over

Continents and seas. I float
Like a child in the womb. Each
Cell of my body is
Penetrated by a
Strange electric life. I glow
In the dark with the moon drenched
Leaves, myself a globe
Of St. Elmo's fire.

I move silently on the
Wet forest path that circles
The shattered tumulus.
The path is invisible.
I am only a dim glow
Like the tumbled and broken
Gravestones of forgotten men
And women that mark the way.
I sit for a while on one
Tumbled sotoba and listen
To the conversations of
Owls and nightjars and tree frogs.
As my eyes adjust to the
Denser darkness I can see
That my seat is a cube and
All around me are scattered
Earth, water, air, fire, ether.
Of these five elements
The moon, the mist, the world, man
Are only fleeting compounds
Varying in power, and
Power is only insight
Into the void – the single
Thought that illuminates the heart.
The heart's mirror hangs in the void.

Do there still rest in the broken
Tumulus ashes and charred

Bones thrown in a corner by
Grave robbers, now just as dead?
She was once a shining flower
With eyebrows like the first night's moon,
Her white face, her brocaded
Robes perfumed with cypress and
Sandalwood; she sang in the Court
Before the Emperor, songs
Of China and Turkestan.
She served him wine in a cup
Of silver and pearls, that gleamed
Like the moonlight on her sleeves.
A young girl with black hair
Longer than her white body –
Who never grew old. Now owls
And nightjars sing in a mist
Of silver and pearls.

The wheel
Swings and turns counterclockwise.
The old graspings live again
In the new consequences.
Yet, still, I walk this same path
Above my cabin in warm
Moonlit mist, in rain, in
Autumn wind and rain of maple
Leaves, in spring rain of cherry
Blossoms, in new snow deeper
Than my clogs. And tonight in
Midsummer, a night enclosed
In an infinite pearl.
Ninety-nine nights over
Yamashina Pass, and the
Hundredth night and the first night
Are the same night. The night
Known prior to consciousness,
Night of ecstasy, night of

Illumination so complete
It cannot be called perceptible.

Winter, the flowers sleep on
The branches. Spring, they awake
And open to probing bees.
Summer, unborn flowers sleep
In the young seeds ripening
In the fruit. The mountain pool
Is invisible in the
Glowing mist. But the mist-drowned
Moon overhead is visible
Drowned in the invisible water.

Mist-drenched, moonlit, the sculpture
Of an orb spider glitters
Across the path. I walk around
Through the bamboo grass. The mist
Dissolves everything else, the
Living and the dead, except
This occult mathematics of light.
Nothing moves. The wind that blows
Down the mountain slope from
The pass and scatters the spring
Blossoms and the autumn leaves
Is still tonight. Even the
Spider's net of jewels has ceased
To tremble. I look back at
An architecture of pearls
And silver wire. Each minute
Droplet reflects a moon, as
Once did the waterpails of
Matsukaze and Murasame.

And I realize that this
Transcendent architecture
Lost in the forest where no one passes

Is itself the Net of Indra,
The compound infinities of infinities,
The Flower Wreath,
Each universe reflecting
Every other, reflecting
Itself from every other,
And the moon the single thought
That populates the Void.
The night grows still more still. No
Sound at all, only a flute
Playing soundlessly in the
Circle of dancing gopis.

Muriel Rukeyser

Muriel Rukeyser published over a dozen books of poetry,
including a *Collected Poems*. She was also known for her translations, particularly of Octavio Paz. She was awarded a Sab-
batical Leave Fellowship in 1966.

EASTER EVE, 1945

WARY OF TIME O it seizes the soul tonight
I wait for the great morning of the west
confessing with every breath mortality.
Moon of this wild sky struggles to stay whole
and on the water silvers the ships of war.
I go alone in the black-yellow light
all night waiting for day, while everywhere the sure
death of light, the leaf's sure return to the root
is repeated in million, death of all man to share.
Whatever world I know shines ritual death,
wide under this moon they stand gathering fire,
fighting with flame, stand fighting in their graves.
All shining with life as the leaf, as the wing shines,
the stone deep in the mountain, the drop in the green wave.
Lit by their energies, secretly, all things shine.
Nothing can black that glow of life;   although
    each part go crumbling down
    itself shall rise up whole.

Now I say there are new meanings;   now I name
death our black honor and feast of possibility
to celebrate casting of life on life. This earth-long day
between blood and resurrection where we wait
remembering sun, seed, fire;   remembering

that fierce Judæan Innocent who risked
every immortal meaning on one life.
Given to our year as sun and spirit are,
as seed we are blessed only in needing freedom.
Now I say that the peace the spirit needs is peace,
not lack of war, but fierce continual flame.
For all man : effort is freedom, effort's peace,
it fights. And along these truths the soul goes home,
    flies in its blazing to a place
      more safe and round than Paradise.

Night of the soul, our dreams in the arms of dreams
dissolving into eyes that look upon us.
Dreams the sources of action, the meeting and the end,
a resting-place among the flight of things.
And love which contains all human spirit, all wish,
the eyes and hands, sex, mouth, hair, the whole woman —
fierce peace I say at last, and the sense of the world.
In the time of conviction of mortality
whatever survive, I remember what I am. —
The nets of this night are on fire with sun and moon
pouring both lights into the open tomb.
Whatever arise, it comes in the shape of peace,
fierce peace which is love, in which move all the stars,
and the breathing of universes, filling, falling away,
and death on earth cast into the human dream.
    What fire survive forever
      myself is for my time.

May Sarton

May Sarton's fifteen collections of poetry include *Letters from Maine* (1984); she has also published 17 novels, eight books of nonfiction and autobiography and two children's books. This is the first publication of "The Silent Minister." She received a Work-in-Progress grant in 1967.

THE SILENT MINISTER

Sहे LOOKS like death," the women in the sewing circle told each other with the excitement, the sheen on their faces that the contemplation of real grief, so rare and exotic, had written there. And although no one of them would have been able to put it into words, they realized that all old Abigail's moans and cries, her brusque appeals that Andrew Hobbins come at once to see her, her scenes of jealousy, her periodic sinkings had been the brilliant, desperate flights of a wild bird in a cage (that cage of impotence and old age), had been in fact signs of life. Now she seemed by contrast to be matter-of-factly dying. She did not hurl her curses at the skies because there was no one to answer. When Andrew Hobbins died so suddenly of a heart attack, so unjustly in Abigail's mind (for he was thirty years younger than she), she lost in that one unforgivable blow a son, religious support, God himself. "Naked to the world," she told herself and, shivering, took to her bed.

Everyone tacitly accepted that it was quite different for Mrs. Hobbins who had her married children to visit, and who had accepted her husband's death with a natural dignity that did not inspire pity so much as admiration and respect.

So the procession of wine jellies and chicken soups did not make their way to the parsonage, but rather past the Florentine urns, up the steep granite steps that led to Abigail Loring's house on the hill...for all the good they did! It was a terrible time for Mary, the old cook. Miss Loring did not have tantrums any more, but *she* did, threatening to leave if her mistress did not eat at least a mouthful, stamping down the stairs with the barely-touched trays and talking loudly to herself in the kitchen, hoping she would be overheard.

"Them as has everything does all the complaining," she would shout to the kettle. "She made his life hell on earth with her goings-on: 'Andrew, come here and talk to me! I'm desperate. You can't go away in August, Andrew, I'm going to die in August.'" And suddenly Mary let out a hoarse cry, something between a laugh and a sob. "You said it, you know you did. You said, 'I'm going to die in August.' Fit as a fiddle the whole time while the good man wore himself out. Oh damn you, why don't you pull yourself together?" Mary banged the kettle down on the stove.

But there was no sound from upstairs where Abigail Loring either lay in bed or sat in a little rocker by the window rocking her grief and reading Christina Rossetti. And after a while Mary would take down Fanny Farmer and console herself by making floating island or some of her special piccalilli, and saying a Hail Mary to give herself courage. For it was no joke when you were past seventy yourself to be catering to a no-appetite, and to see a wild heart like Miss Loring turn into a little old sheep without a spark in its eye.

Would they never find a new minister? And what was the matter with a church that had to wait a year to fill the pulpit? There was a substitute of course. But little good he did. Miss Loring had refused to see him.

"She looks like death," the women in the sewing circle had repeated all through that long year. And then there would be a silence while the thumb of a mitten was rounded, or the heel of a sock, and the unspoken thought roved around them so loudly that no one was conscious that it had not been spoken, "At least he's free now."

Andrew Hobbins had not been a great preacher. He relied largely on the poems of Robert Browning and seemed unable to clarify his ideas to the point where they were communicable. So the descent from the poems he loved to quote to his commentary upon them was swift and disastrous. He had been loved not because of what he had to say, but because of what he was. He was a good man, so good that he seemed wholly unaware of his own goodness. He was a big man with a ruddy face and very blue eyes, awkward in his manners but with delicate skill in the art of listening and then very quietly saying the right word. And he refused to be praised.

"What you don't understand," he said to a sharp-tongued spinster who once attacked Abigail Loring in his presence as a hysterical egotist, "is that I am very fond of Abigail. I enjoy calling on her." He would never take credit for the patience he showed, for she was, everyone knew it, cantankerous, jealous and, more often than not, called him to her only to make a scene. But what he knew and old Mary alone knew was that the reaction to these outbursts was terrible remorse. During one of his first experiences with her tantrums, when he had not been able to keep an engagement for tea, she had railed at him and then quite suddenly had put her hands up to her face – small intense hands that were never still – and said humbly, "The trouble with me is I don't wear well."

After that, they were friends. For he had laughed, and she had laughed, and then she had told him that she felt like a wild bird in a cage, always would and always had, and she knew the cage was of her own making which made it worse. "Pride and my terrible temper," she had said. "I drove them all away, one by one. Cared too much, you know," she had said, giving him one of her brief piercing glances.

She had been a brilliant student at Mt. Holyoke and had a much better mind than most of the men in town, Andrew thought. It was true that he enjoyed seeing her – most of the time. It was also true that she was exhausting and he had often prayed in the last years for light about how to handle what became excessive, unrelenting dependence. For it seemed as if the gentler and more understanding he was with her, the more he gave in to her pleas and demands, the more difficult she became. It had not been easy, but it had not been unrewarding. She made him read all sorts of things he would have missed, sent up to the Athenæum in Boston for new works on theology and philosophy, prodded him about his sermons – and justifiably.

He could hear her saying, "That sermon was a shame, Andrew. You have a mind. Use it." And how could he tell her that he had planned to work at it one evening when she insisted that he come to her and they had talked half the night about the problems of guilt?

The women at the sewing circle did not know all of this, but they knew enough to feel there was something more here than a doddering old lady and a kind minister. They sensed a dimension outside their own experience. Abigail Loring had always seemed a little larger than life, like an actress. How would she react to the new minister, they asked each other aloud? For now at last after the long year of trial sermons and uncomfortable parish dinners when some young man was being looked over, the decision had been made. They had formally invited Leif Andersen to take the place of their beloved Andrew, and he had accepted. He was not young – a good thing in a parish where the old outnumbered the young; he was unmarried – a bad thing in any parish. But he was, at least in the opinion of the majority, a remarkable preacher. Of course it had to be admitted that after his eloquence in the pulpit his excruciating shyness in any social situation was difficult. But they hoped he would warm up and relax when he got to know the community and began to feel more at home.

It was a great day for Mary when she could heave herself up the long flight of stairs and burst in on Miss Abigail without even a knock, to tell her that the whole thing was settled at last and Dr. Leif Andersen had formally accepted the post.

"He'll never replace Andrew," Abigail Loring said, looking up from Christina Rossetti, but Mary noted that the bright, slightly avid look in her eye had come back. "Bring me a jacket, Mary. I'm sick of this old sweater."

Leif Andersen, who dreaded parish visits as if each one were some terrible examination that he could never pass, was soon made aware by the hints, suggestions, and something like pity in people's voices, that before long he would have to pay a call on an old lady called Miss Loring.

"She's royalty in this town. You see, her father founded the mill, Loring & Co. You can see it down at the foot of the hill. Gave the

church a new coat of paint last fall." So one of the church committee told him after the first meeting.

"She's quite a gal," a ruddy-faced businessman spoke across the
table. "Your predecessor found her a handful. You'd better watch
out!"

A discreet smile wove its way round the table like a ribbon being
unrolled. Leif felt a knot in the pit of his stomach. "Why?" he
managed to ask, blushing to the roots of his hair.

"She'll talk your ear off about theology for one thing," a white-
haired gentleman murmured.

But this induced a wave of relief. Leif could handle the imper-
sonal very well. What terrified him was personal contact. At the
sight of human misery, human need, his heart turned over. He
froze with sympathy.

"Don't worry, Dr. Andersen," the rather bluff, red-faced man
said, "I expect a minister always has one or two of these old
spinsters, starved for company, in his parish. It's all in the day's
work, eh?"

"But perhaps we should warn you," the white-haired gentleman
added, "that Miss Loring has been very much upset since Dr.
Hobbins' death, in fact we have some of us feared she would not
survive him."

Leif ran over the advice the course in psychology he had taken
suggested, a grief reaction, they called it. But it did seem somewhat
exaggerated, in this case.

"Dr. Hobbins must have been a very remarkable man," he managed to articulate, and then mercifully the men began to get up.
At least the meeting had involved no responsibility for him. He
had listened and been told whatever they needed to tell him about
business matters. But with Miss Loring, he suddenly realized, he
would be on his own. She would of course, out of loyalty to Dr.
Hobbins, be bound to be critical, and to make comparisons un-
favorable to himself.

At a quarter to four a few days later Leif Andersen put down
with a sigh the volume of Kierkegaard he was studying (yes, he
had better get it over with) and decided to walk the few blocks to
the Loring house. It had been pointed out to him already a dozen

times, and he had an idea that he would be observed through at least one of the curtained windows he passed, and that the news of his visit would travel rather quickly.

It was absurd to be so nervous. After all, all he had to do was to drink a cup of tea and let the old girl do the talking. But his hands felt clammy and that dreadful knot in the pit of his stomach was there, the knot that affected him like an attack of some shameful disease – a seizure of silence.

Miss Abigail Loring had sat in the front parlor in her red velvet Victorian chair with a high back and no arms every afternoon since the first Sunday when Leif Andersen preached. She had made a sort of penance in Andrew's memory by not going to church herself that day, "Curiosity will fill the church today, Mary, and I am going to refrain."

"Foolish old thing," Mary had muttered, "when she's dying to go."

Now it was Wednesday and high time that he made an appearance. She had passed through various phases of excitement, humility, irritation, and finally just plain impatience. And she began to feel too foolish sitting there drinking a cup of tea alone with the two best cups set out on the tray and Mary's little biscuits, all buttered and hot, lying in a white napkin in the silver salver, and a jar of the best marmalade – with no one to eat them but herself.

"Well," Mary called out in triumph at five minutes to four on that Wednesday, "Glory be to God, he's on his way – and my muffins getting harder by the minute."

She hardly noticed that he was unable to say one word as she ushered him in (like a lamb to the slaughter, she thought) and ran to the kitchen to rescue the muffins.

"You are Dr. Andersen, I presume?"

"Yes, Ma'am," he answered, using a locution unfamiliar to New England.

"Do sit down," said Abigail Loring.

For one desperate moment their eyes met, his dark blue, the pupils dilated with apprehension, hers piercing black. It was an accident; it was a shock, as if in the prolonged silence the privacy of each had been invaded, and now there was no retreat. "Mary will bring tea in a moment," she said absent-mindedly, one nervous hand brushing a thread off her tweed skirt. Then she lifted her chin and looked off out the window, as if he were not there, or as if the ghost of someone else was.

Leif Andersen was as aware of her every move, of the essence of her person as an animal is aware. He sensed power, extreme sensibility, pain – I must say something, he thought desperately. "A fine day," he managed to utter after what seemed an interminable pause.

There was no response to this beyond a slight sniff (was it a sniff?) and Mary was astonished to find herself bringing in the immaculate tray to a perfectly silent room. There they sat, frozen, you might say, like two cats just before they make a great hullabaloo. It was enough to give you the willies.

"How do you take your tea, Dr. Andersen?" But at this moment the paroxysm of silence had him fast. He could not bring out a single word. He swallowed twice. His throat was dry. He prayed silently, the one word "Help!" It was not heard.

"Speak up, man!" she said with sudden exasperation. "Have you lost your tongue?" she said, the teapot shaking slightly as she held it prepared to pour, in the air.

"One lump and milk, please." There, it was over. The sweat lay on his forehead like a mask, but the spell was broken. He had managed to speak.

"Eat a muffin with some of Mary's marmalade. Andrew Hobbins loved it," she said sharply. Somehow she had expected anything except this crippled creature – she had imagined Leif Andersen as suave, competent, intellectual, modern; or, on the other hand, perhaps intense and dramatic. She had not imagined that he would have no defense. And they said he was a great preacher! She began to feel herself interested. "I heard fine things about that sermon of yours," she said, " 'fervent' was the word people used. You made an impression."

Andrew swallowed twice and took a long drink of tea. Then he got up to offer Miss Loring a muffin, took one himself, and dropped the butter knife on the floor.

Suddenly he heard the laugh, the laugh of a child, high, gay, challenging. "You're a clumsy boy," she said, "it doesn't matter. Take mine."

"I'm so sorry," he murmured, feeling the blush of shame rising beyond his control before those piercing, amused old eyes.

"Whatever did they tell you about me?" she asked, "that you are so nervous? Never mind. You don't have to tell me. Let's talk," she said, surprising herself, for she suddenly felt in command, obligated. She felt something like responsibility toward this man who had at the same time such power and such weakness, who had talked about goodness (so they had told her) in such a new and startling way. "I've been lonely," she said. "You know that at least."

"Lonely?" He lifted his head as if he had never heard the word before. She saw the panic in his eyes.

"It doesn't matter," she said. "Have another muffin. Tell me about yourself, as they say. Are you always so silent?" She was laughing at him, he saw. He saw also that she was alive with kindness suddenly, that her cheeks were flushed, her eyes bright, that she was prepared for some unknown reason to like him.

"Yes," he bowed his head.

She poured herself another cup of tea. It would never do to allow his infirmity, for she began to suspect that that is what it was, to affect her. She at least must remain in command of the situation. He had a funny solemn face like a little owl, with those wide apart eyes and thin clamped mouth, but she recognized in him the quality she admired most. What was it? Primary intensity perhaps. Prickly, but real. That is what made him able to preach. Then, as an afterthought, she found herself adding, he needs my help. He needs my help – four simple words, but as she articulated them in her mind they became four balloons swelling and swelling within her with something like hope.

"Let me tell you something," she found herself saying to the silence. "They will have told you that I have been ill – Andrew's death came as a fearful shock. I thought I was going to die of it. That is the plain truth. Ridiculous," she added, "wasn't it?" She did not expect an answer, but she found it in the very gentle way he laid his cup down and prepared to listen. She heard him listening.

"It wasn't grief. It was remorse. I made Andrew's life miserable. I behaved like a spoiled child." The words came out, sharp, hard, dry. She had turned them over and over in her heart for months till all the feeling was worn out of them. "It's a relief to tell you."

Then very quickly she filled their two cups again, put in milk and sugar, drank rather loudly.

"I'm grateful," he said quietly. She saw that whatever it was that had possessed him, the seizure was over. "I do understand – about remorse," he said gently, and she felt it was true. Because words came so hard to him they were precious. He spoke the truth. She realized suddenly how very few people do, how very rarely words are used so sparingly as to ring absolutely true. But would the parish understand? Would anyone know this about him? Would they feel it?

"Silence is expensive," she said aloud, though it was half to herself. "It is also in your hands a power. Have you ever considered that it might be?"

"No," he looked at her startled, "it has been for me always a terrible infirmity, really like a disease, paralysis of some nerve."

"It can be your strength. Just now you used it as a strength. Did you know?"

Ntozake Shange

Ntozake Shange's most recent novel is *Betsy Brown*. She received the *Los Angeles Times* Book Award for her poetry and was widely acclaimed for her hit play, *for colored girls who have considered suicide/when the rainbow is enuf*. Her Creative Writing Fellowship was awarded in 1982.

from SASSAFRASS, CYPRESS & INDIGO

WHERE THERE IS a woman there is magic. If there is a moon falling from her mouth, she is a woman who knows her magic, who can share or not share her powers. A woman with a moon falling from her mouth, roses between her legs and tiaras of Spanish moss, this woman is a consort of the spirits.

INDIGO seldom spoke. There was a moon in her mouth. Having a moon in her mouth kept her laughing. Whenever her mother tried to pull the moss off her head, or clip the roses round her thighs, Indigo was laughing.

"Mama, if you pull 'em off, they'll just grow back. It's my blood. I've got earth blood, filled up with the Geechees long gone, and the sea."

SITTING AMONG her dolls, Indigo looked quite mad. As a small child, she stuffed socks with red beans, raw rice, sawdust or palm leaves. Tied ribbons made necks, so they could have heads and torsos. Then eyes from carefully chosen buttons or threads, hair from yarns specially dyed by her sisters and her mama, dresses of the finest silk patches, linen shoes and cotton underskirts, satin mitts or gloves embroidered with the delight of a child's hand. These creatures were still her companions, keeping pace with her changes, her moods and dreams, as no one else could. Indigo heard them talking to her in her sleep. Sometimes when someone else was talking, Indigo excused herself – her dolls were calling for her. There was so much to do. Black people needed so many things. That's why Indigo didn't tell her mama what all she discussed with her friends. It had nothing to do with Jesus. Nothing at all. Even her mama knew that, and she would shake her head the way folks do when they hear bad news, murmuring, "Something's got hold to my child, I swear. She's got too much South in her."

THE SOUTH in her, the land and salt-winds, moved her through Charleston's streets as if she were a mobile sapling, with the gait of a well-loved colored woman whose lover was the horizon in any direction. Indigo imagined tough winding branches growing from her braids, deep green leaves rustling by her ears, doves and macaws flirting above the nests they'd fashioned in the secret, protected niches way high up in her headdress. When she wore this Carolinian costume, she knew the cobblestone streets were really polished oyster shells, covered with pine needles and cotton flowers. She made herself, her world, from all that she came from. She looked around her at the wharf. If there was nobody there but white folks, she made them black folks. In the grocery, if the white folks were buying up all the fresh collards and okra, she made them disappear and put the produce on the vegetable wagons that went round to the Colored. There wasn't enough for Indigo in the world she'd been born to, so she made up what she needed. What she thought the black people needed.

> Access to the moon.
> The power to heal.
> Daily visits with the spirits.

MOON JOURNEYS
cartography by Indigo

Find an oval stone that's very smooth. Wash it in rosewater, 2 times. Lay it out to dry in the night air where no one goes. When dry, hold

stone tightly in the right hand, caress entire face with the left hand.
Repeat the same action with the stone in the left hand. Without halting
the movement, clasp left stone-filled hand with the right. Walk to a tree
that houses a spirit-friend. Sit under the tree facing the direction of
your mother's birthplace. Hold your hands between your bosom, tight.
Take 5 quick breaths and 3 slow ones. Close your eyes. You are on your
way.

ALTERNATIVE MODES OF MOON JOURNEYS
(Winter travel/Inclement weather)

In a thoroughly cleaned bathroom with the window open, burn mag-
nolia incense, preferably, but cinnamon will do. In a handkerchief
handled by some other woman in your family (the further back the
better), put chamomile, an undamaged birthwort leaf, and Lady's
Fern. Tie this with a ribbon from your own hair. Kiss the sachet 3 times.
Drop it gently into a tub of warm water that will cover all your body.
Place two white burning candles at either end of the tub. Float one fully
opened flower in the water. Get in the tub while tickling the water in
circles with the petals of the flower. Lie in the tub, with flower over your
heart. Close your eyes. You are on your way.

NOT ALL black people wanted to go to the moon. But some did.
Aunt Haydee had gone to the moon a lot. She'd told Indigo about
the marvelous parties there were in the very spots the white people
put flags and jumped up and down erratically. They never did learn
how to dance. Been round black folks all these years and still don't
have sense enough to keep in rhythm. But there they were walking
on the moon, like nothing ever went on up there. Like women
didn't sidle up to lunar hills every month. Like seas of menses
could be held back by a rocket launcher. Like the Colored might
disappear with the light of the moon.

"WE AIN'T goin' anywhere, are we?" Indigo sat some of the dolls
on the inside of her thigh. Her very favorites she sat in her lap.
Indigo had made every kind of friend she wanted. African dolls
filled with cotton root bark, so they'd have no more slave children.
Jamaican dolls in red turbans, bodies formed with comfrey leaves
because they'd had to work on Caribbean and American plantations

and their bodies must ache and be sore. Then there were the mammy dolls that Indigo labored over for months. They were almost four feet high, with big gold earrings made from dried sunflowers, and tits of uncleaned cotton. They smelled of fennel, peach leaves, wild ginger, wild yams. She still crawled up into their arms when she was unavoidably lonely, anxious that no living black folks would talk to her the way her dolls and Aunt Haydee did.

Everybody said she was just too ornery to hold a decent conversation. But that wasn't true. What was true was that Indigo had always had to fight Cypress and Sassafrass just to get them to listen to her. They thought they were so grown. So filled up with white folks' ways. They didn't want to hear about the things Aunt Haydee knew. Indigo watched her mother over huge vats of dyes, carrying newly spun yarn from the pots to the lines and back again. Sassafrass, throwing shuttles back and forth and back and forth. Cypress tying off cloth, carrying the cloth to the stairway where she began the appliqués the family was famous for. There was too much back and forth going on for anybody to engage little Indigo in conversations about the haints and the Colored. If the rhythm was interrupted, Sassafrass would just stare at the loom. Cypress would look at her work and not know where to start or what gauge her stitches were. Mama would burn herself with some peculiarly tinted boiling water. Everybody would be mad and not working, so Indigo was sent to talk to the dolls. All the dolls in the house became hers. And the worlds Sassafrass wandered in her weaving, and those Cypress conjured through her body, were lost to Indigo, who handled three-way conversations with her cloth companions all alone.

A girl-child with her dolls is unlikely to arouse attention anywhere, same as little boys with footballs or Davy Crockett hats. So Indigo would sneak from the place she'd been put (the corridor around the back porch), and take her friends out visiting. Old ladies loved for Indigo and Company to pass by. They would give her homemade butter cookies or gingerbread. They offered teas and chocolates, as well as the Scriptures and the legends of their lives. Indigo only had colored dolls and only visited colored ladies.

She didn't like Miz Fitzhugh, who fawned over Cypress and Sassafrass like they were 'most white. No, Mrs. Yancey with the low, secret voice and seventeen million hundred braids was Indigo's friend. And Sister Mary Louise who kept a garden of rose bushes and herbs was Indigo's cut-buddy, down to the Colored Methodist Episcopal Church.

STREETS IN Charleston wind the way old ladies' fingers crochet as they unravel the memories of their girlhoods. One thing about a Charlestonian female is her way with little things. The delicacy of her manner. The force of ritual in her daily undertakings. So what is most ordinary is made extraordinary. What is hard seems simple. Indigo listened to their tales, the short and long ones, with a mind to make herself a doll whose story that was, or who could have helped out. When her father died, Indigo had decided it was the spirit of things that mattered. The humans come and go. Aunt Haydee said spirits couldn't be gone, or the planet would fall apart.
The South in her.

RUMOR WAS that Mrs. Yancey had a way with white folks. They couldn't deny her anything. That's what folks said…that she must honey up to them; leastways, smile a lot. That was the only way the beautiful things she had in her house could be accounted for. Mrs. Yancey couldn't have bought such lace, or that silver tea service. Imagine a colored woman having afternoon tea and crumpets with all that silver. Indigo always carried her doll-friend Miranda over to Mrs. Yancey's. Miranda had better manners than some of her other dolls. Miranda was always clean, too, in a red paisley pinafore and small black sandals. Indigo let Miranda use her parasol to protect her from the sun. What proper young woman would come visiting faint and perspiring? Only some of Indigo's more country dolls would have marched to Mrs. Yancey's with the outdoors all over them.
Indigo walked up to Mrs. Yancey's front porch, pulled her slip up, and fussed with the hair sticking out of her braids. She'd rinsed her hands off, but re-doing her hair for a short chat seemed to make too much of a regular outing. Besides, Miranda was really

dressed up. Indigo had decorated her bonnet with dandelions, and sprayed some of her mama's perfume under her arms and behind her knees. When she was ready, Indigo rang the bell and waited. Sure enough, Mrs. Yancey was coming to the door. She wore slippers with the heels all beat down that made a sound like Bill Bojangles when he did the soft shoe. Opening the bright white door, while pulling the apron from around her neck, Mrs. Yancey bent down to kiss Indigo on the cheek.

"Now ain't you looking mighty fresh today, Indigo. And Miranda must be going to a social, all decked out, huh?"

"No, M'am. We just thought you might want some company. I was talking to Miranda and she told me you were thinking on us real hard."

"Y'all come in and make yourselves at ease in the parlor. Miranda must gotta second sense. She always knows when I wanna see my little girls."

Mrs. Yancey's house smelled like collard greens and corn bread, even when she fried oysters and made red sauce. Indigo nudged Miranda.

"Can ya smell that? Mrs. Yancey's house smells good, doesn't it?" Her house felt good, too. There were so many soft places to sit and smell other things. Mrs. Yancey liked to make pillows. Oval pillows, square pillows, rectangles, triangles, shapes that had no names but were scented, soft, huggable pillows. These pillows were covered with satins and silks, and embroidered in blinding scarlets and golds, and set off with laces, tassels, and cords. Mrs. Yancey told Miranda that she made the pillows now because all her life she had been living between a rock and a hard place. Even though she didn't really need any more, something called her to keep sewing herself comforts. Miranda asked Mrs. Yancey the questions that Indigo considered too forward. Why, one time when Miranda and Indigo were having a bit of pineapple-upside-down cake with their tea, and Mrs. Yancey was talking about how the white folks drove down the Colored, drove the Colored to drink and evil ways, drove decent young gals into lives of sin, chasing them up and down the back stairways from Allendale to Hilton Head, Miranda blurted:

"Well, how come the white people give you so many things? If they so hard-hearted and low-down, why you smile up to 'em?"

Indigo was embarrassed, and gave Miranda a good whack 'cross the face.

"She didn't mean that, M'am."

"Yes, she did, Indigo. She did, and it ain't correct to be slapping on no free somebody. You keep your hands to yourself and listen to what I gotta say."

Indigo settled back in the loveseat, almost disappearing in all the pillows. Miranda finally relaxed and lay next to her, listening.

"Folks in these parts got sucha low idea of the women of the race. They can't imagine how I come by what I come by 'less they weigh my reputation down with they dirty, filthy minds."

"Oh, no M'am, didn't nobody say you did that!" Indigo shot up out of the pillows, dragging Miranda with her to Mrs. Yancey's lap.

"That's not what I mean, sweetheart. Those be shooting words. I was suggesting that whoever be announcing that I grin up in the faces of these folks is out of they minds. All I do is go round the house that I be cleaning, waxing, dusting, ironing, sweeping…my regular chores. And if I come 'cross something that I gotta yen for, I say to the Mrs., 'I sho' do like that.' Then I stare at her, but with my eyes a lil bit going down and in a crooked direction. I look at what it was I wanted and look back at the white lady. I tell my soul to get all in what I want. Next thing you know the white lady can't think of no reason why she should have whatever that is. And she turn round asking me don't I want it, and of course I want it 'cause I done put all my soul in it. And I gotta have my soul in order to come on back round here to my house."

Indigo and Miranda thought about what Mrs. Yancey had said for days, but not nearly so much as they did about Mrs. Yancey and Mr. Henderson, also known as Uncle John the junk man. He was looking bad most of the time. Indigo figured that before she was born, Uncle John would have been called a fine looking man. Mrs. Yancey found no fault with that. Yet every time Uncle John would come round in his horse and wagon with things everybody didn't want, Mrs. Yancey would shudder, like the ugliness of whatall he carted startled her. She'd purse her lips, put her hands on her hips, whisper that cursing whisper Indigo had told Miranda about, or she would throw open her screen door and shout:

"John Henderson get that nasty mess out of my face, get on away from my door with your trash, you hear me!"

Then she'd slam the door shut, brush her hands on her apron and pat her braids, as if she was making sure that nothing about her was as out of order as everything about Uncle John. Still, one day after she had shouted the daylights out the window for Uncle John to go on wherever it was that he laid his pitiful head, he came creeping up the steps.

Miranda and Indigo peeked out the window, being careful to stay behind the curtains. Uncle John was a slight man, copper colored. Indigo explained to Miranda that that was the Indian in him. His eyes had a sly look, like the eyes of those boys that came tearing after Cypress after school; giggling eyes, and a mouth fitting a proud man. Mrs. Yancey looked more like Sister Mary Louise to Indigo. Here she was prancing around, twitching, putting her hair this way and that, because Uncle John was at the door. That didn't make no sense. No sense at all.

Uncle John had to push the bell three times. Finally, Mrs. Yancey slowly opened the wood door, leaving the screen door quite shut.

"Well, John Henderson, what are you doing on my front porch, looking how you look?"

She was right. Uncle John was a mite unkempt: white fuzzies curled from his ear, beneath his chin; his jacket was fraying at the lapels, and his shoes were covered with dirt. Mrs. Yancey hoped it was dirt, anyway. Uncle John, on the other hand, didn't pay no mind to Mrs. Yancey. He just looked at her with those giggling eyes and said:

"I been passing by here more frequent than I usedta, M'am. I'm not a young man no more, an' I been thinking how you collects nice things jus' like I do, an' how you still too smart looking to stay off by yourself all the time. I'm fixing to come calling in the nigh future if you don't mind?"

"John Henderson, you don't even have a place to live. You don't take baths, or shave. And you think you gonna grace my house with your I-don't-care-'bout-nothing-self. You don't even have a place to live."

"I'll just pass by round dinner time, awright." That's all he said, though he was grinning even as he patted his horse, Yoki. He must have been saying sweet things, because Yoki neighed, seemed to blush, and then they were gone.

Miranda had not said much about Mrs. Yancey and Uncle John, but Indigo figured that the way Mrs. Yancey carried on after he left that she set more store by him than she let on. That's why Indigo stole out of her mother's house quickly after their dinner of okra, rice and ham hocks, to see if Uncle John really came back, like he said he would. She carried Marie-Hélène with her, along with Miranda, because Marie-Hélène was so frail that she didn't get out much.

Indigo was really glad both her doll-friends were with her. Otherwise she would never have believed what she saw. Uncle John was there all right. Going up Mrs. Yancey's walk like he would have to, but he was in a tuxedo and top hat. The spats on his shoes gleamed in the lavender sky. He kept his pace up and his back straight with the help of an ebony cane with a gold handle. Plus, when Mrs. Yancey came to the door, her hair wasn't in braids. It was all over the place like those women in the pictures over bars, the mermaids covering their privates, with their hair flowing like seaweed everywhere. She wasn't wearing her slippers, either. She had on high heels and a pale blue dress chiseled onto her form like white on rice. Mrs. Yancey took Uncle John's arm; they virtually floated off the porch, down the walk to the corner.

Indigo kept hearing Mrs. Yancey say, "Uncle John you don't even have a place to live." Everybody knew Uncle John lived in his wagon, but nobody had ever seen what Indigo saw. Uncle John went over to his wagon, pulled out a fine easy chair and set it by the curb, then motioned for Mrs. Yancey to have a seat. Next thing Indigo knew, he had spread a Persian rug in the middle of the street, set a formal table, pulled out a wine bucket, and started dinner on the stove at the back of his wagon. Yoki was all dressed up with flowers woven through her mane and violet feathers tied on her hooves. Uncle John put candles on the table, and pinned a corsage to Mrs. Yancey's dress. She kept looking around like she thought being in the middle of the street in Uncle John's living room was not really safe, when out of nowhere the guys from the Geechee Capitans, a motorcycle gang of disrepute led by Pretty Man, came speeding down the street. Mrs. Yancey 'most jumped to her roof. Uncle John didn't exhibit much concern about these young ruffians on their huffing, humming bikes. He looked up, waved his hand, and the Geechee Capitans, who had never done a good turn by anybody in the city of Charleston, South Carolina, made road blocks on either side of Uncle John's parlor-in-the-middle-of-the-street.

Marie-Hélène told Indigo she thought she would faint. Miranda was speechless. Indigo tried to accept the Geechee Capitans, clad in leather jackets with crossed switchblades painted on their backs, pork-pie hats and black boots, guarding her friend Mrs. Yancey, who was having dinner with Uncle John the junk man in the street. Indigo stayed behind the bushes by the Johnsons' house as long as she could, looking. When Uncle John pulled out a Victrola, played a Fletcher Henderson 78, and asked Mrs. Yancey to dance, Indigo knew it was time to go home. There was too much magic out in the night. Indigo felt the moon in her mouth, singing. The South in her.

SUITORS WITH THE MOON'S BLESSING

Fill a glass that sparkles in sunlight with pure spring water. Place one sprig of fresh mint in the water, and a mouthful of honey. Take your middle finger gently round the curve of your lips as you imagine your beloved might. Kiss the edges of the finger. Take a breath so deep your groin senses it. Hold your breath while envisioning your beloved's face. Release the breath still picturing your beloved. Then with the kissed finger, make a circle round the rim of the glass 12 times, each time repeating your beloved's name. Each time seeing your beloved filled with joy. Close your eyes. Let your beloved fill your heart. Bring the glass to your lips. Drink the gladness that shall be yours.

IF YOUR BELOVED HAS EYES FOR ANOTHER

Sleep on your left side with 6 white roses by your head. Fill your pillow with 2 handfuls of damiana leaves. Do this 3 days in a row. On the fourth day, use one handful of the damiana leaves to make tea. Drink

2 cups; one at dawn, the other at dusk. The other handful of damiana leaves should be mixed with cubeb berries, wrapped in a red or blue piece of cotton (use red if you have passions for your beloved, use blue if you merely desire fidelity). With the damiana-cubeb berry-filled pouch anywhere on your person in the presence of your beloved, your way shall be had.

SEEKING NOTHING /
GIVING THANKS FOR LUNAR GIFTS
(Full moon required)

Bathe casually in a bath scented with cinnamon and vanilla. Wash hair with raspberry tea. Rinse thoroughly, being sure your hands have touched every part of your body as your beloved might. Without adornment of any kind, jewelry or clothing, go to the outside. Lie fully open to the sky, widely, naked. Think of your beloved. Smell your beloved. Allow the Moon to share with you the pleasures your beloved brings you. Hold back nothing. Your thanks are mightily received. (May be executed in the company of your beloved, if he or she stands open over you, or if he or she lies as you lie at least 6 inches from you.) Before rising, you must have surrendered all you know of your beloved to the Moon, or your beloved shall have no more to offer you. (Very advanced. Wait if not sure.)

"...'AND YOUR SONS will become shepherds in the wilderness.' Numbers 14:33. I think that's enough for you to meditate on tonight, Indigo."

"But that doesn't have anything to do with me, Sister Mary Louise!" Indigo squirmed in her seat where she was helping Sister Mary Louise select the flowers for the Little Shepherd of Judea, C.M.E. Church's Young People's Meeting.

"Don't blaspheme, Indigo. The Lord don't take kindly to senseless babblin'."

"I'm not babbling, Sister, really. I'm a girl, that's all. I want to know what I'm supposed to do." Indigo pushed the roses from this side to that, nimbly avoiding the thorns, handling buds with caring alacrity. This one will do. This one will not. Bruised flowers had no place on the altar in Christ's House. Sister Mary Louise was heartened when Indigo came round. Those other two, the one who went off to the North and the other one shaking her ass all the time, they had never learned how to touch flowers or the ways of the Lord. Sister Mary Louise with no children in her house invited Indigo, but not Indigo's doll-friends, to be among her flowers, to join in singing the praises of the Lord Almighty whose blessings are so bountiful we can never give thanks enough, and to bake breads.

"You can take those loaves out the oven, and behave like a good Christian girl, that's what you can do."

Indigo looked at the roses and then at her friend, Mary Louise Murray, who must have been around roses too long. Her face shone like petals with veins glowing, like the opals she wore in her ears. One big plait lay smack in the middle of her head, wound round and round; serpents in the garden. Pale green eyes rushed from her face whenever the Holy Spirit took her, if her bushes were dewy and the sun just coming up. Indigo had a reluctant soul, to Sister Mary's mind. Not that Indigo was a bad child, only she'd been exposed to so many heathenish folks, pagans out there on those islands.

"Christian girls don't do nothing but bake bread?" Indigo peered into the oven. The heat beat her face till she frowned. "Not ready yet," she said, and carefully let the oven door fit back in its latch. Sister Mary Louise was tickled.

"No. Indigo, we don't just bake bread. We tend after beauty in the world. The flowers and the children." For all her Godfearing ways, Sister Mary Murray had been known to get the spirit outside of Church. Sometimes, when she was walking to the fish market or delivering breads, she'd be singing "I Ain't Got Weary Yet," or "Didn't My Lord Deliver Daniel," and she would just get happy in the street. This was not exemplary behavior for a Deaconess. At many a sermon she would be called forth to testify about how the Devil seized her in broad daylight, taking on the movements of the Holy Spirit, tempting the sinner in her. Other folks believed that being without children is what drove Sister Mary to have these fits in public. It only happened when some young boy from the country was within ten feet of her, broad shouldered and raw. Other folks figured that Sister Mary Louise sipped a little bit, and got to feeling so good she couldn't stand it. Indigo knew that

Sister Mary Louise was in fact a Christian woman. Sister didn't allow any dolls that could talk in her house.

"No haints coming in my house. What do you imagine the Lord God Jesus Christ would think, if I set my table for haints?" That's what she'd said to Indigo.

Now Indigo was angry. The bread wasn't ready. Sister's saying little girls make bread and take care of beauty. Indigo thought her stomach was going to jump out of her mouth and knock over all the flowers, stomp the breads, and let hell aloose in Sister Mary's big white kitchen, where Jesus looked down from every wall. The Last Supper. The Annunciation. From way up on Mt. Calvary, there he was waiting for "his sons to shepherd." Indigo was so mad she felt lightheaded; hot all over.

"Sister Mary Louise, when I talked to Miranda she didn't want to bake nothing."

"I told you awready. You too big to be talking to dolls. Good Lord, Indigo, look at yourself." Indigo tried to focus on Sister Mary's face. But she only saw a glimmering. She tried to look at herself, and kept blinking her eyes, rubbing her palms over them, to get some focus. She saw something spreading out of her in a large scarlet pool at her feet. Sister Mary jumped up and down.

"Indigo the Lord's called you to be a woman. Look on High for His Blessing. Look I say. Look to Jesus, who has 'blessed you this day.'" Indigo fell down on her knees like Sister Mary had. And listened and swayed in her growing scarlet lake to the voice of this green-eyed woman singing for the heavens: "Trouble in Mind," "Done Made My Vow," and "Rise and Shine," so that Indigo would know "among whom was Mary Magdalene."

"Speak, child, raise your voice that the Lord May Know You as the Woman You Are."

Then Sister Mary Louise rose, her thin body coated with Indigo's blood. She gently took off Indigo's clothes, dropped them in a pail of cold water. She bathed Indigo in a hot tub filled with rose petals: white, red, and yellow floating around a new woman. She made Indigo a garland of flowers, and motioned for her to go into the back yard.

"There in the garden, among God's other beauties, you should spend these first hours. Eve's curse threw us out the garden. But like I told you, women tend to beauty and children. Now you can do both. Take your blessing and let your blood flow among the roses. Squat like you will when you give birth. Smile like you will when God chooses to give you a woman's pleasure. Go now, like I say. Be not afraid of your nakedness."

Then Sister Mary shut the back door. Indigo sat bleeding among the roses, fragrant and filled with grace.

MARVELOUS MENSTRUATING MOMENTS
(As Told by Indigo to Her Dolls as She Made Each and Every One of Them a Personal Menstruation Pad of Velvet)

A. *Flowing:*

When you first realize your blood has come, smile; an honest smile, for you are about to have an intense union with your magic. This is a private time, a special time, for thinking and dreaming. Change your bedsheet to the ones that are your favorite. Sleep with a laurel leaf under your head. Take baths in wild hyssop, white water lilies. Listen for the voices of your visions; they are nearby. Let annoying people, draining worries, fall away as your body lets what she doesn't need go from her. Remember that you are a river; your banks are red honey where the Moon wanders.

B. *For Disturbance of the Flow:*

Don't be angry with your body if she is not letting go of her blood. Eat strawberries, make strawberry tea with the leaves to facilitate the flow. To increase the flow, drink squaw weed tea. For soothing before your blood flows, drink some black snakeroot or valerian tea. For cramps, chew wild ginger.

"INDIGO, I don't want to hear another word about it, do you understand me. I'm not setting the table with my Sunday china for fifteen dolls who got their period today!"

"But, Mama, I promised everybody we'd have a party because we were growing up and could be more like women. That's what Sister Mary Louise said. She said that we should feast and celebrate with our very best dresses and our very favorite foods."

"Sister Mary Louise needs to get herself married 'fore she's lost what little of her mind she's got left. I don't want you going round that simple woman's house. You take my good velvet from 'tween those dolls' legs. Go to the store and buy yourself some Kotex. Then you come back here and pack those creatures up. Put them in the attic. Bring yourself back here and I'm going to tell you the truth of what you should be worrying about now you sucha grown woman."

"Mama, I can't do that. I can't put them away. I'll have nobody to talk to. Nobody at all."

"Indigo, you're too big for this nonsense. Do like I say, now."

"Mama. What if I stopped carrying Miranda in the street with me, and left my other friends upstairs all the time, could I leave 'em out then, could I? Please Mama, I know they're dollies. I really do. Sassafrass and Cypress kept all the things they made when they were little, didn't they?"

"That's a lie. Don't you have all their dolls? I can't believe a girl as big as you, wearing a training bra and stockings to school, can't think of nothing but make-believe. But if you promise me that you going to leave them in your room and stop asking me to sing to 'em, feed 'em, and talk with 'em, you can leave them out. Now go on to the store."

Indigo left her lesson book on the kitchen table, went to her mother tearing collards by the sink, and gave her a big hug. Her mother's apron always smelled like cinnamon and garlic no matter how many times it was washed. It smelled of times like this when her mother felt a surge in her bosom like her nipples were exploding with milk again, leaving her damp and sweet, but now it was Indigo's tears that softened her spirit.

"Indigo, you're my littlest baby, but you make it hard for me sometimes, you know that."

"Mama, I can make it easier today 'cause I aweady know what it is you were gonna tell me when I came back from the store."

"You do, do you?"

"Yeah, you were going to tell me that since I became a woman, boys were gonna come round more often, 'cause they could follow the trail of stars that fall from between my legs after dark."

"What?"

"The stars that fall from 'tween my legs can only be seen by boys who are pure of mind and strong of body."

"Indigo, listen to me very seriously. This is Charleston, South Carolina. Stars don't fall from little colored girls' legs. Little boys don't come chasing after you for nothing good. White men roam these parts with evil in their blood, and every single thought they have about a colored woman is dangerous. You have gotta stop living this make-believe. Please, do that for your mother."

"Every time I tell you something, you tell me about white folks. 'White folks say you can't go here – white folks say you can't do this – you can't do that.' I didn't make up white folks, what they got to do with me? I ain't white. My dolls ain't white. I don't go round bothering white folks!"

"That's right, they come round bothering us, that's what I'm trying to tell you…"

"Well if they bothering you so much, you do something about 'em."

"Is that some sass comin' out your mouth?"

"No, M'am. It's just I don't understand why any ol' white person from outta nowhere would want to hurt us. That's all."

Indigo moved to her mother, with a seriousness about her that left the kitchen emptied of all its fullness and aroma.

"I love you so much, Mama. & you are a grown colored woman. Some white man could just come hurt you, any time he wants, too? Oh I could just kill 'em, if they hurt you, Mama. I would. I would just kill anybody who hurt you."

Holding her child as tight as she could, as close into herself as she could, the mother whispered as softly as she could, as lovingly as she could: "Well, then we'll both be careful & look after each. Won't we?"

Indigo sort of nodded her head, but all she remembered was that even her mother was scared of white folks, and that she still wrote out the word Kotex on a piece of torn paper wrapped up in a dollar bill to give to Mr. Lucas round to the pharmacy. This, though Indigo insisted Mr. Lucas must know what it is, 'cause he ordered it for his store so all the other colored women could have it when they needed it. After all, even her mother said, this bleeding comes without fail to every good girl once a month. Sometimes her mother made no sense at all, Indigo thought with great consternation. On the other hand, as a gesture of good will & in hopes that her littlest girl would heed her warnings, the mother allowed Indigo one more public jaunt with Miranda, who was, according to Indigo, fraught with grief that their outings were to be curtailed.

Weeping willows curled up from the earth, reaching over Indigo & Miranda on this their last walk in a long friendship, a simple, laughing friendship. Miranda thought the weeping willows were trying to hug them, to pull them up to the skies where whether you were real or not didn't matter. Indigo, in her most grown-up voice, said, "No, they want us to feel real special on this day, that's all." Miranda wasn't convinced, and neither was Indigo, who managed to take the longest walk to the drugstore that her family had ever known.

After following the willows' trellises till there were no more, Indigo reverently passed by Mrs. Yancey's, back round to Sister Mary Louise's, down to the wharf where she and Miranda waved to her father who was living in the sea with mermaids, & then 'cross to the railroad tracks looking for Uncle John. Indigo liked colored folks who worked with things that took 'em some place: colored folks on ships, trains, trolleys, & horses. Yoki was a horse. Uncle John did go places, and after that night with Mrs. Yancey in the street, Indigo figured him mighty powerful.

In between two lone railroad cars was Uncle John's wagon. Sequestered from ill-wishers & the wind, there he was chatting away with the air, the cars, or Yoki. Sometimes men of Color disappear into the beauty of light, especially toward day's end. It's like clouds take on color & get down on the ground & talk to you, or the stars jump in some black man's body & shine all over you. Uncle John was looking like that to Indigo's mind, just brushing away, leaving Yoki's coat glimmering like dusk.

"Good evening, Uncle John."

"Humph." Mr. Henderson turned round knowing full well

who'd come calling, but not wanting to let on. "Oh. If it ain't my girl Indigo. & who's that ya got witcha?"

"This is Miranda. We're going to Mr. Lucas' to pick up something." Indigo was quite careful not to say what she was going to the drugstore for, 'cause her mother had said not to say anything to anybody.

"Indigo, Mr. Lucas' place way off from heah, don't ya think?"

"Well, Uncle John, that's some of it, but not all of it."

Laying down his brush, pulling a stool from the other side of a fire where he was cooking either a chicken or a pigeon, Uncle John motioned for Indigo to take a seat.

"Some of it, but t'aint all of it, ya say? Well, I would be guessin' the rest of it be a matter for discussion."

"Yes, Uncle John. I want you to tell me something. I'm asking you 'cause you been doin' what suits your own mind since I was born."

"No, long fo' that, chile."

"Well, anyway, I want to keep on talkin' with all my dolls. You know they my very best friends." Indigo was talking so fast now, Uncle John started walking in a circle around her so as to understand better. "& Mama wants me to put 'em way 'cause now I am a woman & who will I talk to? I can't seem to get on with the chirren in the school I go ta. I don't like real folks near as much." Indigo had jumped off the stool with Miranda in her arms, much like a woman daring someone to touch her child. Uncle John stood still for a minute, looking at the shadows of the rail cars on Yoki's back.

"Indigo, times catch up on everybody. Me & Yoki heah been catched up by trains & grocery stores. Now you bein' catched up by ya growin' up. That's what ya mama's tryin' to say to ya. Ya gotta try to be mo' in this world. I know, it don't suit me either."

Miranda was crying, nestled in Indigo's elbow. Uncle John mumbled to himself, & climbed in his wagon. Indigo stayed put. Folks said that sometimes, when Uncle John had said all he had to say, he got in his wagon & that was that. Other times folks said Uncle John would get in his wagon and come back out with something to keep your life moving along sweeter. So Indigo didn't move a muscle. Miranda prayed some good would come of all this. They still hadn't gone to Mr. Lucas'. Indigo could hear Uncle John humming to himself, fumbling in that wagon. He was looking for something for her so she could keep talkin' & not have to be with them real folks & all their evil complicated ways of doing. The last of the day's sun settled on Indigo's back, warmed the taut worry out of her limbs, & sat her back down on the stool, jabbering away to Miranda.

"See, you thought that I was gonna just go on & do what Mama said & never play witya no more or go explore & make believe. See, see, ya didn't have no faith. What's that Sister Mary Louise is all the time sayin'?"

"Oh ye of lil faith…" Miranda rejoined.

Uncle John didn't come out of his wagon first. A fiddle did. Uncle John was holding it, of course, but he poked the fiddle out, then one leg, his backside, and the other leg, his precious graying head, and the last arm with a bow in his grasp. Indigo & Miranda were suspicious.

"What we need a violin for?" Miranda sniggled.

"Hush, Miranda, Uncle John knows what he's doin'. Just wait a minute, will ya?"

Uncle John sure nuf had intentions to give this fiddle to Indigo. His face was beaming, arms wide open, with the fiddle & bow tracing the horizons, moving toward Indigo who was smiling with no reason why.

"Indigo, this heah is yo' new talkin' friend."

"A fiddle, Uncle John?" Indigo tried to hide her disappointment, but Miranda hit her in her stomach. "Uh, that's not what I need, Uncle John." She sat back on the stool like she'd lost her backbone. Uncle John was a bit taken back, but not swayed.

"Listen now, girl. I'ma tell ya some matters of the reality of the unreal. In times blacker than these," Uncle John waved the violin & the bow toward the deepening night, "when them slaves was ourselves & we couldn't talk free, or walk free, who ya think be doin' our talkin' for us?"

"White folks, of course," snapped Indigo.

Uncle John's face drew up on his bones like a small furious fire.

His back shot up from his legs like a mahogany log.

"Whatchu say, gal?? I caint believe ya tol' me some white folks was doin' our talkin'. Now, if ya want me to help ya, don't say nary another word to me till I'm tellin' ya I'm finished. Now, listen. Them whites what owned slaves took everythin' was ourselves & didn't even keep it fo' they own selves. Just threw it on away, ya heah. Took them drums what they could, but they couldn't take our feet. Took them languages what we speak. Took off wit our spirits & left us wit they Son. But the fiddle was the talkin' one. The fiddle be callin' our gods what left us/be givin' back some devilment & hope in our bodies worn down & lonely over these fields & kitchens. Why white folks so dumb, they was thinkin' that if we didn't have nothin' of our own, they could come controllin', meddlin', whippin' our sense on outta us. But the Colored smart, ya see. The Colored got some wits to 'em, you & me, we ain't the onliest ones be talkin' wit the unreal. What ya think music is, whatchu think the blues be, & them get happy church musics is about, but talkin' wit the unreal what's mo' real than most folks ever gonna know."

With that Uncle John placed the fiddle in the middle of his left arm & began to make some conversations with Miranda & Indigo. Yes, conversations. Talkin' to 'em. Movin' to an understandin' of other worlds. Puttin' the rhythm in a good sit down & visit. Bringin' the light out a good cry. Chasing the night back round yonder. Uncle John pulled that bow, he bounced that bow, let the bow flirt with those strings till both Miranda & Indigo were most talkin' in tongues. Like the slaves who were ourselves had so much to say, they all went on at once in the voices of the children: this child, Indigo.

When Indigo first tried to hold the fiddle under her neck like the children in the orchestra at school, Uncle John just chuckled, looked away. When she had it placed nearer her armpit & closer to her heart, with the bow tucked indelicately in her palm, he said, "Now talk to us, girl." Indigo hesitated, pulled the bow toward the A string, took a breath, & stopped. "I don't know how to play a violin, Uncle John."

"Yeah, ya do. Tell Miranda somethin' on that fiddle. 'Cause after today, ya won't be able to reach out to her like ya do now. Ya gonna haveta call her out, wit that fiddle."

Indigo looked at Miranda lying on the stool & then back at Uncle John whose eyes were all over her face, the fiddle, the bow. & in a moment like a fever, Indigo carried that bow cross those fiddle strings till Miranda knew how much her friend loved her, till the slaves who were ourselves made a chorus round the fire, till Indigo was satisfied she wasn't silenced. She had many tongues, many spirits who loved her, real & unreal.

The South in her.

It was already so late Mr. Lucas had started to lock up his shop. Only the lights in the very back were still on. Indigo held onto her violin with its musty case religiously, & she beat on the doors of the pharmacy like someone possessed. "Please open up, Mr. Lucas. It's a emergency," she shouted. Mr. Lucas, portly & honey brown, peered out the door thru the lettering: Lucas' Pharmacy, Oldest Negro Drugstore in Charleston, S.C. Between the "S" and the "C" there was Indigo's face, churning & shouting. Mr. Lucas opened up remarking, "An emergency is somebody dyin' or a woman who needs some Kotex." Indigo was stunned. "Hi, Mr. Lucas, how'd you know that?"

"Oh, I been in this business a long time, Indigo. Tell your mother she almost missed me this time."

"Oh, it's not for Mama, it's for me." All of a sudden Indigo blushed & shrank. She'd gone & done what her mother had asked her please not to do. Mr. Lucas took a step toward Indigo, like he was looking for the woman in her. He'd seen younger girls than Indigo who were busy having babies. He'd even seen girls more comely in a grown-woman manner than she who didn't bleed at all. But here was this girl with this child body & woman in her all at once. It was difficult for Mr. Lucas to just go & get the Kotex. He wanted to keep looking at this girl, this woman. He wanted to know what she felt like.

Indigo heard somebody talking to her. She saw Mr. Lucas coming toward her & somebody talking to her. Telling her to get the Kotex & get home quick. Get the Kotex & get home quick. Indigo ran to the back of the store, grabbed the blue box, stuffed it under her arm with Miranda & whipped thru the aisles with Mr. Lucas behind her, lumbering, quiet. The fiddle was knocking all kinds of personal hygiene products off shelves: toothpaste, deodorant, shaving cream. Indigo almost dropped it, but she held tighter, moved faster, heard somebody telling her to get home quick. She got to the doors, started to look back & didn't. She just opened the door as best she could without letting go of anything & ran out.

Mr. Lucas stood in the back of his pharmacy, looking at his S.C. Certification, his diploma from Atlanta University. He knew he might be in some trouble. Didn't know what had got hold to him. Every once in a while, he saw a woman with something he wanted. Something she shouldn't have. He didn't know what it was, an irreverence, an insolence, like the bitch thought she owned the moon.

"Yeah, that's right." Mr. Lucas relaxed. "The whole town knows that child's crazed. If she says a thing, won't a soul put no store in it."

The South in her.

TO RID ONESELF OF THE SCENT OF EVIL*
by Indigo

(Traditional Method)
Though it may cause some emotional disruptions, stand absolutely still & repeat the offender's name till you are overwhelmed with the memory of your encounter. Take 2 deep slow breaths, on a 7 count. Then, waving your arms & hands all about you, so your atmosphere may again be clean, say the name of the offender softly. Each time blowing your own breath into the world that we may all benefit from your renewal. Then in a hot place (your kitchen or out of doors) cover yourself in warm clay poultices. Let them dry on you, taking the poisons of the offender out of

---

* *(Violence or purposeful revenge should not be considered in most cases. Only during wars of national liberation, to restore the honor of the race, or to redress calamitous personal and familial trauma, may we consider brute force/annihilation.)*

your body & spirit. Run a steaming shower over your body, allowing all grime & other to fall from you without using your hands or a cloth. Then, run yourself a new tub full of warm water filled with angelica & chamomile. Bring to your bath a tall clear glass of spring water wherein floats one closed white rose. Lying in your fragrant bath, sip the rose's water, for you are again among nature's flowers.

(For Modern Times)
Drink a strong mix of lemon tea & honey. This, if you've not cheated, should bring sweat to your brow. This is the poison the offender has left lurking. As you sweat, draw a bath that sends steam up toward your face, if you are on your knees. Take a piece of silk or cotton to which you feel attached & that bodes of happier times. Fill it with caraway seeds. Tie it with a ribbon that is your oldest female relative's favorite color. Float it in your bath. Stand naked over your tub. Kiss your right shoulder. Then your left. Step breathing briskly into the water. You shall be cleaned of all the offender's toxic presence.

Isaac Bashevis Singer

Isaac Bashevis Singer won the Nobel Prize for Literature in
1978. Mr. Singer received a Work-in-Progress grant in 1967 and
a publication award for the *American Literary Anthology* in 1968.

THE SLAUGHTERER

Yoineh Meir should have become the Kolo-
mir rabbi. His father and his grandfather had both sat in the rab-
binical chair in Kolomir. However, the followers of the Kuzmir
court had set up a stubborn opposition: this time they would not
allow a Hassid from Trisk to become the town's rabbi. They bribed
the district official and sent a petition to the governor. After long
wrangling, the Kuzmir Hassidim finally had their way and installed
a rabbi of their own. In order not to leave Yoineh Meir without a
source of earnings, they appointed him the town's ritual
slaughterer.

When Yoineh Meir heard of this, he turned even paler than
usual. He protested that slaughtering was not for him. He was
softhearted; he could not bear the sight of blood. But everybody
banded together to persuade him – the leaders of the community;
the members of the Trisk synagogue; his father-in-law, Reb Getz
Frampoler; and Reitze Doshe, his wife. The new rabbi, Reb
Sholem Levi Halberstam, also pressed him to accept. Reb Sholem
Levi, a grandson of the Sondz rabbi, was troubled about the sin
of taking away another's livelihood; he did not want the younger
man to be without bread. The Trisk rabbi, Reb Yakov Leibele,
wrote a letter to Yoineh Meir saying that man may not be more
compassionate than the Almighty, the Source of all compassion.
When you slaughter an animal with a pure knife and with piety,
you liberate the soul that resides in it. For it is well known that

the souls of saints often transmigrate into the bodies of cows, fowl, and fish to do penance for some offense.

After the rabbi's letter, Yoineh Meir gave in. He had been ordained a long time ago. Now he set himself to studying the laws of slaughter as expounded in the "Grain of the Ox," the "Shulchan Aruch," and the Commentaries. The first paragraph of the "Grain of the Ox" says that the ritual slaughterer must be a God-fearing man, and Yoineh Meir devoted himself to the Law with more zeal than ever.

Yoineh Meir – small, thin, with a pale face, a tiny yellow beard on the tip of his chin, a crooked nose, a sunken mouth, and yellow frightened eyes set too close together – was renowned for his piety. When he prayed, he put on three pairs of phylacteries: those of Rashi, those of Rabbi Tam, and those of Rabbi Serirah Gaon. Soon after he had completed his term of board at the home of his father-in-law, he began to keep all fast days and to get up for midnight service.

His wife, Reitze Doshe, already lamented that Yoineh Meir was not of this world. She complained to her mother that he never spoke a word to her and paid her no attention, even on her clean days. He came to her only on the nights after she had visited the ritual bath, once a month. She said that he did not remember the names of his own daughters.

After he agreed to become the ritual slaughterer, Yoineh Meir imposed new rigors upon himself. He ate less and less. He almost stopped speaking. When a beggar came to the door, Yoineh Meir ran to welcome him and gave him his last groschen. The truth is that becoming a slaughterer plunged Yoineh Meir into melancholy, but he did not dare to oppose the rabbi's will. It was meant to be, Yoineh Meir said to himself; it was his destiny to cause torment and to suffer torment. And only Heaven knew how much Yoineh Meir suffered.

Yoineh Meir was afraid that he might faint as he slaughtered his first fowl, or that his hand might not be steady. At the same time, somewhere in his heart, he hoped that he would commit an error. This would release him from the rabbi's command. However, everything went according to rule.

Many times a day, Yoineh Meir repeated to himself the rabbi's words: "A man may not be more compassionate than the Source of all compassion." The Torah says, "Thou shalt kill of thy herd and thy flock as I have commanded thee." Moses was instructed on Mount Sinai in the ways of slaughtering and of opening the animal in search of impurities. It is all a mystery of mysteries – life, death, man, beast. Those that are not slaughtered die anyway of various diseases, often ailing for weeks or months. In the forest, the beasts devour one another. In the seas, fish swallow fish. The Kolomir poorhouse is full of cripples and paralytics who lie there for years, befouling themselves. No man can escape the sorrows of this world.

And yet Yoineh Meir could find no consolation. Every tremor of the slaughtered fowl was answered by a tremor in Yoineh Meir's own bowels. The killing of every beast, great or small, caused him as much pain as though he were cutting his own throat. Of all the punishments that could have been visited upon him, slaughtering was the worst.

BARELY THREE months had passed since Yoineh Meir had become a slaughterer, but the time seemed to stretch endlessly. He felt as though he were immersed in blood and lymph. His ears were beset by the squawking of hens, the crowing of roosters, the gobbling of geese, the lowing of oxen, the mooing and bleating of calves and goats; wings fluttered, claws tapped on the floor. The bodies refused to know any justification or excuse – every body resisted in its own fashion, tried to escape, and seemed to argue with the Creator to its last breath.

And Yoineh Meir's own mind raged with questions. Verily, in order to create the world, the Infinite One had had to shrink His light; there could be no free choice without pain. But since the beasts were not endowed with free choice, why should they have to suffer? Yoineh Meir watched, trembling, as the butchers chopped the cows with their axes and skinned them before they had heaved their last breath. The women plucked the feathers from the chickens while they were still alive.

It is the custom that the slaughterer receives the spleen and tripe of every cow. Yoineh Meir's house overflowed with meat. Reitze Doshe boiled soups in pots as huge as cauldrons. In the large kitchen there was a constant frenzy of cooking, roasting, frying, baking, stirring, and skimming. Reitze Doshe was pregnant again, and her stomach protruded into a point. Big and stout, she had five sisters, all as bulky as herself. Her sisters came with their children. Every day, his mother-in-law, Reitze Doshe's mother, brought new pastries and delicacies of her own baking. A woman must not let her voice be heard, but Reitze Doshe's maidservant, the daughter of a water carrier, sang songs, pattered around barefoot, with her hair down, and laughed so loudly that the noise resounded in every room.

Yoineh Meir wanted to escape from the material world, but the material world pursued him. The smell of the slaughterhouse would not leave his nostrils. He tried to forget himself in the Torah, but he found that the Torah itself was full of earthly matters. He took to the Cabala, though he knew that no man may delve into the mysteries until he reaches the age of forty. Nevertheless, he continued to leaf through the "Treatise of the Hassidim," "The Orchard," the "Book of Creation," and "The Tree of Life." There, in the higher spheres, there was no death, no slaughtering, no pain, no stomachs and intestines, no hearts or lungs or livers, no membranes, and no impurities.

This particular night, Yoineh Meir went to the window and looked up into the sky. The moon spread a radiance around it. The stars flashed and twinkled, each with its own heavenly secret. Somewhere above the World of Deeds, above the constellations, Angels were flying, and Seraphim, and Holy Wheels, and Holy Beasts. In Paradise, the mysteries of the Torah were revealed to souls. Every holy *Tsadik* inherited three hundred and ten worlds and wove crowns for the Divine Presence. The nearer to the Throne of Glory, the brighter the light, the purer the radiance, the fewer the unholy host.

Yoineh Meir knew that man may not ask for death, but deep within himself he longed for the end. He had developed a repugnance for everything that had to do with the body. He could not even bring himself to go to the ritual bath with the other men.

Under every skin he saw blood. Every neck reminded Yoineh Meir of the knife. Human beings, like beasts, had loins, veins, guts, buttocks. One slash of the knife and those solid householders would drop like oxen. As the Talmud says, all that is meant to be burned is already as good as burned. If the end of man was corruption, worms, and stench, then he was nothing but a piece of putrid flesh to start with.

Yoineh Meir understood now why the sages of old had likened the body to a cage – a prison where the soul sits captive, longing for the day of its release. It was only now that he truly grasped the meaning of the words of the Talmud: "Very good, this is death." Yet man was forbidden to break out of his prison. He must wait for the jailer to remove the chains, to open the gate.

Yoineh Meir returned to his bed. All his life he had slept on a feather bed, under a feather quilt, resting his head on a pillow; now he was suddenly aware that he was lying on feathers and down plucked from fowl. In the other bed, next to Yoineh Meir's, Reitze Doshe was snoring. From time to time a whistle came from her nostrils and a bubble formed on her lips. Yoineh Meir's daughters kept going to the slop pail, their bare feet pattering on the floor. They slept together, and sometimes they whispered and giggled half the night.

Yoineh Meir had longed for sons who would study the Torah, but Reitze Doshe bore girl after girl. While they were small, Yoineh Meir occasionally gave them a pinch on the cheek. Whenever he attended a circumcision, he would bring them a piece of cake. Sometimes he would even kiss one of the little ones on the head. But now they were grown. They seemed to have taken after their mother. They had spread out in width. Reitze Doshe complained that they ate too much and were getting too fat. They stole tidbits from the pots. The eldest, Bashe, was already sought in marriage. At one moment, the girls quarrelled and insulted each other, at the next they combed each other's hair and plaited it into braids. They were forever babbling about dresses, shoes, stockings, jackets, panties. They cried and they laughed. They looked for lice, they fought, they washed, they kissed.

When Yoineh Meir tried to chide them, Reitze Doshe cried, "Don't butt in! Let the children alone!" Or she would scold, "You had better see to it that your daughters shouldn't have to go around barefoot and naked!"

Why did they need so many things? Why was it necessary to clothe and adorn the body so much, Yoineh Meir would wonder to himself.

Before he had become a slaughterer, he was seldom at home and hardly knew what went on there. But now he began to stay at home, and he saw what they were doing. The girls would run off to pick berries and mushrooms; they associated with the daughters of common homes. They brought home baskets of dry twigs. Reitze Doshe made jam. Tailors came for fittings. Shoemakers measured the women's feet. Reitze Doshe and her mother argued about Bashe's dowry. Yoineh Meir heard talk about a silk dress, a velvet dress, all sorts of skirts, cloaks, fur coats.

Now that he lay awake, all those words reëchoed in his ears. They were rolling in luxury because he, Yoineh Meir, had begun to earn money. Somewhere in Reitze Doshe's womb a new child was growing, but Yoineh Meir sensed clearly that it would be another girl. "Well, one must welcome whatever Heaven sends," he warned himself.

He had covered himself, but now he felt too hot. The pillow under his head became strangely hard, as though there were a stone among the feathers. He, Yoineh Meir, was himself a body: feet, a belly, a chest, elbows. There was a stabbing in his entrails. His palate felt dry.

Yoineh Meir sat up. "Father in Heaven, I cannot breathe!"

ELUL IS a month of repentence. In former years, Elul would bring with it a sense of exalted serenity. Yoineh Meir loved the cool breezes that came from the woods and the harvested fields. He could gaze for a long time at the pale-blue sky with its scattered clouds that reminded him of the flax in which the citrons for the Feast of Tabernacles were wrapped. Gossamer floated in the air. On the trees the leaves turned saffron yellow. In the twittering of the birds he heard the melancholy of the Solemn Days, when man takes an accounting of his soul.

But to a slaughterer Elul is quite another matter. A great many beasts are slaughtered for the New Year. Before the Day of Atonement, everybody offers a sacrificial fowl. In every courtyard, cocks crowed and hens cackled, and all of them had to be put to death. Then comes the Feast of Booths, the Day of the Willow Twigs, the Feast of Azereth, the Day of Rejoicing in the Law, the Sabbath of Genesis. Each holiday brings its own slaughter. Millions of fowl and cattle now alive were doomed to be killed.

Yoineh Meir no longer slept at night. If he dozed off, he was immediately beset by nightmares. Cows assumed human shape, with beards and side locks, and skullcaps over their horns. Yoineh Meir would be slaughtering a calf, but it would turn into a girl. Her neck throbbed, and she pleaded to be saved. She ran to the study house and spattered the courtyard with her blood. He even dreamed that he had slaughtered Reitze Doshe instead of a sheep.

In one of his nightmares, he heard a human voice come from a slaughtered goat. The goat, with his throat slit, jumped on Yoineh Meir and tried to butt him, cursing in Hebrew and Aramaic, spitting and foaming at him. Yoineh Meir awakened in a sweat. A cock crowed like a bell. Others answered, like a congregation answering the cantor. It seemed to Yoineh Meir that the fowl were crying out questions, protesting, lamenting in chorus the misfortune that loomed over them.

Yoineh Meir could not rest. He sat up, grasped his side locks with both hands, and rocked.

Reitze Doshe woke up. "What's the matter?"

"Nothing, nothing."

"What are you rocking for?"

"Let me be."

"You frighten me!"

After a while Reitze Doshe began to snore again. Yoineh Meir got out of bed, washed his hands, and dressed. He wanted to put ash on his forehead and recite the midnight prayer, but his lips refused to utter the holy words. How could he mourn the destruction of the Temple when a carnage was being readied here in Kolomir, and he, Yoineh Meir, was the Titus, the Nebuchadnezzar!

The air in the house was stifling. It smelled of sweat, fat, dirty underwear, urine. One of his daughters muttered something in her sleep, another one moaned. The beds creaked. A rustling came from the closets. In the coop under the stove were the sacrificial fowls that Reitze Doshe had locked up for the Day of Atonement. Yoineh Meir heard the scratching of a mouse, the chirping of a cricket. It seemed to him that he could hear the worms burrowing through the ceiling and the floor. Innumerable creatures surrounded man, each with its own nature, its own claims on the Creator.

Yoineh Meir went out into the yard. Here everything was cool and fresh. The dew had fallen. In the sky, the midnight stars were glittering. Yoineh Meir inhaled deeply. He walked on the wet grass, among the leaves and shrubs. His socks grew damp above his slippers. He came to a tree and stopped. In the branches there seemed to be some nests. He heard the twittering of awakened fledglings. Frogs croaked in the swamp beyond the hill. "Don't they sleep at all, those frogs?" Yoineh Meir asked himself. "They have the voices of men."

Since Yoineh Meir had begun to slaughter, his thoughts were obsessed with living creatures. He grappled with all sorts of questions. Where did flies come from? Were they born out of their mother's womb, or did they hatch from eggs? If all the flies died out in winter, where did the new ones come from in summer? And the owl that nested under the synagogue roof—what did it do when the frosts came? Did it remain there? Did it fly away to warm countries? And how could anything live in the burning frost, when it was scarcely possible to keep warm under the quilt?

An unfamiliar love welled up in Yoineh Meir for all that crawls and flies, breeds and swarms. Even the mice – was it their fault that they were mice? What wrong does a mouse do? All it wants is a crumb of bread or a bit of cheese. Then why is the cat such an enemy to it?

Yoineh Meir rocked back and forth in the dark. The rabbi may be right. Man cannot and must not have more compassion than the Master of the universe. Yet he, Yoineh Meir, was sick with pity. How could one pray for life for the coming year, or for a favorable writ in Heaven, when one was robbing others of the breath of life?

Yoineh Meir thought that the Messiah Himself could not redeem

the world as long as injustice was done to beasts. By rights, everything should rise from the dead: every calf, fish, gnat, butterfly.
Even in the worm that crawls in the earth there glows a divine
spark. When you slaughter a creature, you slaughter God....

"Woe is me, I am losing my mind!" Yoineh Meir muttered.

A week before the New Year, there was a rush of slaughtering.
All day long, Yoineh Meir stood near a pit, slaughtering hens,
roosters, geese, ducks. Women pushed, argued, tried to get to the
slaughterer first. Others joked, laughed, bantered. Feathers flew,
the yard was full of quacking, gabbling, the screaming of roosters.
Now and then a fowl cried out like a human being.

Yoineh Meir was filled with a gripping pain. Until this day he
had still hoped that he would get accustomed to slaughtering. But
now he knew that if he continued for a hundred years his suffering
would not cease. His knees shook. His belly felt distended. His
mouth was flooded with bitter fluids. Reitze Doshe and her sisters
were also in the yard, talking with the women, wishing each a
blessed New Year, and voicing the pious hope that they would
meet again next year.

Yoineh Meir feared that he was no longer slaughtering according
to the Law. At one moment, a blackness swam before his eyes; at
the next, everything turned golden green. He constantly tested the
knife blade on the nail of his forefinger to make sure it was not
nicked. Every fifteen minutes he had to go to urinate. Mosquitoes
bit him. Crows cawed at him from among the branches.

He stood there until sundown, and the pit became filled with
blood.

After the evening prayers, Reitze Doshe served Yoineh Meir
buckwheat pudding with pot roast. But though he had not tasted
any food since morning, he could not eat. His throat felt con-
stricted, there was a lump in his gullet, and he could scarcely
swallow the first bite. He recited the Shema of Rabbi Isaac Luria,
made his confession, and beat his breast like a man who was
mortally sick.

Yoineh Meir thought that he would be unable to sleep that
night, but his eyes closed as soon as his head was on the pillow
and he had recited the last benediction before sleep. It seemed to

him that he was examining a slaughtered cow for impurities, slitting open its belly, tearing out the lungs and blowing them up. What did it mean? For this was usually the butcher's task. The lungs grew larger and larger; they covered the whole table and swelled upward toward the ceiling. Yoineh Meir ceased blowing, but the lobes continued to expand by themselves. The smaller lobe, the one that is called "the thief," shook and fluttered, as if trying to break away. Suddenly a whistling, a coughing, a growling lamentation broke from the windpipe. A dybbuk began to speak, shout, sing, pour out a stream of verses, quotations from the Talmud, passages from the Zohar. The lungs rose up and flew, flapping like wings. Yoineh Meir wanted to escape, but the door was barred by a black bull with red eyes and pointed horns. The bull wheezed and opened a maw full of long teeth.

Yoineh Meir shuddered and woke up. His body was bathed in sweat. His skull felt swollen and filled with sand. His feet lay on the straw pallet, inert as logs. He made an effort and sat up. He put on his robe and went out. The night hung heavy and impenetrable, thick with the darkness of the hour before sunrise. From time to time a gust of air came from somewhere, like a sigh of someone unseen.

A tingling ran down Yoineh Meir's spine, as though someone brushed it with a feather. Something in him wept and mocked. "Well, and what if the rabbi said so?" he spoke to himself. "And even if God Almighty had commanded, what of that? I'll do without rewards in the world to come! I want no Paradise, no Leviathan, no Wild Ox! Let them stretch me on a bed of nails. Let them throw me into the Hollow of the Sling. I'll have none of your favors, God! I am no longer afraid of your Judgment! I am a betrayer of Israel, a willful transgressor!" Yoineh Meir cried. "I have more compassion than God Almighty – more, more! He is a cruel God, a Man of War, a God of Vengeance. I will not serve Him. It is an abandoned world!" Yoineh Meir laughed, but tears ran down his cheeks in scalding drops.

Yoineh Meir went to the pantry where he kept his knives, his whetstone, the circumcision knife. He gathered them all and dropped them into the pit of the outhouse. He knew that he was blaspheming, that he was desecrating the holy instruments, that he was mad, but he no longer wished to be sane.

He went outside and began to walk toward the river, the bridge, the wood. His prayer shawl and phylacteries? He needed none! The parchment was taken from the hide of a cow. The cases of the phylacteries were made of calf's leather. The Torah itself was made of animal skin. "Father in Heaven, Thou art a slaughterer!" a voice cried in Yoineh Meir. "Thou art a slaughterer and the Angel of Death! The whole world is a slaughterhouse!"

A slipper fell off Yoineh Meir's foot, but he let it lie, striding on in one slipper and one sock. He began to call, shout, sing. I am driving myself out of my mind, he thought. But this is itself a mark of madness....

He had opened a door to his brain, and madness flowed in, flooding everything. From moment to moment, Yoineh Meir grew more rebellious. He threw away his skullcap, grasped his prayer fringes and ripped them off, tore off pieces of his vest. A strength possessed him, the recklessness of one who had cast away all burdens.

Dogs chased him, barking, but he drove them off. Doors were flung open. Men ran out barefoot, with feathers clinging to their skullcaps. Women came out in their petticoats and nightcaps. All of them shouted, tried to bar his way, but Yoineh Meir evaded them.

The sky turned red as blood, and a round skull pushed up out of the bloody sea as out of the womb of a woman in childbirth.

Someone had gone to tell the butchers that Yoineh Meir had lost his mind. They came running with sticks and rope, but Yoineh Meir was already over the bridge and was hurrying across the harvested fields. He ran and vomited. He fell and rose, bruised by the stubble. Shepherds who take the horses out to graze at night mocked him and threw horse dung at him. The cows at pasture ran after him. Bells tolled as for a fire.

Yoineh Meir heard shouts, screams, the stamping of running feet. The earth began to slope and Yoineh Meir rolled downhill. He reached the wood, leaped over tufts of moss, rocks, running brooks. Yoineh Meir knew the truth: this was not the river before him; it was a bloody swamp. Blood ran from the sun, staining the tree trunks. From the branches hung intestines, livers, kidneys. The forequarters of beasts rose to their feet and sprayed him with gall and slime. Yoineh Meir could not escape. Myriads of cows and fowls encircled him, ready to take revenge for every cut, every wound, every slit gullet, every plucked feather. With bleeding throats, they all chanted, "Everyone may kill, and every killing is permitted."

Yoineh Meir broke into a wail that echoed through the wood in many voices. He raised his fist to Heaven: "Fiend! Murderer! Devouring beast!"

FOR TWO DAYS the butchers searched for him, but they did not find him. Then Zeinvel, who owned the water mill, arrived in town with the news that Yoineh Meir's body had turned up in the river by the dam. He had drowned.

The members of the burial society immediately went to bring the corpse. There were many witnesses to testify that Yoineh Meir had behaved like a madman, and the rabbi ruled that the deceased was not a suicide. The body of the dead man was cleansed and given burial near the graves of his father and his grandfather. The rabbi himself delivered the eulogy.

Because it was the holiday season and there was danger that Kolomir might remain without meat, the community hastily dispatched two messengers to bring a new slaughterer.

(TRANSLATED BY MIRRA GINSBURG)

Alice Walker

Alice Walker won the Pulitzer Prize and an American Book Award in 1983 for *The Color Purple*. She has published collections of her short stories and her poetry. She received a Discovery Award from the N.E.A. in 1970 and Creative Writing Fellowships in 1973 and 1978.

THE ABORTION

THEY HAD DISCUSSED it, but not deeply, whether they wanted the baby she was now carrying. "I don't *know* if I want it," she said, eyes filling with tears. She cried at anything now, and was often nauseous. That pregnant women cried easily and were nauseous seemed banal to her, and she resented banality.

"Well, think about it," he said, with his smooth reassuring voice (but with an edge of impatience she now felt) that used to soothe her.

It was all she *did* think about, all she apparently *could*; that he could dream otherwise enraged her. But she always lost, when they argued. Her temper would flare up, he would become instantly reasonable, mature, responsible, if not responsive precisely, to her mood, and she would swallow down her tears and hate herself. It was because she believed him "good." The best human being she had ever met.

"It isn't as if we don't already have a child," she said in a calmer tone, carelessly wiping at the tear that slid from one eye.

"We have a perfect child," he said with relish, "thank the Good Lord!"

Had she ever dreamed she'd marry someone humble enough to go around thanking the Good Lord? She had not.

Now they left the bedroom, where she had been lying down on their massive king-size bed with the forbidding ridge in the middle, and went down the hall – hung with bright prints – to the cheerful, spotlessly clean kitchen. He put water on for tea in a bright yellow pot.

She wanted him to want the baby so much he would try to save its life. On the other hand, she did not permit such presumptuousness. As he praised the child they already had, a daughter of sunny disposition and winning smile, Imani sensed subterfuge, and hardened her heart.

"What am I talking about," she said, as if she'd been talking about it. "Another child would kill me. I can't imagine life with two children. Having a child is a good experience *to have had*, like graduate school. But if you've had one, you've had the experience and that's enough."

He placed the tea before her and rested a heavy hand on her hair. She felt the heat and pressure of his hand as she touched the cup and felt the odor and steam rise up from it. Her throat contracted.

"I can't drink that," she said through gritted teeth. "Take it away."

THERE WERE days of this.

CLARICE, their daughter, was barely two years old. A miscarriage brought on by grief (Imani had lost her fervidly environmentalist mother to lung cancer shortly after Clarice's birth; the asbestos ceiling in the classroom where she taught first graders had leaked for twenty years) separated Clarice's birth from the new pregnancy. Imani felt her body had been assaulted by these events and was, in fact, considerably weakened, and was also, in any case, chronically anæmic and run down. Still, if she had wanted the baby more than she did not want it, she would not have planned to abort it.

They lived in a small town in the South. Her husband, Clarence, was, among other things, legal adviser and defender of the new black mayor of the town. The mayor was much in their lives because of the difficulties being the first black mayor of a small town assured, and because, next to the major leaders of black struggles in the South, Clarence respected and admired him most.

Imani reserved absolute judgment, but she did point out that

Mayor Carswell would never look at her directly when she made a comment or posed a question, even sitting at her own dinner table, and would instead talk to Clarence as if she were not there. He assumed that as a woman she would not be interested in, or even understand, politics. (He would comment occasionally on her cooking or her clothes. He noticed when she cut her hair.) But Imani understood every shade and variation of politics: she understood, for example, why she fed the mouth that did not speak to her; because for the present she must believe in Mayor Carswell, even as he could not believe in her. Even understanding this, however, she found dinners with Carswell hard to swallow.

But Clarence was dedicated to the mayor, and believed his success would ultimately mean security and advancement for them all.

On the morning she left to have the abortion, the mayor and Clarence were to have a working lunch, and they drove her to the airport deep in conversation about municipal funds, racist cops, and the facilities for teaching at the chaotic, newly integrated schools. Clarence had time for the briefest kiss and hug at the airport ramp.

"Take care of yourself," he whispered lovingly as she walked away. He was needed, while she was gone, to draft the city's new charter. She had agreed this was important; the mayor was already being called incompetent by local businessmen and the chamber of commerce, and one inferred from television that no black person alive even knew what a city charter was.

"Take care of myself." Yes, she thought. I see that is what I have to do. But she thought this self-pityingly, which invalidated it. She had expected *him* to take care of her, and she blamed him for not doing so now.

Well, she was a fraud, anyway. She had known after a year of marriage that it bored her. "The Experience of Having a Child" was to distract her from this fact. Still, she expected him to "take care of her." She was lucky he didn't pack up and leave. But he seemed to know, as she did, that if anyone packed and left, it would be her. Precisely *because* she was a fraud and because in the end he would settle for fraud and she could not.

On the plane to New York her teeth ached and she vomited bile

—bitter, yellowish stuff she hadn't even been aware her body produced. She resented and appreciated the crisp help of the stewardess, who asked if she needed anything, then stood chatting with the cigarette-smoking white man next to her, whose fat hairy wrist, like a large worm, was all Imani could bear to see out of the corner of her eye.

Her first abortion, when she was still in college, she frequently remembered as wonderful, bearing as it had all the marks of a supreme coming of age and a seizing of the direction of her own life, as well as a comprehension of existence that never left her: that life—what one saw about one and called Life—was not a façade. There was nothing behind it which used "Life" as its manifestation. Life was itself. Period. At the time, and afterwards, and even now, this seemed a marvelous thing to know.

The abortionist had been a delightful Italian doctor on the Upper East Side in New York, and before he put her under he told her about his own daughter who was just her age, and a junior at Vassar. He babbled on and on until she was out, but not before Imani had thought how her thousand dollars, for which she would be in debt for years, would go to keep her there.

When she woke up it was all over. She lay on a brown Naugahyde sofa in the doctor's outer office. And she heard, over her somewhere in the air, the sound of a woman's voice. It was a Saturday, no nurses in attendance, and she presumed it was the doctor's wife. She was pulled gently to her feet by this voice and encouraged to walk.

"And when you leave, be sure to walk as if nothing is wrong," the voice said.

Imani did not feel any pain. This surprised her. Perhaps he didn't do anything, she thought. Perhaps he took my thousand dollars and put me to sleep with two dollars' worth of ether. Perhaps this is a racket.

But he was so kind, and he was smiling benignly, almost fatherly, at her (and Imani realized how desperately she needed this "fatherly" look, this "fatherly" smile). "Thank you," she murmured sincerely: she was thanking him for her life.

Some of Italy was still in his voice. "It's nothing, nothing," he said. "A nice, pretty girl like you; in school like my own daughter, you didn't need this trouble."

"He's nice," she said to herself, walking to the subway on her way back to school. She lay down gingerly across a vacant seat, and passed out.

She hemorrhaged steadily for six weeks, and was not well again for a year.

.　　　.　　　.

BUT THIS WAS seven years later. An abortion law now made it possible to make an appointment at a clinic, and for seventy-five dollars a safe, quick, painless abortion was yours.

Imani had once lived in New York, in the Village, not five blocks from where the abortion clinic was. It was also near the Margaret Sanger clinic, where she had received her very first diaphragm, with utter gratitude and amazement that someone apparently understood and actually cared about young women as alone and ignorant as she. In fact, as she walked up the block, with its modern office buildings side by side with older, more elegant brownstones, she felt how close she was still to that earlier self. Still not in control of her sensuality, and only through violence and with money (for the flight, for the operation itself) in control of her body.

SHE FOUND that abortion had entered the age of the assembly line. Grateful for the lack of distinction between herself and the other women – all colors, ages, states of misery or nervousness – she was less happy to notice, once the doctor started to insert the catheter, that the anesthesia she had been given was insufficient. But assembly lines don't stop because the product on them has a complaint. Her doctor whistled, and assured her she was all right, and carried the procedure through to the horrific end. Imani fainted some seconds before that.

They laid her out in a peaceful room full of cheerful colors. Primary colors: yellow, red, blue. When she revived she had the feeling of being in a nursery. She had a pressing need to urinate.

A nurse, kindly, white-haired and with firm hands, helped her to the toilet. Imani saw herself in the mirror over the sink and was alarmed. She was literally gray, as if all her blood had leaked out. "Don't worry about how you look," said the nurse. "Rest a bit here and take it easy when you get back home. You'll be fine in a week or so."

She could not imagine being fine again. Somewhere her child – she never dodged into the language of "fetuses" and "amorphous growths" – was being flushed down a sewer. Gone all her or his chances to see the sunlight, savor a fig.

"Well," she said to this child, "it was you or me, Kiddo, and I chose me."

There were people who thought she had no right to choose herself, but Imani knew better than to think of those people now.

It was a bright, hot Saturday when she returned.

Clarence and Clarise picked her up at the airport. They had brought flowers from Imani's garden, and Clarice presented them with a stout-hearted hug. Once in her mother's lap she rested content all the way home, sucking her thumb, stroking her nose with the forefinger of the same hand, and kneading a corner of her blanket with the three fingers that were left.

"How did it go?" asked Clarence.

"It went," said Imani.

THERE WAS no way to explain abortion to a man. She thought castration might be an apt analogy, but most men, perhaps all, would insist this could not possibly be true.

"The anesthesia failed," she said. "I thought I'd never faint in time to keep from screaming and leaping off the table."

Clarence paled. He hated the thought of pain, any kind of violence. He could not endure it; it made him physically ill. This was one of the reasons he was a pacifist, another reason she admired him.

She knew he wanted her to stop talking. But she continued in a flat, deliberate voice.

"All the blood seemed to run out of me. The tendons in my legs felt cut. I was gray."

He reached for her hand. Held it. Squeezed.

"But," she said, "at least I know what I don't want. And I intend never to go through any of this again."

They were in the living room of their peaceful, quiet and colorful house. Imani was in her rocker, Clarice dozing on her lap. Clarence sank to the floor and rested his head against her knees. She felt he was asking for nurture when she needed it herself. She felt the two of them, Clarence and Clarice, clinging to her, using her. And that the only way she could claim herself, feel herself distinct from them, was by doing something painful, self-defining but self-destructive.

She suffered the pressure of his head as long as she could.

"Have a vasectomy," she said, "or stay in the guest room. Nothing is going to touch me anymore that isn't harmless."

He smoothed her thick hair with his hand. "We'll talk about it," he said, as if that was not what they were doing. "We'll see. Don't worry. We'll take care of things."

She had forgotten that the third Sunday in June, the following day, was the fifth memorial observance for Holly Monroe, who had been shot down on her way home from her high school graduation ceremony five years before. Imani *always* went to these memorials. She liked the reassurance that her people had long memories, and that those people who fell in struggle or innocence were not forgotten. She was, of course, too weak to go. She was dizzy and still losing blood. The white lawgivers attempted to get around assassination – which Imani considered extreme abortion – by saying the victim provoked it (there had been some difficulty saying this about Holly Monroe, but they had tried) but were anti-abortionist to a man. Imani thought of this as she resolutely showered and washed her hair.

Clarence had installed central air conditioning their second year in the house. Imani had at first objected. "I want to smell the trees, the flowers, the natural air!" she cried. But the first summer of 110-degree heat had cured her of giving a damn about any of that. Now she wanted to be cool. As much as she loved trees, on a hot day she would have sawed through a forest to get to an air conditioner.

In fairness to him, she had to admit he asked her if she thought she was well enough to go. But even to be asked annoyed her. She was not one to let her own troubles prevent her from showing proper respect and remembrance toward the dead, although she understood perfectly well that once dead, the dead do not exist. So respect, remembrance was for herself, and today her self needed rest. There was something mad about her refusal to rest, and she felt it as she tottered about getting Clarice dressed. But she did not stop. She ran a bath, plopped the child in it, scrubbed her plump body on her knees, arms straining over the tub awkwardly in a way that made her stomach hurt – but not yet her uterus – dried her hair, lifted her out and dried the rest of her on the kitchen table.

"You are going to remember as long as you live what kind of people they are," she said to the child, who, gurgling and cooing, looked into her mother's stern face with light-hearted fixation.

"You are going to hear the music," Imani said. "The music they've tried to kill. The music they try to steal." She felt feverish and was aware she was muttering. She didn't care.

"They think they can kill a continent – people, trees, buffalo – and then fly off to the moon and just forget about it. But you and me we're going to remember the people, the trees and the fucking buffalo. Goddammit."

"Buffwoe," said the child, hitting at her mother's face with a spoon.

She placed the baby on a blanket in the living room and turned to see her husband's eyes, full of pity, on her. She wore pert green velvet slippers and a lovely sea green robe. Her body was bent within it. A reluctant tear formed beneath his gaze.

"Sometimes I look at you and I wonder 'What is this man doing in my house?'"

This had started as a joke between them. Her aim had been never to marry, but to take in lovers who could be sent home at dawn, freeing her to work and ramble.

"I'm here because you love me," was the traditional answer. But Clarence faltered, meeting her eyes, and Imani turned away.

It was a hundred degrees by ten o'clock. By eleven, when the memorial service began, it would be ten degrees hotter. Imani staggered from the heat. When she sat in the car she had to clench her teeth against the dizziness until the motor prodded the air conditioning to envelop them in coolness. A dull ache started in her uterus.

The church was not of course air conditioned. It was authentic Primitive Baptist in every sense.

Like the previous four memorials this one was designed by Holly Monroe's classmates. All twenty-five of whom – fat and thin – managed to look like the dead girl. Imani had never seen Holly Monroe, though there were always photographs of her dominating the pulpit of this church where she had been baptized and where she had sung in the choir – and to her, every black girl of a certain vulnerable age *was* Holly Monroe. And an even deeper truth was that Holly Monroe was herself. Herself shot down, aborted on the eve of becoming herself.

She was prepared to cry and to do so with abandon. But she did not. She clenched her teeth against the steadily increasing pain and her tears were instantly blotted by the heat.

Mayor Carswell had been waiting for Clarence in the vestibule of the church, mopping his plumply jowled face with a voluminous handkerchief and holding court among half a dozen young men and women who listened to him with awe. Imani exchanged greetings with the mayor, he ritualistically kissed her on the cheek, and kissed Clarice on the cheek, but his rather heat-glazed eye was already fastened on her husband. The two men huddled in a corner away from the awed young group. Away from Imani and Clarice, who passed hesitantly, waiting to be joined or to be called back, into the church.

There was a quarter hour's worth of music.

"Holly Monroe was five feet, three inches tall, and weighed one hundred and eleven pounds," her best friend said, not reading from notes, but talking to each person in the audience. "She was a stubborn, loyal Aries, the best kind of friend to have. She had black kinky hair that she experimented with a lot. She was exactly the color of this oak church pew in the summer; in the winter she was the color [pointing up] of this heart pine ceiling. She loved green. She did not like lavender because she said she also didn't like pink. She had brown eyes and wore glasses, except when she was meeting someone for the first time. She had a sort of rounded nose. She had beautiful large teeth, but her lips were always chapped so she didn't smile as much as she might have if she'd ever gotten used to carrying Chap Stick. She had elegant feet.

"Her favorite church song was 'Leaning on the Everlasting

Arms.' Her favorite other kind of song was 'I Can't Help Myself – I Love You and Nobody Else.' She was often late for choir rehearsal though she loved to sing. She made the dress she wore to her graduation in Home Ec. She *hated* Home Ec...."

Imani was aware that the sound of low, murmurous voices had been the background for this statement all along. Everything was quiet around her, even Clarice sat up straight, absorbed by the simple friendliness of the young woman's voice. All of Holly Monroe's classmates and friends in the choir wore vivid green. Imani imagined Clarice entranced by the brilliant, swaying color as by a field of swaying corn.

Lifting the child, her uterus burning, and perspiration already a stream down her back, Imani tiptoed to the door. Clarence and the mayor were still deep in conversation. She heard "board meeting... aldermen...city council." She beckoned to Clarence.

"Your voices are carrying!" she hissed.

She meant: How dare you not come inside.

They did not. Clarence raised his head, looked at her, and shrugged his shoulders helplessly. Then, turning, with the abstracted air of priests, the two men moved slowly toward the outer door, and into the church yard, coming to stand some distance from the church beneath a large oak tree. There they remained throughout the service.

TWO YEARS later, Clarence was furious with her: What is the matter with you? he asked. You never want me to touch you. You told me to sleep in the guest room and I did. You told me to have a vasectomy I didn't want and *I did*. (Here, there was a sob of hatred for her somewhere in the anger, the humiliation: he thought of himself as a eunuch, and blamed her.)

She was not merely frigid, she was remote.

She had been amazed after they left the church that the anger she'd felt watching Clarence and the mayor turn away from the Holly Monroe memorial did not prevent her accepting a ride home with him. A month later it did not prevent her smiling on him fondly. Did not prevent a trip to Bermuda, a few blissful days of very good sex on a deserted beach screened by trees. Did not prevent her listening to his mother's stories of Clarence's youth as though she would treasure them forever.

And yet. From that moment in the heat at the church door, she had uncoupled herself from him, in a separation that made him, except occasionally, little more than a stranger.

And he had not felt it, had not known.

"What have I done?" he asked, all the tenderness in his voice breaking over her. She smiled a nervous smile at him, which he interpreted as derision — so far apart had they drifted.

They had discussed the episode at the church many times. Mayor Carswell — whom they never saw anymore — was now a model mayor, with wide biracial support in his campaign for the legislature. Neither could easily recall him, though television frequently brought him into the house.

"It was so important that I help the mayor!" said Clarence. "He was our *first*!"

Imani understood this perfectly well, but it sounded humorous to her. When she smiled, he was offended.

She had known the moment she left the marriage, the exact second. But apparently that moment had left no perceptible mark.

They argued, she smiled, they scowled, blamed and cried — as she packed.

Each of them almost recalled out loud that about this time of the year their aborted child would have been a troublesome, "terrible" two-year-old, a great burden on its mother, whose health was by now in excellent shape, each wanted to think aloud that the marriage would have deteriorated anyway, because of that.

Tobias Wolff

Tobias Wolff's most recent book is *The Barracks Thief*, which won the P.E.N./Faulkner Award for 1985. He received Creative Writing Fellowships in 1978 and 1985.

THE LIAR

My MOTHER read everything except books. Advertisements on buses, entire menus as we ate, billboards; if it had no cover it interested her. So when she found a letter in my drawer that was not addressed to her she read it. "What difference does it make if James has nothing to hide?" – that was her thought. She stuffed the letter in the drawer when she finished it and walked from room to room in the big empty house, talking to herself. She took the letter out and read it again to get the facts straight. Then, without putting on her coat or locking the door, she went down the steps and headed for the church at the end of the street. No matter how angry and confused she might be, she always went to four o'clock Mass and now it was four o'clock.

It was a fine day, blue and cold and still, but Mother walked as though into a strong wind, bent forward at the waist with her feet hurrying behind in short, busy steps. My brother and sisters and I considered this walk of hers funny and we smirked at one another when she crossed in front of us to stir the fire, or water a plant. We didn't let her catch us at it. It would have puzzled her to think that there might be anything amusing about her. Her one concession to the fact of humor was an insincere, startling laugh. Strangers often stared at her.

While Mother waited for the priest, who was late, she prayed. She prayed in a familiar, orderly, firm way: first for her late husband, for my father's parents (just touching base; she had disliked them) and finally for her children in order of their ages, ending with me. Mother did not consider originality a virtue and until my name came up her prayers were exactly the same as on any other day.

But when she came to me she spoke up boldly. "I thought he wasn't going to do it any more. Murphy said he was cured. What am I supposed to do now?" There was reproach in her tone. Mother put great hope in her notion that I was cured. She regarded my cure as an answer to her prayers and by way of thanksgiving sent a lot of money to the Thomasite Indian Mission, money she had been saving for a trip to Rome. She felt cheated and she let her feelings be known. When the priest came in Mother slid back on the seat and followed the Mass with concentration. After communion she began to worry again and went straight home without stopping to talk to Frances, the woman who always cornered Mother after Mass to tell about the awful things done to her by Communists, devil-worshippers, and Rosicrucians. Frances watched her go with narrowed eyes.

Once in the house, Mother took the letter from my drawer and brought it into the kitchen. She held it over the stove with her fingernails, looking away so that she would not be drawn into it again, and set it on fire. When it began to burn her fingers she dropped it in the sink and watched it blacken and flutter and close upon itself like a fist. Then she washed it down the drain and called Dr. Murphy.

THE LETTER was to my friend Ralphy in Arizona. He used to live across the street from us but he had moved. Most of the letter was about a tour we, the junior class, had taken of Alcatraz. That was all right. What got Mother was the last paragraph where I said that she had been coughing up blood and the doctors weren't sure what was wrong with her, but that we were hoping for the best.

This wasn't true. Mother took pride in her physical condition, considered herself a horse: "I'm a regular horse," she would reply when people asked about her health. For several years now I had been saying unpleasant things that weren't true and this habit of mine irked Mother greatly, enough to persuade her to send me to

Dr. Murphy, in whose office I was sitting when she burned the letter. Dr. Murphy was our family physician and had no training in psychoanalysis but he took an interest in "things of the mind," as he put it. He had treated me for appendicitis and tonsilitis and Mother thought that he could put the truth into me as easily as he took things out of me, a hope Dr. Murphy did not share. He was basically interested in getting me to understand what I did, and lately he had been moving toward the conclusion that I understood what I did as well as I ever would.

DR. MURPHY listened to Mother's account of the letter, and what she had done with it. He was curious about the wording I had used and became irritated when Mother told him she had burned it. "The point is," she said, "he was supposed to be cured and he's not."

"Margaret, I never said he was cured."

"You certainly did. Why else would I have sent over a thousand dollars to the Thomasite Mission?"

"I said that he was responsible. That means that James knows what he's doing, not that he's going to stop doing it."

"I'm sure you said he was cured."

"Never. To say that someone is cured you have to know what health is. With this kind of thing that's impossible. What do you mean by curing James, anyway?"

"You know."

"Tell me anyway."

"Getting him back to reality, what else?"

"Whose reality? Mine or yours?"

"Murphy, what are you talking about? James isn't crazy, he's a liar."

"Well, you have a point there."

"What am I going to do with him?"

"I don't think there's much you can do. Be patient."

"I've been patient."

"If I were you, Margaret, I wouldn't make too much of this. James doesn't steal, does he?"

"Of course not."

"Or beat people up or talk back."

"No."

"Then you have a lot to be thankful for."

"I don't think I can take any more of it. That business about leukemia last summer. And now this."

"Eventually he'll outgrow it, I think."

"Murphy, he's sixteen years old. What if he doesn't outgrow it? What if he just gets better at it?"

Finally Mother saw that she wasn't going to get any satisfaction from Dr. Murphy, who kept reminding her of her blessings. She said something cutting to him and he said something pompous back and she hung up. Dr. Murphy stared at the receiver. "Hello," he said, then replaced it on the cradle. He ran his hand over his head, a habit remaining from a time when he had hair. To show that he was a good sport he often joked about his baldness, but I had the feeling that he regretted it deeply. Looking at me across the desk, he must have wished that he hadn't taken me on. Treating a friend's child was like investing a friend's money.

"I don't have to tell you who that was."

I nodded.

Dr. Murphy pushed his chair back and swiveled it around so he could look out the window behind him, which took up most of the wall. There were still a few sailboats out on the Bay, but they were all making for shore. A woolly gray fog had covered the bridge and was moving in fast. The water seemed calm from this far up, but when I looked closely I could see white flecks everywhere, so it must have been pretty choppy.

"I'm surprised at you," he said. "Leaving something like that lying around for her to find. If you really have to do these things you could at least be kind and do them discreetly. It's not easy for your mother, what with your father dead and all the others somewhere else."

"I know. I didn't mean for her to find it."

"Well." He tapped his pencil against his teeth. He was not convinced professionally, but personally he may have been. "I think you ought to go home now and straighten things out."

"I guess I'd better."

"Tell your mother I might stop by, either tonight or tomorrow. And James – don't underestimate her."

WHILE MY FATHER was alive we usually went to Yosemite for three or four days during the summer. My mother would drive and Father would point out places of interest, meadows where boom towns once stood, hanging trees, rivers that were said to flow upstream at certain times. Or he read to us; he had that grown-ups' idea that children love Dickens and Sir Walter Scott. The four of us sat in the back seat with our faces composed, attentive, while our hands and feet pushed, pinched, stomped, goosed, prodded, dug, and kicked.

One night a bear came into our camp just after dinner. Mother had made a tuna casserole and it must have smelled to him like something worth dying for. He came into the camp while we were sitting around the fire and stood swaying back and forth. My brother Michael saw him first and elbowed me, then my sisters saw him and screamed. Mother and Father had their backs to him but Mother must have guessed what it was because she immediately said, "Don't scream like that. You might frighten him and there's no telling what he'll do. We'll just sing and he'll go away."

We sang "Row Row Row Your Boat" but the bear stayed. He circled us several times, rearing up now and then on his hind legs to stick his nose into the air. By the light of the fire I could see his doglike face and watch the muscles roll under his loose skin like rocks in a sack. We sang harder as he circled us, coming closer and closer. "All right," Mother said, "enough's enough." She stood abruptly. The bear stopped moving and watched her. "Beat it," Mother said. The bear sat down and looked from side to side. "Beat it," she said again, and leaned over and picked up a rock.

"Margaret, don't," my father said.

She threw the rock hard and hit the bear in the stomach. Even in the dim light I could see the dust rising from his fur. He grunted and stood to his full height. "See that?" Mother shouted: "He's filthy. Filthy!" One of my sisters giggled. Mother picked up another rock. "Please, Margaret," my father said. Just then the bear turned and shambled away. Mother pitched the rock after him. For the rest of the night he loitered around the camp until he found the tree where we had hung our food. He ate it all. The next day we drove back to the city. We could have bought more supplies in the valley, but Father wanted to go and would not give in to any argument. On the way home he tried to jolly everyone up by making jokes, but Michael and my sisters ignored him and looked stonily out the windows.

Things were never easy between my mother and me, but I didn't underestimate her. She underestimated me. When I was little she suspected me of delicacy, because I didn't like being thrown into the air, and because when I saw her and the others working themselves up for a roughhouse I found somewhere else to be. When they did drag me in I got hurt, a knee in the lip, a bent finger, a bloody nose, and this too Mother seemed to hold against me, as if I arranged my hurts to get out of playing.

Even things I did well got on her nerves. We all loved puns except Mother, who didn't get them, and next to my father I was the best in the family. My specialty was the Swifty – " 'You can bring the prisoner down,' said Tom condescendingly." Father encouraged me to perform at dinner, which must have been a trial for outsiders. Mother wasn't sure what was going on, but she didn't like it.

She suspected me in other ways. I couldn't go to the movies without her examining my pockets to make sure I had enough money to pay for the ticket. When I went away to camp she tore my pack apart in front of all the boys who were waiting in the bus outside the house. I would rather have gone without my sleeping bag and a few changes of underwear, which I had forgotten, than be made such a fool of. Her distrust was the thing that made me forgetful.

And she thought I was cold-hearted because of what happened the day my father died and later at his funeral. I didn't cry at my father's funeral, and showed signs of boredom during the eulogy, fiddling around with the hymnals. Mother put my hands into my lap and I left them there without moving them as though they were things I was holding for someone else. The effect was ironical and she resented it. We had a sort of reconciliation a few days later after I closed my eyes at school and refused to open them. When several teachers and then the principal failed to persuade me to look at them, or at some reward they claimed to be holding, I was handed over to the school nurse, who tried to pry the lids open and scratched one of them badly. My eye swelled up and I went rigid. The principal panicked and called Mother, who fetched me home. I wouldn't talk to her, or open my eyes, or bend, and they had to lay me on the back seat and when we reached the house Mother had to lift me up the steps one at a time. Then she put me on the couch and played the piano to me all afternoon. Finally I opened my eyes. We hugged each other and I wept. Mother did not really believe my tears, but she was willing to accept them because I had staged them for her benefit.

My lying separated us, too, and the fact that my promises not to lie any more seemed to mean nothing to me. Often my lies came back to her in embarrassing ways, people stopping her in the street and saying how sorry they were to hear that such and such had happened. No one in the neighborhood enjoyed embarrassing Mother, and these situations stopped occurring once everybody got wise to me. There was no saving her from strangers, though. The summer after Father died I visited my uncle in Redding and when I got back I found to my surprise that Mother had come to meet my bus. I tried to slip away from the gentleman who had sat next to me but I couldn't shake him. When he saw Mother embrace me he came up and presented her with a card and told her to get in touch with him if things got any worse. She gave him his card back and told him to mind his own business. Later, on the way home, she made me repeat what I had said to the man. She shook her head. "It's not fair to people," she said, "telling them things like that. It confuses them." It seemed to me that Mother had confused the man, not I, but I didn't say so. I agreed with her that I shouldn't say such things and promised not to do it again, a promise I broke three hours later in conversation with a woman in the park.

It wasn't only the lies that disturbed Mother; it was their morbidity. This was the real issue between us, as it had been between her and my father. Mother did volunteer work at Children's

Hospital and St. Anthony's Dining Hall, collected things for the St. Vincent de Paul Society. She was a lighter of candles. My brother and sisters took after her in this way. My father was a curser of the dark. And he loved to curse the dark. He was never more alive than when he was indignant about something. For this reason the most important act of the day for him was the reading of the evening paper.

Ours was a terrible paper, indifferent to the city that bought it, indifferent to medical discoveries – except for new kinds of gases that made your hands fall off when you sneezed – and indifferent to politics and art. Its business was outrage, horror, gruesome coincidence. When my father sat down in the living room with the paper Mother stayed in the kitchen and kept the children busy, all except me, because I was quiet and could be trusted to amuse myself. I amused myself by watching my father.

He sat with his knees spread, leaning forward, his eyes only inches from the print. As he read he nodded to himself. Sometimes he swore and threw the paper down and paced the room, then picked it up and began again. Over a period of time he developed the habit of reading aloud to me. He always started with the society section, which he called the parasite page. This column began to take on the character of a comic strip or a serial, with the same people showing up from one day to the next, blinking in chiffon, awkwardly holding their drinks for the sake of Peninsula orphans, grinning under sunglasses on the deck of a ski hut in the Sierras. The skiers really got his goat, probably because he couldn't understand them. The activity itself was inconceivable to him. When my sisters went to Lake Tahoe one winter weekend with some friends and came back excited about the beauty of the place, Father calmed them right down. "Snow," he said, "is overrated."

Then the news, or what passed in the paper for news: bodies unearthed in Scotland, former Nazis winning elections, rare animals slaughtered, misers expiring naked in freezing houses upon mattresses stuffed with thousands, millions; marrying priests, divorcing actresses, high-rolling oilmen building fantastic mausoleums in honor of a favorite horse, cannibalism. Through all this my father waded with a fixed and weary smile.

Mother encouraged him to take up causes, to join groups, but he would not. He was uncomfortable with people outside the family. He and my mother rarely went out, and rarely had people in, except on feast days and national holidays. Their guests were always the same, Dr. Murphy and his wife and several others whom they had known since childhood. Most of these people never saw each other outside our house and they didn't have much fun together. Father discharged his obligations as host by teasing everyone about stupid things they had said or done in the past and forcing them to laugh at themselves.

Though Father did not drink, he insisted on mixing cocktails for the guests. He would not serve straight drinks like rum-and-Coke or even Scotch-on-the-rocks, only drinks of his own devising. He gave them lawyerly names like "The Advocate," "The Hanging Judge," "The Ambulance Chaser," "The Mouthpiece," and described their concoction in detail. He told long, complicated stories in a near-whisper, making everyone lean in his direction, and repeated important lines; he also repeated the important lines in the stories my mother told, and corrected her when she got something wrong. When the guests came to the ends of their own stories, he would point out the morals.

Dr. Murphy had several theories about Father, which he used to test on me in the course of our meetings. Dr. Murphy had by this time given up his glasses for contact lenses, and lost weight in the course of fasts which he undertook regularly. Even with his baldness he looked years younger than when he had come to the parties at our house. Certainly he did not look like my father's contemporary, which he was.

One of Dr. Murphy's theories was that Father had exhibited a classic trait of people who had been gifted children by taking an undemanding position in an uninteresting firm. "He was afraid of finding his limits," Dr. Murphy told me: "As long as he kept stamping papers and making out wills, he could go on believing that he didn't *have* limits." Dr. Murphy's fascination with Father made me uneasy, and I felt traitorous listening to him. While he lived, my father would never have submitted himself for analysis; it seemed a betrayal to put him on the couch now that he was dead.

I did enjoy Dr. Murphy's recollections of Father as a child. He told me about something that happened when they were in the Boy Scouts. Their troop had been on a long hike and Father had fallen behind. Dr. Murphy and the others decided to ambush him as he came down the trail. They hid in the woods on each side and waited. But when Father walked into the trap none of them moved or made a sound and he strolled on without even knowing they were there. "He had the sweetest look on his face," Dr. Murphy said, "listening to the birds, smelling the flowers, just like Ferdinand the Bull." He also told me that my father's drinks tasted like medicine.

WHILE I rode my bicycle home from Dr. Murphy's office Mother fretted. She felt terribly alone but she didn't call anyone because she also felt like a failure. My lying had that effect on her. She took it personally. At such times she did not think of my sisters, one happily married, the other doing brilliantly at Fordham. She did not think of my brother Michael, who had given up college to work with runaway children in Los Angeles. She thought of me. She thought that she had made a mess of her family.

Actually she managed the family well. While my father was dying upstairs she pulled us together. She made lists of chores and gave each of us a fair allowance. Bedtimes were adjusted and she stuck by them. She set regular hours for homework. Each child was made responsible for the next eldest, and I was given a dog. She told us frequently, predictably, that she loved us. At dinner we were each expected to contribute something, and after dinner she played the piano and tried to teach us to sing in harmony, which I could not do. Mother, who was an admirer of the Trapp family, considered this a character defect.

Our life together was more orderly, healthy, while Father was dying than it had been before. He had set us rules to follow, not much different really than the ones Mother gave us after he got sick, but he had administered them in a fickle way. Though we were supposed to get an allowance we always had to ask him for it and then he would give us too much because he enjoyed seeming magnanimous. Sometimes he punished us for no reason, because he was in a bad mood. He was apt to decide, as one of my sisters was going out to a dance, that she had better stay home and do something to improve herself. Or he would sweep us all up on a Wednesday night and take us ice-skating.

He changed after he learned about the cancer, and became more calm as the disease spread. He relaxed his teasing way with us, and from time to time it was possible to have a conversation with him which was not about the last thing that had made him angry. He stopped reading the paper and spent time at the window.

He and I became close. He taught me to play poker and sometimes helped me with my homework. But it wasn't his illness that drew us together. The reserve between us had begun to break down after the incident with the bear, during the drive home. Michael and my sisters were furious with him for making us leave early and wouldn't talk to him or look at him. He joked: though it had been a grisly experience we should grin and bear it — and so on. His joking seemed perverse to the others, but not to me. I had seen how terrified he was when the bear came into the camp. He had held himself so still that he had begun to tremble. When Mother started pitching rocks I thought he was going to bolt, really. I understood — I had been frightened too. The others took it as a lark after they got used to having the bear around, but for Father and me it got worse through the night. I was glad to be out of there, grateful to Father for getting me out. I saw that his jokes were how he held himself together. So I reached out to him with a joke: "'There's a bear outside,' said Tom intently." The others turned cold looks on me. They thought I was sucking up. But Father smiled.

When I thought of other boys being close to their fathers I thought of them hunting together, tossing a ball back and forth, making birdhouses in the basement, and having long talks about girls, war, careers. Maybe the reason it took us so long to get close was that I had this idea. It kept getting in the way of what we really had, which was a shared fear.

TOWARD THE END Father slept most of the time and I watched him. From below, sometimes, faintly, I heard Mother playing the piano. Occasionally he nodded off in his chair while I was reading to him; his bathrobe would fall open then, and I would see the long new scar on his stomach, red as blood against his white skin. His ribs all showed and his legs were like cables.

I once read in a biography of a great man that he "died well." I assume the writer meant that he kept his pain to himself, did not set off false alarms, and did not too much inconvenience those who were to stay behind. My father died well. His irritability gave way to something else, something like serenity. In the last days he became tender. It was as though he had been rehearsing the scene, that the anger of his life had been a kind of stage fright. He managed his audience – us – with an old trouper's sense of when to clown and when to stand on his dignity. We were all moved, and admired his courage, as he intended we should. He died downstairs in a shaft of late afternoon sunlight on New Year's Day, while I was reading to him. I was alone in the house and didn't know what to do. His body did not frighten me but immediately and sharply I missed my father. It seemed wrong to leave him sitting up and I tried to carry him upstairs to the bedroom but it was too hard, alone. So I called up my friend Ralphy across the street. When he came over and saw what I wanted him for he started crying but I made him help me anyway. A couple of hours later Mother got home and when I told her that Father was dead she ran upstairs, calling his name. A few minutes later she came back down. "Thank God," she said, "at least he died in bed." This seemed important to her and I didn't tell her otherwise. But that night Ralphy's parents called. They were, they said, shocked at what I had done and so was Mother when she heard the story, shocked and furious. Why? Because I had not told her the truth? Or because she had learned the truth, and could not go on believing that Father had died in bed? I really don't know.

"MOTHER," I said, coming into the living room, "I'm sorry about the letter. I really am."

She was arranging wood in the fireplace and did not look at me or speak for a moment. Finally she finished and straightened up and brushed her hands. She stepped back and looked at the fire

she had laid. "That's all right," she said. "Not bad for a consump-
tive."

"Mother, I'm sorry."

"Sorry? Sorry you wrote it or sorry I found it?"

"I wasn't going to mail it. It was a sort of joke."

"Ha ha." She took up the whisk broom and swept bits of bark
into the fireplace, then closed the drapes and settled on the couch.
"Sit down," she said. She crossed her legs. "Listen, do I give you
advice all the time?"

"Yes."

"I do?"

I nodded.

"Well, that doesn't make any difference. I'm supposed to. I'm
your mother. I'm going to give you some more advice, for your
own good. You don't have to make all these things up, James.
They'll happen anyway." She picked at the hem of her skirt. "Do
you understand what I'm saying?"

"I think so."

"You're cheating yourself, that's what I'm trying to tell you.
When you get to be my age you won't know anything at all about
life. All you'll know is what you've made up."

I thought about that. It seemed logical.

She went on. "I think maybe you need to get out of yourself
more. Think more about other people."

The doorbell rang.

"Go see who it is," Mother said. "We'll talk about this later."

It was Dr. Murphy. He and Mother made their apologies and
she insisted that he stay for dinner. I went to the kitchen to fetch
ice for their drinks, and when I returned they were talking about
me. I sat on the sofa and listened. Dr. Murphy was telling Mother
not to worry. "James is a good boy," he said. "I've been thinking
about my oldest, Terry. He's not really dishonest, you know, but
he's not really honest either. I can't seem to reach him. At least
James isn't furtive."

"No," Mother said, "he's never been furtive."

Dr. Murphy clasped his hands between his knees and stared at
them. "Well, that's Terry. Furtive."

Before we sat down to dinner Mother said grace; Dr. Murphy bowed his head and closed his eyes and crossed himself at the end, though he had lost his faith in college. When he told me that, during one of our meetings, in just those words, I had the picture of a raincoat hanging by itself outside a dining hall. He drank a good deal of wine and persistently turned the conversation to the subject of his relationship with Terry. He admitted that he had come to dislike the boy. Then he mentioned several patients of his by name, some of them known to Mother and me, and said that he disliked them too. He used the word "dislike" with relish, like someone on a diet permitting himself a single potato chip. "I don't know what I've done wrong," he said abruptly, and with reference to no particular thing. "Then again maybe I haven't done anything wrong. I don't know what to think any more. Nobody does."

"I know what to think," Mother said.

"So does the solipsist. How can you prove to a solipsist that he's not creating the rest of us?"

This was one of Dr. Murphy's favorite riddles, and almost any pretext was sufficient for him to trot it out. He was a child with a card trick.

"Send him to bed without dinner," Mother said. "Let him create that."

Dr. Murphy suddenly turned to me. "Why do you do it?" he asked. It was a pure question, it had no object beyond the satisfaction of his curiosity. Mother looked at me and there was the same curiosity in her face.

"I don't know," I said, and that was the truth.

Dr. Murphy nodded, not because he had anticipated my answer but because he accepted it. "Is it fun?"

"No, it's not fun. I can't explain."

"Why is it all so sad?" Mother asked. "Why all the diseases?"

"Maybe," Dr. Murphy said, "sad things are more interesting."

"Not to me," Mother said.

"Not to me, either," I said. "It just comes out that way."

After dinner Dr. Murphy asked Mother to play the piano. He particularly wanted to sing "Come Home Abbie, the Light's on the Stair."

"That old thing," Mother said. She stood and folded her napkin deliberately and we followed her into the living room. Dr. Murphy stood behind her as she warmed up. Then they sang "Come Home Abbie, the Light's on the Stair," and I watched him stare down at Mother intently, as if he were trying to remember something. Her own eyes were closed. After that they sang "O Magnum Mysterium." They sang it in parts and I regretted that I had no voice, it sounded so good.

"Come on, James," Dr. Murphy said as Mother played the last chords. "These old tunes not good enough for you?"

"He just can't sing," Mother said.

WHEN DR. MURPHY left, Mother lit the fire and made more coffee. She slouched down in the big chair, sticking her legs straight out and moving her feet back and forth. "That was fun," she said.

"Did you and Father ever do things like that?"

"A few times, when we were first going out. I don't think he really enjoyed it. He was like you."

I wondered if Mother and Father had had a good marriage. He admired her and liked to look at her; every night at dinner he had to move the candlesticks slightly to the right and left of center so he could see down the length of the table. And every evening when she set the table she put them in the center again. She didn't seem to miss him very much. But I wouldn't really have known if she did, and anyway I didn't miss him all that much myself, not the way I had. Most of the time I thought about other things.

"James?"

I waited.

"I've been thinking that you might like to go down and stay with Michael for a couple of weeks or so."

"What about school?"

"I'll talk to Father McSorley. He won't mind. Maybe this problem will take care of itself if you start thinking about other people."

"I do."

"I mean helping them, like Michael does. You don't have to go if you don't want to."

"It's fine with me. Really. I'd like to see Michael."

"I'm not trying to get rid of you."

"I know."

Mother stretched, then tucked her feet under her. She sipped noisily at her coffee. "What did that word mean that Murphy used? You know the one?"

"Paranoid? That's where somebody thinks everyone is out to get him. Like that woman who always grabs you after Mass – Frances."

"Not paranoid. Everyone knows what that means. Sol-something."

"Oh. Solipsist. A solipsist is someone who thinks he creates everything around him."

Mother nodded and blew on her coffee, then put it down without drinking from it. "I'd rather be paranoid. Do you really think Frances is?"

"Of course. No question about it."

"I mean really *sick?*"

"That's what paranoid *is*, is being sick. What do you think, Mother?"

"What are you so angry about?"

"I'm not angry." I lowered my voice. "I'm not angry. But you don't believe those stories of hers, do you?"

"Well, no, not exactly. I don't think she knows what she's saying, she just wants someone to listen. She probably lives all by herself in some little room. So she's paranoid. Think of that. And I had no idea. James, we should pray for her. Will you remember to do that?"

I nodded. I thought of Mother singing "O Magnum Mysterium,'" saying grace, praying with easy confidence, and it came to me that her imagination was superior to mine. She could imagine things as coming together, not falling apart. She looked at me and I shrank; I knew exactly what she was going to say. "Son," she said, "do you know how much I love you?"

THE NEXT afternoon I took the bus to Los Angeles. I looked forward to the trip, to the monotony of the road and the empty fields by the roadside. Mother walked with me down the long concourse. The station was crowded and oppressive. "Are you sure this is the right bus?" she asked at the loading platform.

"Yes."

"It looks so old."

"Mother – "

"All right." She pulled me against her and kissed me, then held me an extra second to show that her embrace was sincere, not just like everyone else's, never having realized that everyone else does the same thing. I boarded the bus and we waved at each other until it became embarrassing. Then Mother began checking through her handbag for something. When she had finished I stood and adjusted the luggage over my seat. I sat and we smiled at each other, waved when the driver gunned the engine, shrugged when he got up suddenly to count the passengers, waved again when he resumed his seat. As the bus pulled out my mother and I were looking at each other with plain relief.

I had boarded the wrong bus. This one was bound for Los Angeles but not by the express route. We stopped in San Mateo, Palo Alto, San Jose, Castroville. When we left Castroville it began to rain, hard; my window would not close all the way, and a thin stream of water ran down the wall onto my seat. To keep dry I had to stay away from the wall and lean forward. The rain fell harder. The engine of the bus sounded as though it were coming apart.

In Salinas the man sleeping beside me jumped up but before I had a chance to change seats his place was taken by an enormous woman in a print dress, carrying a shopping bag. She took possession of her seat and spilled over onto half of mine, backing me up to the wall. "That's a storm," she said loudly, then turned and looked at me. "Hungry?" Without waiting for an answer she dipped into her bag and pulled out a piece of chicken and thrust it at me. "Hey, by God," she hooted, "look at him go to town on that drumstick!" A few people turned and smiled. I smiled back around the bone and kept at it. I finished that piece and she handed me another, and then another. Then she started handing out chicken to the people in the seats near us.

Outside of San Luis Obispo the noise from the engine grew suddenly louder and just as suddenly there was no noise at all. The driver pulled off to the side of the road and got out, then got on again dripping wet. A few moments later he announced that the bus had broken down and they were sending another bus to pick us up. Someone asked how long that might take and the driver said he had no idea. "Keep your pants on!" shouted the woman next to me. "Anybody in a hurry to get to L.A. ought to have his head examined."

The wind was blowing hard around the bus, driving sheets of rain against the window on both sides. The bus swayed gently. Outside the light was brown and thick. The woman next to me pumped all the people around us for their itineraries and said whether or not she had ever been where they were from or where they were going. "How about you?" She slapped my knee. "Parents own a chicken ranch? I hope so!" She laughed. I told her I was from San Francisco. "San Francisco, that's where my husband was stationed." She asked me what I did there and I told her I worked with refugees from Tibet.

"Is that right? What do you do with a bunch of Tibetans?"

"Seems like there's plenty of other places they could've gone," said a man in front of us. "Coming across the border like that. We don't go there."

"What do you do with a bunch of Tibetans?" the woman repeated.

"Try to find them jobs, locate housing, listen to their problems."

"You understand that kind of talk?"

"Yes."

"Speak it?"

"Pretty well. I was born and raised in Tibet. My parents were missionaries over there."

Everyone waited.

"They were killed when the Communists took over."

The big woman patted my arm.

"It's all right," I said.

"Why don't you say some of that Tibetan?"

"What would you like to hear?"

"Say 'The cow jumped over the moon.'" She watched me, smiling, and when I finished she looked at the others and shook her head. "That was pretty. Like music. Say some more."

"What?"

"Anything."

They bent toward me. The windows suddenly went blind with rain. The driver had fallen asleep and was snoring gently to the swaying of the bus. Outside the muddy light flickered to pale yellow, and far off there was thunder. The woman next to me leaned back and closed her eyes and then so did all the others as I sang to them in what was surely an ancient and holy tongue.

Charles Wright

Charles Wright's *Country Music* was co-winner of the American Bood Award in poetry in 1983. His most recent collection if *The Other Side of the River*. He received Creative Writing Fellowships in 1975 and 1984.

THE OTHER SIDE OF THE RIVER

EASTER AGAIN, and a small rain falls
On the mockingbird and the housefly,
                              on the Chevrolet
In its purple joy
And the TV antennas huddled across the hillside –

Easter again, and the palm trees hunch
Deeper beneath their burden,
                              the dark puddles take in
Whatever is given them,
And nothing rises more than halfway out of itself –

Easter with all its little mouths open into the rain.

There is no metaphor for the spring's disgrace,
No matter how much the rose leaves look like bronze dove hearts,
No matter how much the plum trees preen in the wind.

For weeks I've thought about the Savannah River,
For no reason,
                 and the winter fields around Garnett, South
Carolina
My brother and I used to hunt
At Christmas,

Princess and Buddy working the millet stands
And the vine-lipped face of the pine woods
In their languorous zig-zags,
The quail, when they flushed, bursting like shrapnel points
Between the trees and the leggy shrubs
                                into the undergrowth,
Everything else in motion as though under water,
My brother and I, the guns, their reports tolling from far away
Through the aqueous, limb-filtered light,
December sun like a single tropical fish
Uninterested anyway,
                        suspended and holding still
In the coral stems of the pearl-dusked and distant trees...

There is no metaphor for any of this,
Or the meta-weather of April,
The vinca blossoms like deep bruises among the green.

———————

It's linkage I'm talking about,
                        and harmonies and structures
And all the various things that lock our wrists to the past.

Something infinite behind everything appears,
                                and then disappears.

It's all a matter of how
                    you narrow the surfaces.
It's all a matter of how you fit in the sky.

———————

Often, at night, when the stars seem as close as they do now,
    and as full,
And the trees balloon and subside in the way they do
                                when the wind is right,
As they do now after the rain,
                    the sea way off with its false sheen,

And the sky that slick black of wet rubber,
I'm 15 again, and back on Mt. Anne in North Carolina
Repairing the fire tower,
Nobody else around but the horse I packed in with,
                                    and five days to finish the job.
Those nights were the longest nights I ever remember,
The lake and pavilion 3,000 feet below
                                    as though modeled in tinfoil,
And even more distant than that,
The last fire out, the after-reflection of Lake Llewellyn
Aluminum glare in the sponged dark,
Lightning bugs everywhere,
                            the plump stars
Dangling and falling near on their black strings.

These nights are like that,
The silvery alphabet of the sea
                        increasingly difficult to transcribe,
And larger each year, everything farther away, and less clear,
Than I want it to be,
                    not enough time to do the job,
And faint thunks in the earth,
As though somewhere nearby a horse was nervously pawing the
    ground.

                    _____

I want to sit by the bank of the river,
                                in the shade of the evergreen tree
And look in the face of whatever,
                        the whatever that's waiting for me.

                    _____

There comes a point when everything starts to dust away
More quickly than it appears,
                        when what we have to comfort the dark
Is just that dust, and just its going away.

25 years ago I used to sit on this jut of rocks
As the sun went down like an offering through the glaze
And backfires of Monterey Bay,
And anything I could think of was mine because it was there
                              in front of me, numinously everywhere,
Appearing and piling up...

So to have come to this,
                remembering what I did do, and what I didn't do,
The gulls whimpering over the boathouse,
                                        the monarch butterflies
Cruising the flower beds,
And all the soft hairs of spring thrusting up through the wind,
And the sun, as it always does,
                dropping into its slot without a click,
Is a short life of trouble.

Appendix

WINNERS OF CREATIVE WRITING
FELLOWSHIPS AND AWARDS, 1966-1985

In 20 YEARS, the types and names of awards and fellowships granted by the Literature Program of the National Endowment for the Arts have changed. The earliest grants were awarded for Distinguished Service, for inclusion in the *American Literary Anthology*, for Works-in-Progress or for short sabbaticals from work. For a brief time in the 1970s, drama writing grants were awarded through the Literature Program; now, they are awarded through the Endowment's Theater Program. Once the primary grant category was called Creative Writing Fellowship; now the grant is called Fellowship in Creative Writing. Grant amounts have ranged from $500 for inclusion in the *American Literary Anthology* to the $20,000 presently awarded to writers who receive Fellowships in Creative Writing.

Fellowships in Creative Writing are awarded yearly to poets and prose writers who meet certain minimum publication requirements. Writers are invited to submit a sample of their writing to the Literature Program. The work is read by panels of consultants – one each in poetry and prose – who are experienced writers and editors whose job it is to make the often difficult selections as to who will receive grants in any particular year. In 1985, 100 fellowships were awarded (49 in prose, 51 in poetry) as well as four Senior Fellowships.

For a list of current guidelines, write to Literature Program, National Endowment for the Arts, 1100 Pennsylvania Avenue N.W., Washington, D.C. 20506.

The writers listed below have all been honored by their peers as artists whose courage and determination and ability are superior.

A

CHESTER AARON
JONATHAN AARON
LEE K. ABBOTT
LOUISE HARDIMAN ABBOTT
RAYMOND K. ABBOTT
ROBERT H. ABEL
WALTER ABISH
THOMAS D. ABSHER
DIANE ACKERMAN
DUANE W. ACKERSON
ALICE ADAMS
DOCK ADAMS
GLENDA ADAMS
LEONIE ADAMS
ELIZABETH S. ADCOCK
JONIS AGEE
THOMAS F. AHERN
PELORHANKHE OGAWA AI
SANDRA B. ALCOSSER
DAISY ALDAN
NELSON ALGREN
JODY ALIESAN
DICK S. ALLEN
PAULA GUNN ALLEN
SAMUEL W. ALLEN
JOHN R. ALLMAN
JUAN M. ALONSO
S. KEITH ALTHAUS
A. R. AMMONS
RUDOLPHO A. ANAYA
CALVIN ANDERSON
JACK ANDERSON
JAMES C. ANDERSON
JON V. ANDERSON
MARGARET A. ANDERSON
RODNEY L. ANDERSON
BRUCE E. ANDREWS
JEANNE R. ANDREWS
BIM B. A. ANGST
MAX APPLE
PHILIP APPLEMAN
JAMES W. APPLEWHITE
RAY ARANHA
ANTHONY V. ARDIZZONE
LINDA ARKING
JOSE ARMAS
CARROLL ARNETT
ELIZABETH A. ARTHUR
XAM SA ASANTEWA
JOHN ASHBERY
SANDRA F. ASHER
DAPHNE ATHAS
ALVIN AUBERT
W. H. AUDEN
JESSICA L. AUERBACH
PAUL AUSTER

B

ROBERT E. BAGG
DAVID BAKER
DONALD W. BAKER
SHERIDAN BAKER
WILLIAM E. BAKER
JOHN BALABAN
TONI CADE BAMBARA

RUSSELL E. BANKS
AMIRI BARAKA
COLEMAN B. BARKS
ANNA MARIE BARLOW
DJUNA BARNES
JIM W. BARNES
WILLIS BARNSTONE
HELEN BAROLINI
JOHN BARRY
FREDERICK BARTHELME
ELIZABETH BARTLETT
SCOTT BATES
JONATHAN BAUMBACH
RICHARD S. BAUSCH
CHARLES M. BAXTER
PETER S. BEAGLE
LAURA J. BEAUSOLIEL
STEPHEN BECKER
BARRY E. BECKHAM
JOHN BEECHER
BEN BELITT
MARVIN H. BELL
JOE DAVID BELLAMY
LANCE S. BELVILLE
MICHAEL BENEDIKT
GEORGE HOWARD BENNETT
PAUL BENNETT
BETH BENTLEY
STEPHEN BERG
CAROL BERGE
LOU G. BERGER
DEIDRE L. BERGSON
WILLIAM C. BERKSON
KENNETH BERNARD
ALAN W. BERNHEIMER
CHARLES K. BERNSTEIN
JANE BERNSTEIN
TED BERRIGAN
DAVID A. BERRY
WENDELL BERRY

JOHN BERRYMAN
LEO BERSANI
MEI-MEI BERSSENBRUGGE
JAMES D. BERTOLINO
ALVAH BESSIE
HARVEY S. BIALY
FRANK BIDART
WAYNE B. BIDDLE
LAUREL ELLEN BIRD
PHYLLIS T. BIRNBAUM
ANN BIRSTEIN
JOHN D. BISHOP
TRIM BISSELL
DAVID BLACK
CLARK L. BLAISE
GUS BLAISDELL
ROBIN BLASER
RICHARD BLESSING
CORINNE DEMAS BLISS
MICHAEL C. BLUMENTHAL
ELAINE FORD BOATIN
ALAN N. BOATMAN
VICTOR F. BOCKRIS
DEBORAH L. BOE
LOUISE BOGAN
ISABEL BOLTON
HAROLD BOND
PHILIP BOOTH
AUDREY BORENSTEIN
MARIANNE J. BORUCH
PHILIP BOSAKOWSKI
MALCOLM BOSSE
DAVID L. BOSWORTH
MARILYN S. BOUCHER
VANCE BOURJAILLY
FAUBION BOWERS
PAUL BOWLES
JOHN D. BOYD
JAMES BOYER
KAY BOYLE

T. C. BOYLE
BARRY BOYS
JOHN L. BRANDI
SAMUEL P. BRASFIELD
RICHARD BRAUTIGAN
DONALD G. BREDES
JACK BRENNER
LEE BREUER
RICHARD P. BRICKNER
BESMILR BRIGHAM
JOHN MALCOLM BRINNIN
LUCIE BROCK-BROIDO
HAROLD BRODKEY
LESLIE D. BRODY
DAVID BROMIGE
ESTHER M. BRONER
DONNA BROOK
CHANDLER BROSSARD
T. ALAN BROUGHTON
OLGA C. BROUMAS
BROCK BROWER
CLAUDE BROWN
JAMES W. BROWN
KENNETH H. BROWN
LENNOX BROWN
LINDA J. BROWN
RITA MAE BROWN
ROBERT BROWN
ROSELLEN BROWN
STERLING BROWN
WILLIAM BROWN, JR.
MICHAEL DENNIS BROWNE
MICHAEL BROWNSTEIN
DEBRA M. BRUCE
JOSEPH E. BRUCHAC
C. D. B. BRYAN
JAMES V. BRUMMELS
THOMAS A. BRUSH
CHRISTOPHER F. BUCKLEY

FREDERICK BUELL
CHARLES BUKOWSKI
EDWARD A. BULLINS
JERALD BULLIS
R. MICHAEL BUNDGAARD
MICHAEL P. BURKARD
CLIFFORD BURKE
KENNETH BURKE
GERALD P. BURNS
RALPH M. BURNS
ROBERT GRANT BURNS
TIMOTHY W. BURNS
MADELEINE H. BURNSIDE
JANET G. BURROWAY
CHRISTOPHER BURSK
FREDERICK BUSCH
BARNEY BUSH
NAOMI A. BUSHMAN
GRACE BUTCHER
BILL BUTLER

C

MARY P. CABLE
MICHAEL J. CADNUM
JACK CADY
CONYUS L. CALHOUN
HORTENSE CALISHER
ROBERT O. CALLAHAN
KATHY J. CALLAWAY
FRANCOIS CAMION
BEBE MOORE CAMPBELL
JAMES CAMPBELL
STEVE CANNON
ALVARA CARDONA-HINE
GUY A. CARDWELL
DAVID C. CARKEET
HENRY CARLILE
RONALD F. CARLSON
JOHN CARPENTER

WILLIAM M. CARPENTER

WAYNE CARRIER

HAYDEN CARRUTH

HORACE L. CARTER

JARED R. CARTER

LONNIE CARTER

PAUL CARTER

RANDOLPH CARTER

RAYMOND CARVER

JANE CASEY

JOHN D. CASEY

TURNER CASSITY

JOANN CATTONER

ANN CAVALLARO

MAURA STANTON CECIL

JOSEPH CERAVOLO

LORNA D. CERVANTES

MYRTHA O. CHABRAN

MARISHA CHAMBERLAIN

GEORGE J. CHAMBERS

MARIANNE H. CHAMETZKY

JEAN VALENTINE CHANCE

LESLIE CHAPMAN

JEROME CHARYN

E. HALE CHATFIELD

THALIA CHERONIS-SELZ

KELLY CHERRY

LAURA CHESTER

ALAN S. CHEUSE

FRANK C. CHIN

MARILYN MEI LING CHIN

YVONNE C. CHISM

JOHN F. CHRISTGAU

SANDRA CISNEROS

SIBYL CLAIBORNE

DAVID ULYSSES CLARK

THOMAS W. CLARK

TOM CLARK

JAN L. CLAUSEN

JOHN J. CLAYTON

MICHELLE C. CLIFF

LUCILLE CLIFTON

WILLIAM COBB

GEORGE CODEGAN

ANDREI CODRESCU

L. KEITH COHEN

CHARLES T. COLE

LEWIS COLE

JAMES A. COLEMAN

WANDA COLEMAN

MICHAEL R. COLLIER

PETER A. COLLIER

JACK COLLUM

BETSEY COLQUITT

LAURIE E. COLWIN

LEO CONNELAN

FRANK CONROY

JACK W. CONROY

CLARK COOLIDGE

JANE COOPER

JANE M. COOPER

ROBERT COOVER

WILLIAM CORBETT

BARBARA A. CORCORAN

RAYMOND COREIL

CID CORMAN

ALFRED D. CORN

SAM CORNISH

JAMES CORPORA

MARY E. CORRIGAN

J. W. CORRINGTON

JAYNE CORTEZ

GERALD P. COSTANZO

MARK P. COSTELLO

JANE E. COTTRELL

HENRI COULETTE

MARY E. COUNSELMAN

MICHAEL F. COVINO

MALCOLM COWLEY

JAMES W. COX

LOUIS O. COXE
STEPHEN A. CRAMER
MAX CRAWFORD
STANLEY G. CRAWFORD
THOMAS P. CRAWFORD
BOBBIE L. CREELEY
ROBERT CREELEY
FREDERICK C. CREWS
HARRY CREWS
JAMES CROSS (HUGH J. PARRY)
MARY F. CROW
DOUGLAS E. CROWELL
VICTOR H. CRUZ
ELIZABETH CULLINAN
JAMES V. CUNNINGHAM
GEORGE CUOMO
RICHARD A. CURREY
DAVID L. CURRY

D

RICHARD L. DABNEY
JOHN P. DACEY
EDWARD DAHLBERG
RAE DALVEN
ROBERT DANA
ROSEMARY F. DANIELL
JAMES P. DANIELS
ORESTE D'ARCONTE
ANN DARR
TINA DARRAGH
MICK DAUGHERTY
JOHN P. DAVIDSON
MICHAEL DAVIDSON
ALFRED I. DAVIS
ALLEN DAVIS, III
CHRISTOPHER DAVIS
KATHRYN DAVIS
CECIL DAWKINS
RICHARD DAY
ROBERT DAY

ANN F. DEAGON
DAVID DECK
JOHN A. DECK
BILL DEEMER
MADELINE M. DeFREES
TOM DeHAVEN
CONSTANCE DE JONG
JAMES L. DE JONGH
ADELE S. DE LA BARRE
NICHOLAS F. DELBANCO
RICK DeMARINIS
JAMES D. DEN BOER
REVEL DENNY
ALFREDO DE PALCHI
TOI M. DERRICOTTE
ALEXIS DE VEAUX
PETER DEXTER
WILLIAM DICKEY
PIETRO DI DONATO
MONICA DI EMIDIO
ANNIE DILLARD
RAY DI PALMA
DIANE DI PRIMA
MELVIN DIXON
STEPHEN B. DIXON
CHARLES DIZENZO
PATRICIA A. DOBLER
STEPHEN J. DOBYNS
WAYNE C. DODD
HARRIET H. DOERR
IVAN DOIG
JOHN A. DOMINI
D. W. DONZELLA
EDWARD DORN
RITA F. DOVE
PHILLIP DOW
ALBERT D. DRAKE
BARBARA DRAKE
JOEL DRESSLER
JOHN F. DRISCOLL

NORMAN E. DUBIE
ANDRÉ J. DUBUS
JOSEPH M. DUEMER
E. NORMAN DUKES
MARGARET M. DUKORE
HARRIS P. DULANY
JEFFREY L. DUNCAN
ROBERT DUNCAN
STEPHEN E. DUNN
STEPHEN R. DUNN
STUART J. DYBECK

E

JOAN EADES
CORNELIUS R. EADY
PATRICIA A. EAKINS
ROBERT B. EARLY
RUSSELL EDSON
MARGARET F. EDWARDS
WILLIAM EDYVEAN
GRETEL EHRLICH
SERGIO D. ELIZONDO
STANLEY ELKIN
C. LEWIS ELLINGHAM
RICHARD ELLMAN
KENWARD ELMSLIE
LYNN C. EMANUEL
CAROLYN F. EMSHWILLER
JOHN D. ENGELS
MARY J. ENGH
TED ENSLIN
GEORGE GARRETT EPPS
PHILLIP ANTHONY EPRILE
DANIEL M. EPSTEIN
LESLIE EPSTEIN
SANDRA EPSTEIN
PAMELA M. ERBE
LOUISE ERDRICH
STEPHEN C. ERHART
CLAYTON ESHLEMAN

DAVID A. EVANS
GEORGE E. EVANS
WELCH D. EVERMAN
WILLIAM O. EVERSON
PETER P. EVERWINE

F

LARRY FAGIN
RONALD L. FAIR
NANCY FALES
THOMAS DAVID FARBER
JAMES T. FARRELL
RAYMOND FEDERMAN
CHERYL J. FEIN
ROSS A. FELD
JOHN FELSTINER
MARGARET L. FERGUSON
ANDREW FETLER
JAMES M. FETLER
JULIA FIELDS
JAMES L. FILES
WARREN L. FINE
DONALD FINKEL
CAROLINE FINKELSTEIN
JOHN M. FINLAY
DAVID L. FISHER
HARRISON M. FISHER
ROBERT FITZGERALD
THOMAS FITZSIMMONS
ROBERT J. FLANAGAN
JANE FLANDERS
DANIEL E. FLESHLER
ROLAND W. FLINT
CALVIN L. FORBES
CAROLYN FORCHÉ
RICHARD FORD
MARIA IRENE FORNES
PAUL FOSTER
GENE FOWLER
RICHARD X. FRANCE

DONALD M. FRANE
JOSEPH FRANK
SHELDON FRANK
JENNIE E. FRANKLIN
KATHLEEN J. FRASER
STUART FRIEBERT
ALAN H. FRIEDMAN
CAROL K. FROST
CHARLES FULLER
VIRGINIA FURTWANGLER

G

WILLIAM GADDIS
FRANK J. GAGLIANO
ERNEST J. GAINES
FRED GAINES
TESS GALLAGHER
RICHARD J. GALLUP
BRENDAN J. GALVIN
JAMES A. GALVIN
CATHERINE GAMMON
BRUCE M. GANS
EUGENE K. GARBER
CECILIO GARCIA
JOHN R. GARDINER
JOHN C. GARDNER, JR.
LEONARD GARDNER
JACK GARLINGTON
GEORGE GARRETT
BARBARA GARSON
THOMAS M. GAVIN
JACK GELBER
DANIEL F. GERBER, JR.
REGINALD GIBBONS
MARGARET F. GIBSON
PATRICIA J. GIBSON
BARRY C. GIFFORD
JACK GILBERT
VIRGINIA L. GILBERT
GARY GILDNER
JOHN C. GILHOOLEY

LAURA C. GILPIN
ALLEN GINSBERG
MARISA E. GIOFFRE
NIKKI GIOVANNI
ELTON GLASER
JOANNA M. GLASS
MYRA GLAZER
JUDITH I. GLEASON
JOSEPH G. GLOVER
LOUISE GLUCK
GAIL GODWIN
PATRICIA GOEDICKE
IVAN GOLD
LLOYD GOLD
ALBERT GOLDBARTH
LESTER GOLDBERG
SIDNEY GOLDFARB
MARTIN M. GOLDSMITH
STANFORD M. GOLDSTEIN
IVY H. GOODMAN
STEPHEN GOODWIN
CAROLINE GORDON
JAIMY GORDON
CHARLES E. GORDONE
ANGELINE W. GOREAU
GARY GOSS
DELCIE S. GOURDINE
DOUGLAS W. GOWER
JORIE GRAHAM
JUDITH RAE GRAHN
MARCUS J. GRAPES
ERNEST A. GRAY, III
GAYLE GRAY
SPALDING GRAY
STEPHEN R. GRECCO
ELY GREEN
HANNAH GREEN
ALVIN GREENBERG
PAULA FOX GREENBERG
JONATHAN E. GREENE
THEODORE M. GREENWALD

DEBORA GREGER

LINDA GREGERSON

CHARLES GREGORY

ROBERT B. GRENIER

SUSAN GRIFFIN

PATRICIA B. GRIFFITH

LAWRENCE M. GROBEL

RICHARD GROSSINGER

ALLEN R. GROSSMAN

JAMES LELAND GROVE

LEE M. GRUE

ALBERT GUERARD

BRUCE GUERNSEY

BARBARA GUEST

KEITH R. GUNDERSON

STEPHANIE C. GUNN

ALLAN GURGANUS

RAMON GUTHRIE

LEE GUTKIND

H

MARILYN T. HACKER

PAMELA W. HADAS

ROBERT S. HAHN

JOHN HAINES

WILLIAM HAIRSTON

JAMES BAKER HALL

OAKLEY HALL, III

RICHARD G. HALL

WALTER HALL

DANIEL HALPERN

SAM HAMILL

PATRICIA M. HAMPL

ALLEN B. HANNAY

JOSEPH W. HANSEN

KATHRYN G. HANSEN

RONALD T. HANSEN

KENNETH HANSON

PAULINE HANSON

C. G. HANZLICEK

ROBERT D. HARBISON

ELIZABETH L. HARDWICK

DONALD D. HARINGTON

NAOMI JOY HARJO

MICHAEL S. HARPER

STEPHEN M. HARRIGAN

GRACE HARRIMAN

JAMES HARRIS

MARIE HARRIS

MARK HARRIS

PHYLLIS MASEK HARRIS

BARBARA G. HARRISON

JAMES T. HARRISON

WILLIAM N. HARRISON

RICHARD HARTEIS

CHARLES O. HARTMAN

ANNE C. HARVEY

LOLA B. HASKINS

LINDA M. HASSELSTROM

BAXTER HATHAWAY

JAMES B. HATHAWAY

STEPHEN HATHAWAY

WILLIAM T. HAUPTMAN

MARIANNE HAUSER

JOHN HAWKES

JOSEPHINE HAXTON

JOHN WILLIAMS HAY

JULIE HAYDEN

ROBERT HAYDEN

ROBERT HAZEL

SHELBY HEARON

ERNEST V. HEBERT

ANN LEVY HEBSEN

ROBERT HEDIN

CHARLES HENLEY

MICHAEL J. HEFFERNAN

MARCY G. HEIDISH

JACK L. HEIFNER

LARRY C. HEINEMANN

STEVE F. HELLER

ROBERT W. HEMENWAY
DON F. HENDRIE, JR.
DeWITT F. HENRY
JOHN JACOB HERMAN
LUZ C. HERNANDEZ
JUAN F. HERRERA
WILLIAM L. HERRIN
ROBERT HERSHON
WILLIAM HEYEN
ARLENE HEYMAN
JAMES A. HEYNEN
BEN L. HIATT
LELAND HICKMAN
JOHN HICKS
ROBERT HIGHTOWER
OSCAR HIJUELOS
PATI HILL
RICHARD F. HILL
ROBERTA J. HILL
CONRAD HILLBERRY
BRENDA L. HILLMAN
DARYL HINE
DENNIS HINRICHSEN
EDWARD M. HIRSCH
GEORGE HITCHCOCK
WILLIAM HJORTSBERG
EDWARD HOAGLAND
GEARY HOBSON
HENRY WILLIAM HOFFMAN
WILLIAM M. HOFFMAN
MICHAEL HOGAN
JAMES M. HOGGARD
JONATHAN HOLDEN
ANSELM A. HOLLO
JAMES A. HOLMSTRAND
GARRETT K. HONGO
EDWARD HONIG
PAUL A. HOOVER
ISRAEL HOROVITZ
JAMES HOUSTON

RICHARD HOWARD
FANNY HOWE
CHRISTOPHER L. HOWELL
EDWARD HOWER
BETTE HOWLAND
DAVID R. HUDDLE
MARCUS A. HUDSON
MARY GRAY HUGHES
JOHN R. HUMPHREYS
DEL M. HUNT
WILLIAM HUNT
CYNTHIA D. HUNTINGTON
ANNE HUSSEY
W. LEWIS HYDE

I

DAVID IGNATOW
MOMOKO IKO
LAWSON INADA
COLETTE INEZ
ELIZABETH A. INNESS-BROWN
JOHN W. IRVING

J

MARVIN X. JACKMON
ANGELA R. JACKSON
LAURA JACKSON
RICHARD P. JACKSON
SANDRA J. JACKSON-OPOKU
HARVEY J. JACOBS
HAROLD JAFFE
PHYLLIS W. JANOWITZ
TAMA JANOWITZ
MARK F. JARMAN
EMMETT JARRETT
RODERICK H. JELLEMA
LEN R. JENKIN
LAURA JENSEN
CHARLES R. JOHNSON
CURTIS L. JOHNSON

DENIS JOHNSON
RONALD T. JOHNSON
THOMAS JOHNSON
CATHERINE H. JONES
DARYL E. JONES
GAYL JONES
PAULA L. JONES
RODNEY G. JONES
WILLIAM BRUCE JONES
ERICA JONG
JUNE JORDAN
ERNEST A. JOSELOVITZ
LAWRENCE M. JOSEPH
ALLEN JOSEPHS
DONALD A. JUNKINS
DONALD R. JUSTICE

K

PAUL D. KAHN
ROBERTA KALECHOFSKY
JERRY KAMSTRA
LONNY KANEKO
JOHANNAH KAPLAN
MARY M. KARR
JAMES G. KATES
STEVE KATZ
JANET KAUFFMAN
STANLEY KAUFFMAN
BOB G. KAUFMAN
SHIRLEY KAUFMAN
REBECCA KAVALER
LAWRENCE M. KEARNEY
EDMUND L. KEELEY
BARBARA J. KEILER
TIM KELLEY
DAVID M. KELLY
ROBERT KELLY
BRIGID P. KELLY-MADONICK
PAUL F. KENNEBECK
ADRIENNE KENNEDY

RICHARD S. KENNEDY
WILLIAM J. KENNEDY
X. J. KENNEDY
TAMARA J. KENNELLY
SUSAN M. KENNEY
JANE KENYON
BAINE P. KERR
JOHN J. KESSEL
WENDY A. KESSELMAN
JASCHA KESSLER
STEPHEN KESSLER
KEORAPETSE KGOSITSILE
FAIZUL R. A. KHAN
FAYE KICKNOSWAY
JOHN T. KIDDER
JOHN OLIVER KILLENS
RICHARD E. KIM
YONG IK KIM
CHUCK KINDER
MAXINE HONG KINGSTON
GALWAY KINNELL
WILLIAM L. KINTER
DAVID K. KIRBY
TRINA KIRK
M. SMITH KIRKPATRICK
GARY R. KISSICK
VERA P. KISTLER
WILLIAM KITTREDGE
PETER KLAPPERT
MILTON KLONSKY
STEPHEN C. KNAUTH
ETHERIDGE KNIGHT
HILLARY KNIGHT
JOHN I. KNOEPFLE
WILLIAM KNOTT
KENNETH KOCH
STEPHEN KOCH
HERBERT R. KOHL
JAMES A. KOLLER
YUSEF KOMUNYAKAA

HANS KONINGSBERGER
THEODORE KOOSER
ARTHUR L. KOPIT
HENRY J. KORN
JOYCE KORNBLATT
SR. MARY NORBERT KORTE
NORMAN KOTKER
ZANE H. KOTKER
ROBERT KOTLOWITZ
WILLIAM KOTZWINKLE
STEVE M. KOWIT
ELAINE KRAF
JOHN K. KRICH
JUDITH KROLL
JAMES A. KRUSOE
KENNETH W. KUHLKEN
ELLEN G. KULLMAN
MAXINE KUMIN
STANLEY KUNITZ
CLEVELAND KURTZ
GREG S. KUZMA
JOANNE KYGER

L

EDWARD T. LAHEY
MICHAEL D. LALLY
ARTHUR D. LANGE
ELINOR LANGER
JOSEPH LANGLAND
WAYNE BANKS LANIER, JR.
GEORGE LANNING
MARINA DEB. LAPALMA
JEREMY LARNER
ERLING LARSEN
PETER LaSALLE
JOHN A. LATTA
LOIS LAUTNER
NORMAN LAVERS
DOUGLAS LAWDER
ROBERT LAX

NAOMI LAZARD
PETER J. LEACH
DAVID A. LEAVITT
DAVID LeCOUNT
DON L. LEE
LANCE LEE
BARBARA F. LEFCOWITZ
DIANE LEFER
MARY J. LEITHAUSER
CORNELL LENGYEL
MERIDEL LE SUEUR
DONALD W. LEVERING
DENISE LEVERTOV
CURT LEVIANT
ROBERT A. LEVIN
ALLEN LEVINE
PHILIP LEVINE
LARRY M. LEVINGER
LARRY LEVIS
GROVER LEWIS
IRA LEWIS
JAMES F. LEWISOHN
JOHN L'HEUREUX
MORTON J. LICHTER
LAURENCE LIEBERMAN
RENÉE B. LIEBERMAN
HERBERT LIEBMAN
KATHLEEN E. LIGNELL
LUCY LIM
ROMULUS LINNEY
LEWIS LIPSITZ
LEO E. LITWAK
STEPHEN S. LIU
LUCIA A. LOCKERT
RONALD W. LOEWINSOHN
JOHN B. LOGAN
WILLIAM LOGAN
ROY L. LONDON
BARBARA A. LONG
PHILIP LOPATE

AUDRÉ G. LORDE
DICK LOURIE
DAVID LOW
BEVERLY F. LOWRY
SUSAN G. LUDVIGSON
EDWARD G. LUEDERS
GLENNA B. LUSCHEI
THOMAS LUX
SVERRE LYNGSTAD
EUGENE LYONS
RICHARD M. LYONS
ANDREW LYTLE

M

CYNTHIA MacDONALD
DAVID R. MacDONALD
SUSAN. MacDONALD
JAMIE MacINNES
DONNA B. MACK
NORMAN W. MacLEOD
JACKSON MacLOW
BEN MADDOW
PHILIP MAGDALANY
JAMES L. MAGNUSON
JOSEPH C. MAIOLO
GEORGE MALKO
HENRY MALONE
MICHAEL PATRICK MALONE
F. S. MANALLI
MARVIN L. MANDEL
FREDERICK F. MANFRED
FREYA F. MANFRED
MARY E. MARCHANT
　(ROBERTSON)
ADRIANNE MARCUS
BRUCE MARCUS
LAURA A. MARELLO
PETER MARIN
WALLACE MARKFIELD
PAUL L. MARIANI

JULIA MARKUS
JACK MARLANDO
CHARLES MAROWITZ
PAULE B. MARSHALL
JAMES MARTIN
RICHARD J. MARTIN
MICHAEL A. MARTONE
MARY W. MARVIN
BOBBIE ANN MASON
CLIFFORD L. MASON
TIM MASON
HARRY MATHEWS
CLEOPATRA MATHIS
DENNIS L. MATHIS
DAVID C. C. MATTHEW
WILLIAM P. MATTHEWS
BERNADETTE F. MAYER
JESSICA M. MAXWELL
GAIL B. MAZUR
J. THOMAS McAFEE
MARY E. McANALLY
SARA McAULAY
JAMES J. McAULEY
MEKEEL McBRIDE
DONALD R. McCAIG
LINDA J. McCARRISTON
SEN. EUGENE McCARTHY
JAMES McCARTIN
LOUIS McCARTY
MICHAEL McCLURE
JAMES McCONKEY
PATRICIA E. McCONNEL
FRANK D. McCONNELL
MALCOLM McCONNELL
HOWARD L. McCORD
MAIRI C. McCORMICK
EMILY A. McCULLY
KENNETH McCULLOUGH
WALTER R. McDONALD
TOM. McDONOUGH

COLLEEN J. McELROY
DAVID F. McELROY
JOSEPH McELROY
JULIET McGRATH
THOMAS McGRATH
HEATHER McHUGH
KEVIN CHARLES McILOY
RALPH M. McINERNY
DAVID W. McKAIN
JAMES L. McMANUS
WESLEY C. McNAIR
JAMES McPHERSON
SANDRA McPHERSON
ROBERT T. McQUILKIN
JANET McREYNOLDS
MARY E. MEBANE
RUBEN MEDINA
MURRAY MEDNICK
E. JAY MEEK
PETER MEINKE
WILLIAM MEISSNER
DAVID MELTZER
IFEANYI MENKITI
DON C. MEREDITH
WILLIAM MEREDITH
LOUISE M. MERIWETHER
ANNE HAMILTON MERKLEY
JAMES MERSMANN
W. S. MERWIN
JOANNE M. MESCHERY
DEENA METZGER
MICHAEL F. MEWSHAW
THOMAS MEYER
BERTRAM MEYERS
LUCAS MEYERS
ROBERT MEZEY
LEONARD MICHAELS
PETER MICHELSON
CHRISTOPHER MIDDLETON
BARTON MIDWOOD

JOSEPHINE MILES
SARA MILES
BROWN MILLER
HEATHER ROSS MILLER
JANE R. MILLER
SUSAN MILLER
ARTHENIA MILLICAN
PAMELA MILLWARD
JOHN MILTON
JOHN M. MINCZESKI
STEPHEN MINOT
GARY L. MIRANDA
MARTIN S. MITCHELL
SUSAN MITCHELL
JAMES MASAO MITSUI
RAY MIZER
JUDITH L. MOFFETT
URSULE MOLINARO
DOROTHY MONET
ROBERT S. MONTGOMERY
JOSÉ E. MONTOYA
MICHAEL MOODY
MICHAEL M. MOONEY
HONOR MOORE
ROD V. MOORE
MICHAEL C. MOOS
ALEJANDRO MORALES
FRED T. MORGAN
FREDERICK MORGAN
RICHARD O. MORGAN
ROBERT R. MORGAN
ROBIN MORGAN
HELEN V. S. MORPURGO
MARY MORRIS
J. MADISON MORRISON
HOWARD MOSS
JULIAN MOYNAHAN
ROBERT MULLEN
JACQUELINE PIERCE MUNGAI
DAVID A. MURA

MORNA MURPHY
CAROL A. MUSKE
BERNARD MYERS
JACK E. MYERS
WALTER M. MYERS

N

SENA J. NASLUND
LAWRENCE NAUMOFF
GLORIA NAYLOR
JANET L. NEIPRIS
KENT NELSON
PAUL S. NELSON, JR.
RICHARD J. NELSON
HOWARD NEMEROV
JAY NEUGEBOREN
MICHAEL D. NEVILLE
SUSAN S. NEVILLE
MARGARET NEWLIN
CHARLES H. NEWMAN
REBECCA NEWTH
MARIS NICHOLS
JOSEPH NICHOLSON
M. MICHAEL NIFLIS
NONA V. NIMNICHT
JOHN FREDERICK NIMS
HUGH NISSENSON
JAMES E. NOLAN
LOU (BINK) NOLL
JOHN FORD NOONAN
HAROLD G. NORSE
CHARLES L. NORTH
ALICE E. NOTLEY
CRAIG NOVA
ALAN D. NURKSE

O

JOYCE CAROL OATES
DANIEL H. O'BRIEN
JOHN A. O'BRIEN

JOHN C. O'BRIEN
WILLIAM O'BRIEN
EDWIN F. OCHESTER
SHAUN O'CONNELL
MARY K. O'DONNELL
LOUIS D. OHLE
RICHARD O'KEEFE
SHARON OLDS
CAROLE OLES
CAROLE OLIGARIO
EVE OLITSKY
MARY OLIVER
TILLIE OLSEN
CHARLES OLSON
MERLE T. OLSON
KEVIN O'MORRISON
JOHN B. OMWAKE
ROBERT ONOPA
GEORGE OPPEN
JOEL L. OPPENHEIMER
SALLY A. ORDWAY
STEVEN L. ORLEN
JOHN M. ORLOCK
PETER ORLOVSKY
WILLIAM A. O'ROURKE
GREGORY S. ORR
SIMON ORTIZ
MARK S. OSAKI
ALICIA OSTRIKER
JOHN L. O'TOOLE
RON OVERTON
MAUREEN A. OWEN
ROCHELLE OWENS
CYNTHIA OZICK

P

HENRY PACHTER
ROBERT PACK
NANCY H. PACKER
RON PADGETT

CHARLOTTE PAINTER
GRACE PALEY
GEORGE MICHAEL PALMER
J. E. PALMER
GREG L. PAPE
RONNIE PARIS
LINDA PASTEN
KENNETH PATCHEN
JEFF L. PATE
WILLIAM B. PATRICK
LINDSAY PATTERSON
RAYMOND R. PATTERSON
JOHN PAUKER
HARRY PEARSON, JR.
WILLIAM G. PELFREY
JOHNATHAN PENNER
MINDY PENNYBACKER
VICTOR H. PERERA
DAVID H. PERKINS
JOHN PERRAULT
JOYCE E. PESEROFF
BETTE PESETSKY
ROBERT L. PETERS
QUINTON PETERSON
ROBERT PETERSON
CATHERINE G. PETROSKI
ANTHONY R. PETROSKY
ANN L. PETRY
MICHAEL E. PETTIT
JOHN F. PFEIL
ROGER C. PFINGSTON
ARTHUR PFISTER
ROBERT D. PHARR
MARIE E. PHEMSTER
JAYNE ANNE PHILLIPS
WILLIAM PHILLIPS
CONSTANCE M. PIERCE
JAMES F. PIERCE
MARGE PIERCY
DRURY L. PIFER

JOHN PIJEWSKI
ROBERT PINSKY
NANCY K. PIORE
LAWRENCE J. PITKETHLY
ALLEN J. PLANZ
GEORGE PLIMPTON
RICHARD PLOETZ
STANLEY R. PLUMLY
RICHARD POIRIER
CARLENE HATCHER POLITE
KATHA S. POLLITT
MARIE PONSOT
MELINDA POPHAM
BERNARD H. PORTER
JOE A. PORTER
ANDREW POTOK
NANCY A. POTTER
A. POULIN, JR.
EZRA POUND
CHARLES E. POVERMAN
REYNOLDS PRICE
RICHARD J. PRICE
WILLIAM PRICE
ROBIN J. PRISING
MELISSA B. PRITCHARD
FREDERIC PROKOSCH
FRANCINE C. PROSE
CATERINA F. PROVOST

Q

GEORGE F. QUASHA
SR. M. BERNETTA QUINN
LEROY V. QUINTANA

R

LAWRENCE RAAB
ARNOLD M. RABIN
NAHID RACHLIN
HENRY RAGO
SONIA RAIZISS

CARL RAKOSI

JEROLD RAMSEY

DUDLEY F. RANDALL

JULIA V. N. RANDALL

JOHN CROWE RANSOM

WILLIAM RANSOM

KATHERINE RAO

BARBARA J. RASKIN

MICHAEL D. RATTEE

DAVID E. RAY

SHREELA RAY

JOHN RECHY

RONALD E. RECTOR

EUGENE D. REDMOND

ISHMAEL REED

ARTHUR REEL

MARSHALL H. REESE

TOVA REICH

JAN C. REID

LOUIS A. REILE

JAMES ALAN REISS

ETTORE RELLA

LISA RESS

KENNETH REXROTH

JOHN C. REZMERSKI

JEWELL P. RHODES

RICHARD L. RHODES

JOSEPH P. RIBAR

RONALD RIBMAN

STANLEY RICE

ADRIENNE RICH

CAROLYN A. RICHARDS

SUSAN N. RICHARDS

ROBERT S. RICHE

NOEL RICO

JOHN RIDLAND

DAVID E. RIGSBEE

ALBERTO A. RIOS

EDWARD RIVERA

ANDRES RIVERO

LEONARD R. ROBERTS

MOSS P. ROBERTS

JILL ROBINSON

JOHN L. ROBINSON

KIT L. ROBINSON

CAROLYN M. RODGERS

ALEIDA M. RODRIGUEZ

WILLIAM A. ROECKER

DEL MARIE ROGERS

PATTIANN ROGERS

THOMAS N. R. ROGERS

LEO ROMERO

ORLANDO A. ROMERO

LEON ROOKE

WILLIAM PITT ROOT

NED ROREM

LOUISE B. ROSE

WENDY E. ROSE

MICHAEL J. ROSEN

JESSIE ROSENBERG

MICHAEL ROSSMAN

JEROME ROTHENBERG

MICHAEL ROTHSCHILD

DAVID A. ROUNDS

ANN ROWER

GIBBONS RUARK

CAROL P. RUBENSTEIN

DAVID G. RUBIN

MICHAEL RUBIN

RICK RUBIN

MARY L. RUEFLE

EUGENE RUGGLES

MURIEL RUKEYSER

NORMAN H. RUSSELL

VERN A. RUTSALA

MICHAEL RYAN

S

IRA SADOFF

EDWARD W. SAID

DAVID ST. JOHN
PRIMUS ST. JOHN
J. R. SALAMANCA
FLOYD F. SALAS
I. L. SALOMON
BENJAMIN SALTMAN
ROSAURA SANCHEZ
SAUL O. SANCHEZ
SONIA B. SANCHEZ
THOMAS SANCHEZ
ED SANDERS
IVAN SANDERS
SCOTT R. SANDERS
REG SANER
ANNETTE A. SANFORD
BIENVENIDO N. SANTOS
ARAM SAROYAN
MAY SARTON
ROGER SAULS
TEO SAVORY
JULIA RANDALL SAWYER
NORA C. SAYRE
LESLIE SCALAPINO
DAVID SCHAFF
RICHARD SCHECHNER
HARRIS SCHIFF
PETER SCHJELDAHL
DENNIS SCHMITZ
NANCY J. SCHOENBERGER
MICHAEL J. SCHOLNICK
KARINE SCHOMER
PETER SCHRAG
PHILIP S. SCHULTZ
MICHAEL P. SCHULZE
JAMES SCHUYLER
LYNN SHARON SCHWARTZ
ARMAND SCHWERNER
CAROLYNNE B. SCOTT
HERBERT SCOTT
JAMES SCULLY

ALLAN SEAGER
JAN L. SEALE
PETER SEATON
ROBERTA SEBENTHALL
CAROLYN SEE
LORE SEGAL
MICHAEL SEIDE
FREDERICK SEIDEL
HUGH SEIDMAN
RAMON SENDER, JR.
   (MORNINGSTAR)
FRED S. SETTERBURG
ROBERT G. SHACOCHIS
ANDERS SHAFER
NTOZAKE SHANGE
ALAN R. SHAPIRO
DAVID J. SHAPIRO
RICHARD O. SHAW
LAURIE A. SHECK
MARC J. SHEEHAN
EVELYN SHEFNER
MARSHA SHEINESS
RICHARD SHELTON
MICHAEL J. SHERIDAN
MARTIN G. SHERMAN
JUDITH J. SHERWIN
DAVID J. SHIELDS
JANE SHORE
SUSAN R. SHREVE
ALIX KATES SHULMAN
ROBERT H. SIEGEL
LESLIE MARMON SILKO
RONALD G. SILLIMAN
ROBERTA SILMAN
RANDALL G. SILVIS
L. SEYMOUR SIMCKES
JAMES SIMMERMAN
CHARLES SIMIC
LYDIA SIMMONS
MINA LEWITON SIMON

LOUIS SIMPSON

PATSY SIMS

THOMAS SINCLAIR

ISAAC BASHEVIS SINGER

DONALD L. SINGLETON

ROGER D. SKILLINGS, JR.

JOHN SKINNER

KNUTE SKINNER

MYRA W. SKLAREW

JOHN SKOYLES

ROBERT SLATER

BERNICE SLOTE

JANE G. SMILEY

ARTHUR E. SMITH

BRUCE SMITH

C. W. SMITH

DAVID J. SMITH

DINITIA E. R. SMITH

EBBE R. SMITH

JORDAN F. SMITH

MARK R. SMITH

MASON E. SMITH

WILLIAM J. SMITH

SUSAN R. SNIVELY

W. D. SNODGRASS

EDWARD SNOW

ANTHONY G. SOBIN

BARBARA P. SOLOMON

TED SOLOTAROFF

SCOTT R. SOMMER

ROBERT T. SORRELLS

HELEN SORRELS

GILBERT SORRENTINO

GARY A. SOTO

DAVID SOUTHERN

MARCIA SOUTHWICK

RONALD M. SPATZ

ROBERTA L. SPEARE

ELIZABETH SPENCER

PETER SPIELBERG

MAUREEN F. SPIKE

PAUL SPIKE

ELIZABETH K. SPIRES

KATHLEEN D. SPIVACK

DAVID STACTON

KIM STAFFORD

WILLIAM STAFFORD

SUE STANDING

ANN STANFORD

DONALD STANFORD

GEORGE STANLEY

MAURA STANTON

CLAUDE I. STANUSH

LAURENCE STAPLETON

BRADFORD STARK

PAT STATEN

MARK S. STEADMAN

ARJYRA J. STEDMAN

JACK STEELE

MAX STEELE

FELIX STEFANILE

PAGE STEGNER

CHARLES F. STEIN

MEREDITH L. STEINBACH

ROBERT STEINER

DAVID STEINGASS

LISA STEINMAN

STEPHEN STEPANCHEV

GERALD STERN

RICHARD STERN

ALEX STEVENS

JOHN STEWART

SUSAN A. STEWART

GLORIA J. STILL

MILAN STITT

CAROLYN STOLOFF

ALMA STONE

ROBERT A. STONE

MARK STRAND

MARY PETERSON STRATER

JONATHAN STRONG, JR.
LYN STRONGIN
JEAN STROUSE
DAN M. STRYK
LUCIEN H. STRYK
DABNEY STUART
FLOYD STUART
HAROLD STUART
LYNN L. SUKENICK
RON SUKENICK
NANCY SULLIVAN
HOLLIS SUMMERS
LINDA SVENDSEN
HARVEY SWADOS
LAURELL J. SWAILS
BRIAN SWANN
JEFFREY W. SWEET
MAY SWENSON
JOAN SWIFT
THOMAS B. SWISS
ARTHUR C. SZE
BARBARA SZERLIP

T

JOHN TAGGART
ELIZABETH TALLENT
STEPHEN J. TAPSCOTT
BARRY D. TARGAN
JAMES V. TATE
RONALD TAVEL
HARRY TAYLOR
HENRY S. TAYLOR
MARY ANN TAYLOR
MICHAEL TAYLOR
PATRICIA E. TAYLOR
PETER TAYLOR
RICHARD TAYLOR
MEGAN TERRY
STEVE TESICH
GEORGE TETER

JULIA THACKER
MICHAEL M. THELWELL
ALEXANDER THEROUX
JAMES W. THOMAS
LORENZO THOMAS
TOM THOMAS
CHARLES W. THOMPSON
GARY R. THOMPSON
JEAN LOUISE THOMPSON
MARILYN D. THOMPSON
NANCY PRICE THOMPSON
ROBERT S. THOMPSON
MONA VAN DUYN THURSTON
RUTHVEN TODD
JOAN E. TORRES
ANTHONY R. TOWLE
WILLARD TRASK
BERNARD W. TREISTER
WILLIAM A. TREMBLAY
EVE TRIEM
CECILIA LIANG TRIPI
DENNIS TRUDELL
FREDERICK W. TURNER
RALPH TUTT
GEORGE K. TYSH

U

LAURA ULEWICZ
ROBERT ULLIAN
LESLIE ULLMAN
JOHN E. UNTERECKER
CONSTANCE URDANG

V

NANOS J. VALAORITIS
MICHAEL VAN WALLEGHEN
PEDRO O. VASQUEZ
EDWARD VASTA
STEPHANIE R. VAUGHN
JON E. VEINBERG

THOMAS M. VEITCH

EVANGELINA S. VIGIL

DAVID VIGODA

MARK L. VINZ

PAUL R. VIOLI

ARTURO VIVANTE

MAI VO-DINH

SARA A. VOGAN

PAULA A. VOGEL

SHARON VOGEL

ARTHUR VOGELSANG

ELLEN VOIGT

JOHN VON HARTZ

DIANE VREULS

W

DAN WAKEFIELD

DIANE WAKOSKI

ANNE WALDMAN

ROSEMARY WALDROP

ALICE WALKER

EVAN K. WALKER

GRANVILLE WALKER, JR.

DAVID R. WALLACE

GERALD W. WALLACE

ROBERT WALLACE

MARGARET B. WALSH

THOMAS N. WALTERS

MARTIN L. WAMPLER

MARION R. WANIEK

IRENE E. WANNER

JEFFREY M. WANSHEL

DIANE L. WARD

ROBERT WARD

LARKIN A. WARREN

ROBERT PENN WARREN

LEWIS D. WARSH

FRANK WATERS

MICHAEL WATERS

ELLEN WATSON

ROBERT W. WATSON

BARRETT J. WATTEN

GORDON A. WEAVER

MICHAEL S. WEAVER

IGOR M. WEBB

JOHN WEBB

RAMONA WEEKS

THEODORE W. WEESNER

ROGER WEINGARTEN

DAVID F. WEISS

THEODORE WEISS

SARAH BROWN WEITZMAN

JAMES WELCH

BERNARD WELT

ELINOR H. WELT

PAUL WEST

NANCY G. WESTERFIELD

WALTER D. WETHERELL

DOUG N. WHEELER

EDGAR WHITE

JOHN E. WHITE

MARY J. WHITE

SHARON A. WHITE

RUTH WHITMAN

THOMAS WHITBREAD

REED WHITTEMORE

GEORGE A. WICKES

JOHN WIENERS

ALLEN WIER

DARA WIER

EUGENE WILDMAN

SILVIA WILKINSON

NANCY WILLARD

MARY L. WILLEY

C. K. WILLIAMS

EDWARD G. WILLIAMS

JOHN WILLIAMS

JOHN A. WILLIAMS

JONATHAN C. WILLIAMS

JOY WILLIAMS

CONSTANCE E. WILLIS
MEREDITH SUE WILLIS
ALAN B. WILLIAMSON
ELEANOR WILNER
EDWARD D. WILSON
KEITH C. WILSON
ROBERT E. WILSON
JOYCE M. WINSLOW
PETE WINSLOW
YVOR WINTERS
WILLIAM WISER
WILLIAM WITHERUP
JOHN C. WITTE
WARREN WOESSNER
DAVID C. WOJAHN
JACK C. WOLF
GEOFFREY WOLFF
TOBIAS WOLFF
HILMA WOLITZER
ROY S. WOLPER
SHAWN H. WONG
SUSAN M. WOOD
JOHN WOODS
WILLIAM C. WOODS
MARTIN WORMAN
CAROLYN D. WRIGHT
CHARLES D. WRIGHT
CHARLES P. WRIGHT
FRANZ P. WRIGHT
JAMES WRIGHT
JAY WRIGHT
ROBERT A. WRIGLEY
SYBIL WULETICH

Y

SUSAN K. YANKOWITZ
RICHARD YATES
JOHN YAU
JOSE YGLESIAS
AL YOUNG

DAVID P. YOUNG
GARY E. YOUNG
GEOFFREY M. YOUNG
RAY YOUNG BEAR
JOHN YOUNT

Z

LELA A. ZACHARIAS
SAUL ZACHARY
WAYNE ZADE
MARC A. ZAGOREN
BILL ZAVATSKY
CHRISTINE ZAWADIWSKY
EILEEN M. ZEITZ
JOHN F. ZEUGNER
PAUL J. ZIMMER
LLOYD A. ZIMPEL
JOEL R. ZOSS
AHMOS ZU-BOLTON
LOUIS ZUKOVSKY
PAUL L. ZWEIG

THE TYPE IS GALLIARD, A FACE DESIGNED BY MATTHEW CARTER.

BOOK DESIGN BY TREE SWENSON.

COVER PHOTO BY PAUL BOYER.

MANUFACTURED BY FAIRFIELD GRAPHICS.